WINTER DREAMS

WINTER DREAMS

A Historical Guide to Old Age

BARBARA H. ROSENWEIN

REAKTION BOOKS

*To the memory of Ruth, Sylvia and Roz,
my Elegant Three*

Published by
REAKTION BOOKS LTD
2–4 Sebastian Street
London EC1V 0HE, UK
www.reaktionbooks.co.uk

First published 2025
Copyright © Barbara H. Rosenwein 2025

All rights reserved

EU GPSR Authorised Representative
Logos Europe, 9 rue Nicolas Poussin, 17000, La Rochelle, France
email: contact@logoseurope.eu

No part of this publication may be reproduced, stored in a retrieval system, or transmitted, in any form or by any means, electronic, mechanical, photocopying, recording or otherwise, without the prior permission of the publishers. No part of this publication may be used or reproduced in any manner for the purpose of training artificial intelligence technologies or systems.

Printed and bound by Bell & Bain, Glasgow

A catalogue record for this book is available from the British Library

ISBN 978 1 83639 091 6

Contents

NOTE TO READERS 6

Introduction 7
One Enjoyment 17
Two Acceptance 56
Three Reciprocity 94
Four Work 150
Five Dignity 193
Conclusion 233

REFERENCES 241
FURTHER READING 253
ACKNOWLEDGEMENTS 255
PHOTO ACKNOWLEDGEMENTS 256
INDEX 257

NOTE TO READERS

All translations are mine unless otherwise indicated. I have lightly edited and updated the orthography, punctuation and capitalization of early modern English and explained obsolete words within brackets. Biblical quotations are from *The New Oxford Annotated Bible*, 5th edition. All dates are CE (AD) unless noted as BCE (BC).

Introduction

When my grandmother turned sixty, she said that she was old. She coiffed and sprayed her silver hair once a week at a beauty parlour. She played canasta with her 'girlfriends'. When she was widowed, she happily moved to a retirement apartment. Yet from my point of view, she was not old: until her abrupt death in her eighties, she remained independent and in good health.

Fifty years later, when my mother-in-law was in her eighties, she thought of herself as young. She dyed her short hair red and swam every day. She enjoyed her volunteer work teaching art to 'old people' (her term) in an old-age home. When her husband died, she remained alone in their house and, as she entered her nineties, she hired a helper. Every night before dinner, she had a martini. Her 'girlfriends', all her age, called themselves the Elegant Eight, and went to movies and concerts together.

But my own widowed mother, at around age eighty, developed dementia. She could no longer take care of herself, although she insisted that she could. She fought tooth and nail against moving to an assisted living facility, but once there, she quickly adjusted and called her tiny room there 'home'. She recognized me, but in general she lived in a fantasy world. She told me, for example, that she was in love with a man who loved her in turn. They would wed as soon as he divorced his wife, a terrible woman who was making all sorts of trouble for him. No, my mother couldn't remember his name, but so what? She was in the winter of her life, and her love with this phantasmal man was chief among her pleasures. I cruelly tried to disabuse her of him, and she rightly became furious at me. She was happy; she was in love; she had a new life ahead of her.

Did she dream of this lover at night? Scientific literature today declares that 'dreams have usually little subjective importance in the mental life of aged persons.'[1] But I myself, by now well along in age, have more vivid and emotionally charged dreams than I had ten years ago. Just the other night, for example, I dreamt I was back at the University of Chicago, my alma mater, and could not find my classroom. I was already late and evidently in the wrong building. But the right one was across a river. I panicked and woke up with my heart pounding. This certainly had 'subjective importance' to me. The terrifying feeling that I am lost is all too familiar to me. Perhaps scientists and I differ on what 'subjective' means. Or, it may be that scientific studies are overly dependent on the artificial environment of sleep laboratories.

My daughter suggested that my mother didn't have a dream at all but rather saw a sentimental drama on television and internalized the story. Or maybe my mother mistook a man's friendly visit for an amorous tryst. In any case, this fantasy, this winter dream in the last season of her life, gave her great joy.

Whether dreamt at night or part of waking life, 'winter dreams' are precious. They tell us that no matter how old people are, they continue to have fantasies and feelings. And we who partake in the ageism of our day (a feeling shared by young and old alike) should school ourselves to have the patience and fortitude to take these reveries and emotions seriously. To this end, I mean for this historical guide, which covers many centuries, to reprogram our assumptions, our prejudices and our fears.

Introduction

The passing of time makes us old, but what constitutes 'old age' is largely a cultural and individual construct. My grandmother was a totally capable woman in her sixties, but she and her friends thought of themselves as old. By contrast, my mother and mother-in-law were heirs of Betty Friedan, a leading light of the women's rights movement of the 1960s. They thought of themselves (and wanted others to see them) as vibrant, competent and independent, no matter their age.

Thus the times we live in have much to do with how we feel about being old. And there is a wealth of material about the old in past centuries because, contrary to popular opinion, most people in the past did *not* die around the age of thirty. Thirty was the 'mean average' age of human beings until the 1950s.[2] It tells us that as many people lived beyond thirty as died before it. Once people survived infancy and early childhood, they might live well into their sixties or later. Without records of chronological age, which became routine in the West only in the eighteenth century, scholars of the past are hard put to make exact estimates.[3] Many surveys of the historical evidence end their age categories with 45+, which means that people in their sixties, seventies and eighties are grouped with everyone over age 45.

Some researchers, however, have attempted to counter this imprecision. Michael Gurven and Hillard Kaplan studied the available 'mortality profiles of all extant hunter-gatherers' revealing 'an average modal adult life span of about 72 years'. That meant that most of those people died around the age of 72. However, between 24 to 35 per cent of the adult population lived beyond that age.[4]

Objective numbers are useful, if problematic. A more subjective way to approach the matter is to ask, when did people seem – and consider themselves – old? When Socrates was condemned to death, he was seventy years old. According to one eyewitness report, he was glad to accept his sentence because it released him from the *future* indignities of old age. He didn't consider himself to be old yet, or at least not *very* old. In fifth-century BCE Athens (where Socrates grew up and plied his philosophical trade), men were deemed fit for warfare between the ages of 20 and 58. At that point they were excused from military service, but they could still serve on governing bodies. At Sparta they could be elected to the governing body *only* once they were sixty. They were certainly 'mature' by then, but whether or not they were deemed old is harder to ascertain.

One persistent tradition divides human life into stages, or 'ages of man' ending with the 'old man'. These were symbolic as well as biological; the model of Seven Ages was popular because it was also said to be consistent with the number of the planets and the organs of the body. Three was special because it had a beginning, middle and end. Four was particularly favoured because it had unique arithmetical properties (equal to both 2 + 2 and 2 × 2) and because it underlay the four humours of the body, the four seasons and so on.

The Roman poet Ovid (d. *c.* 17 CE) lamented the final age, when man 'slides down the sloping path of declining old age/ that weakens and demolishes the strength of former years', and when Helen, known for her ravishing looks, sees her 'ageing wrinkles' in the mirror and weeps (15.221–33).[5] Ovid's reference to Helen was a rare inclusion of women's experience within 'man's' ages.

Later, as Christianity conquered much of Western thought, ancient ideas were joined to scriptural exegesis and moralizing schemes – the Six days of Creation, the four Gospel books, the ten Steps of Ageing, which showed the contrasting fates that awaited the righteous and the sinful (illus. 1). In Shakespeare, the Ages of Man were turned into a seven-act performance. Already in the sixth act, the man is so shrunken that his trousers, once tight, bag around his legs, and his voice 'pipes and whistles'. In the seventh act,

> Last scene of all,
> That ends this strange, eventful history,
> Is second childishness and mere oblivion,
> Sans teeth, sans eyes, sans taste, sans everything.
> (*As You Like It*, 2.7.162–5)

In the role of a disinterested observer, Shakespeare had an ironic take on the whole sequence. He didn't much care how

1 Unknown artist, *The Ages of Man and Woman*, c. 1642–5, engraving. Both men and women climb and descend the steps of ageing, which end at age 100. Their progress is accompanied by pious poems in the cartouches, while below are cautionary verses explaining that in 'the rise and fall of human beings, one declines sweetly and the other in fear'.

the shrunken man felt about shrinking nor what it felt like to be 'sans everything'.

Closer to our own time, however, psychologist Erik Erikson proposed 'eight stages of man', each with its own psychological and emotional task. A baby's achievement was to feel trust rather than mistrust. That of the toddler, whose task was to be toilet-trained, was to gain 'autonomy' rather than succumb to 'shame and doubt'. For later stages, Erikson posited that the adult had to successfully 'generate' children, things and ideas, while the elderly had to accept themselves as 'something that had to be'.[6]

This achievement-oriented schema reflected its time. Looking back on it from our own era, I find it well suited to the emphasis in the 1950s on the domestic sphere and the production of babies. Erikson was not interested in *all* emotions but rather in a few life-task feelings. And he pronounced judgements on them: this one was good, that one bad. As if in life's court of law, he opposed plaintiffs and defendants: trust vs basic mistrust; autonomy vs shame and doubt; initiative vs guilt; industry vs inferiority; identity vs role diffusion; intimacy vs isolation; generativity vs stagnation; lastly, ego integrity vs despair.

My own quest in this book, however, is to chronicle variety rather than to prescribe. I want to understand what our emotional responses to old age might be in the present given our cultural and intellectual legacies. I am interested in two issues: how people in the past felt *about* the old, and how the old themselves felt about *being* old. These are not really separate matters, since the feelings people have about themselves affect how others see them – and vice versa.

Today, gerontologists separate the elderly into 'young old' and 'old old'. The young old are active, participate in consumer society, and are generally admired together with an admixture of surprise, as in, 'Wow, she's eighty years old and she still goes skydiving!' The old old are weak, dependent and decrepit.

But 'young old' and 'old old' are in many ways judgmental adjectives rather than scientific facts. For one thing, they are not connected to any precise chronological age. I would say that my mother-in-law and grandmother were 'young old' in their eighties, but my mother at the same age was 'old old'.

No matter the adjectives, all of these older women had feelings – often very strong ones. I was with my mother just as she lay dying and was in great pain. 'Do you know who this is?', the nurse attending her asked. She looked up at me. 'Barbara!', she said, her face lighting up. Shakespeare was wrong. Even at the last, people are not 'sans everything': they still have emotions.

AS A HISTORIAN of emotions, I try to capture the feelings of the past from the traces that people have left behind. I maintain that all human beings are so constituted as to feel what I (and probably you) call emotions. All of us have the potential to feel affectively or emotionally. But not all of us classify, understand and value feelings in the same way. That same variety was also true in the past. Emotions may be studied historically precisely because they have been attached to different things, evaluated in numerous ways and given culturally relevant meanings.[7]

When my historical approach allows it, I sometimes talk about 'emotional communities'. I mean groups of people who implicitly agree (or agreed) on which emotions are important, unimportant or dismaying. They tacitly harmonize as well in their expression, suppression or denial of those feelings. I generally use the terms 'emotions' and 'feelings' synonymously. The difference, in my view, is that 'feelings' is a more informal, less scientifically loaded word. It is congenial to use it for cultures that do not (or did not) talk about emotions per se yet which, in my view, nevertheless had them in some form.

To access the feelings of the elderly in the past, the historian must rely on the sources that the past leaves behind. We cannot interview or distribute questionnaires to people who lived before us. Diaries and the like were (with a few exceptions) products of the early modern period, introduced during a particular moment in which psychological self-examination became desirable.

However, even if interviews, questionnaires and diaries had always been available, they would even so pose problems for historians. For one thing, people are not always honest with themselves or others, and, for another, they don't always know or have a name for how they feel. Furthermore, feelings are always embedded in contexts that include personal and cultural expectations, political and family structures, and particular vocabularies of words and gestures. These are self-evident to the writer but must be teased out by the reader.

Consider, for example, the letters of the Renaissance humanist Petrarch, many of which were about old age. Petrarch wanted to present old age, and in particular *his* old age, as he thought best, right and appropriate. That doesn't mean that the feelings he expressed in his letters were not valuable for the historian of emotions. Even the musings of a young girl in a diary meant for her eyes alone will reflect not just her innermost thoughts but the emotional norms that come from the values and traditions of her family, community and larger society. All that is grist for the historian's mill.

Indeed, if properly used, there is only a fine line between 'historical' and 'fictive' materials. Authors of fiction must create whole worlds in which to make their characters believable and meaningful to an audience. They must, in short, create a context within which their works will be read, watched and heard. In addition, playwrights, novelists and fantasists speak to a public; they don't spin out their tales in a vacuum. Indeed, they *cannot* do so because they themselves belong to their own society and culture.

Those societies and cultures change over time, and so do the feelings of the elderly, as we shall see in the chapters to come. In the first, we explore the emotions of (and about) the old in ancient Greece and China, where sons were expected to care for their parents, a practice that engendered love, resentment and joy. Turning in Chapter Two to ancient Rome, we confront a patriarchal culture that so elevated the power and status of the old father that intergenerational tensions provoked rumours of patricide. In the Middle Ages (Chapter Three), regional traditions asserted themselves even as Christianity and Islam inspired feelings suited to their ideals and ideologies. The early modern period (Chapter Four) insisted on the value of labour and had little sympathy for those who did not or could not work. Yet, around the same time in the North American Great Lakes region, the tribes speaking Anishinaabemowin (Ojibwe dialects) accorded to the elderly special and honourable roles. Chapter Five looks at the old in our own day, the heir of all of these traditions. That final chapter chronicles the slow implementation of social security and the fragile claim that the elderly have today on dignity and worth.

In the course of this book, we will see the importance of individual contexts. We will come to understand (for example) why the emotions expressed by the ageing Roman Seneca were very different from those of the late medieval poet Petrarch and why neither had the feelings of Italo Svevo in the twentieth century. Seneca balanced his strong commitment to Stoic calm with service to an impulsive and autocratic emperor. As an old man, he tried to retire from the imperial court in the hopes of cultivating his wisdom. He had to commit suicide instead. Petrarch was part of an affectively connected yet geographically far-flung circle of Italian intellectual elites. He knew about the pains of loneliness and weak joints, but that was not what he emphasized. Rather, he put stress on his tranquil and happy feelings when reading ancient Roman authors. Like them, he hoped to gain fame and glory and to give similar joy to future generations. So along with his tranquillity came admiration and ambition. But Svevo had no imperial privileges and few like-minded friends or ancient companions to give him comfort. He lived when the Italian fascists were on the rise. These were men and women who gloried in violence and dismissed the relevance of the old. Svevo's fictional 'very old man' withdrew into himself in that context, letting off steam and complaints in his secret notebooks.

Yet Seneca, Petrarch and Svevo were alike in at least one way: both faced the last stage of life. Old age comes to us all, gently to some, harshly to others, and (today) often as a shocking surprise. We gain new perspective on this, the final challenge of our lives, by exploring how people in the past felt about their own ageing and that of others. Above all, we learn from history that old age – like all other stages of life – is an emotional enterprise, happy and sad, grateful and bitter, wise and foolish, intense and depleted, full of fear, anger and love.

One
Enjoyment

My grandmother came to the United States from Poland as a teenager. She started to work in a factory, saved money and bought a small candy store in Chicago with my grandfather (another factory worker, he an immigrant from Ukraine). In a few years, they exchanged the candy store for one selling dry goods. All the while, they raised my mother in small living quarters at the back of the store. Eventually, they purchased an apartment building, with my grandfather doubling as the janitor. After my grandfather died, my grandmother sold the building and retired. Around that time, in her sixties, she told me, 'Work hard when you're young, and you can relax when you're old.'

Her notion of a life of leisure – getting a tan, eating out, playing cards with her friends – was nothing like that of the 'noble swineherd' Eumaeus, slave of the Trojan war hero Odysseus. Yet he might have quoted a similar aphorism. We know about him from 'Homer', the name we give to the person or persons who produced the epic poems *Iliad* and *Odyssey* in roughly the form we now have. That written version was probably fixed in the seventh century BCE, even as its long-evolving oral tradition continued.

Unlike my grandmother, Eumaeus lived in a largely agricultural world in which he was one of many pig-herders. Nevertheless, he knew about cities of a sort – called *poleis* (sing. *polis*). Each constituted a walled community organized into households with common laws, customs and cults. Each was ruled by a leader (*basileus*), the man pre-eminent among the elites of the city. Eumaeus' master was the leader Odysseus. Owner of extensive farms and many herds (including the pigs tended by Eumaeus), Odysseus commanded numerous dependents and followers. When he went to war, they went with him. By the time we meet Eumaeus in the poem, Odysseus had been away from Ithaca with his men for twenty years – ten fighting the Trojan War, another ten in adventures both dangerous and amorous on his way home. Meanwhile, his position in Ithaca was being challenged by many suitors of his wife, Penelope. Rarest of women, she has managed to hold them off by clever ruses.

Although Homer rarely mentioned free farmers, there must have been many such in the Homeric age. Eumaeus hoped to join them one day. Although he was only a lowly pig-herder and a slave, he earned the poet's epithet 'noble' (*dios*), and he demonstrated that innate nobility with the fine pens he built for his animals and with his loyalty to the absent leader. As he ruefully told a decrepit old visitor (Odysseus at last back home, but in disguise),

> My real lord is kept from home by gods.
> He would have taken care of me, and given
> what kindly owners give to loyal slaves:
> a house with land, and a wife whom many men
> would want – as recompense for years of labor
> which gods have blessed and made to prosper. Master
> would have been good to me, if he had stayed
> here till old age.[1] (*Od.* 14.61–9)

My grandmother relied on her savings; Eumaeus on his master. But both looked forward to a reward for their hard work in their final years. Eumaeus may have spent his life taking care of his master's pigs, but his winter dream was a farm of his own and a beautiful, virtuous wife.

For his part, Odysseus had a very different – though equally pleasurable – vision of his own final years. He was *already* well-endowed with property, and his wife, Penelope, was indeed 'a woman whom many men would' – and did – 'want'. He could have chosen to remain 'ageless and immortal' with the beautiful nymph Calypso, whom he met on his return journey from Troy, but he chose otherwise (*Od.* 5.136). True, at first, he was happy to stay with her, and *she* wanted him to become her husband and remain with her forever. But eventually he tired of her and longed to go back home. Calypso couldn't understand him. She knew that he would suffer many more hardships if he left her. And as for seeing his wife, who was there waiting for him, well, the goddess could justly boast, 'I know my body is better than hers is' (*Od.* 5.211–12). Odysseus agreed:

> You are quite right. I know my modest wife
> Penelope could never match your beauty.
> She is a human; you are deathless, ageless.
> But even so, I want to go back home. (*Od.* 5.216–19)

Didn't he know that ageing brings frailty, diminution of strength and eventually death? Of course he did! But, a bit like Eumaeus in his own way, he looked forward to a status that younger men could not have, what the shade of Tiresias prophetically described as a 'gentle death . . . of comfortable old age, your people flourishing' (*Od.* 11.136). Old age gave men like Odysseus – heroes on the battlefield; leaders of other men; owners of slaves, servants and animals; wedded to a faithful wife – satisfactions that no eternal life with Calypso could offer.

Odysseus' old father, Laertes, might have exemplified a 'comfortable old age' if he had not missed his son so badly over their twenty-year separation that he deteriorated conspicuously, dressing like a peasant and 'wallowing in grief' (*Od.* 24.233). But once his son arrived, he revived. At Odysseus' behest, he bathed, and then the goddess Athena 'made him grow taller and more muscular' (*Od.* 24.367). He had formerly been a glorious warrior, and now his strength returned for one final triumph: when Odysseus' enemies attacked, it was Laertes who hurled the spear that killed the leader of Penelope's erstwhile suitors, a happy winter dream indeed.

Thus, while the Homeric slave dreamt of a farm and a wife, the Homeric warrior's dream was to remain a force on the battlefield. That ideal continued to have an allure long after military heroes were outmoded. But even ageing Homeric warriors usually realized that they could no longer throw spears. They had to find a different talent, that of the wise counsellor. In the *Iliad*, old Nestor took on that role with pleasure. Though still keeping his war-gear near his bed, he excelled as the calm conciliator of headstrong young fighters. If he regretted losing the strength of his younger years, he nevertheless appreciated the dignity of his new role:

> No way do the gods grant mortals all things at once –
> Then I was young, but now old age is my companion.
> Even so, I shall go round the mounted fighters, instruct them
> with words of counsel: that is an old man's right.[2]
> (*Il.* 4.320–4)

Only an old man could – and would – take the time to find the right words to soothe impulsive youths. Sometimes the younger set found Nestor irritating. Telemachus, Odysseus' son, was one. He stopped off at the old king's palace to get news of his long-absent father, but Nestor's insistent hospitality got on his nerves. That 'persistence', however, was another privilege of ancient Greek elders. They were *expected* to slow down and do the right thing. In the case of Nestor, that meant offering excessive hospitality.

And in the case of Priam, the old king of Troy in the *Iliad*, it meant humbling himself when he had to. That moment came when Achilles, the great Greek hero, killed and desecrated the body of Priam's dearest son, Hector. To give his son proper funeral rites, Priam had to reclaim the corpse (illus. 8). Taking his life in his hands, entering enemy territory with a 'heart of iron', he 'approached Achilles,/ embraced his knees, and kissed his hands – those terrible/ murderous hands, that had killed so many of his sons' (*Il.* 24.477–9). Achilles was amazed. How had Priam penetrated Greek defences as if they were soft butter? How could he humiliate himself so? Nor did Priam stop with the embrace. Like Nestor, he found just the right words to move the young warrior. 'Remember your own father, godlike Achilles,/ whose years equal mine, on old age's deathly threshold' (*Il.* 24.485–6). In that way, the Homeric old man worked a sort of magic that no warrior's strength could accomplish. For, just as Nestor knew how to persuade, so Priam

> stirred in Achilles the urge to weep for his father:
> he took the old man by the hand, gently pushed him away.
> Both had their memories . . .
> their joint mourning resounded throughout the hut.
> (*Il.* 24.507–12)

Like a great actor, Priam was capable of arousing overwhelming feelings in both himself and his audience. That, too, was an old man's – and a poet's – prerogative.

After he had had his fill of grief, Achilles consoled the old king by reminding him of the bleak human condition in general, for all were subject to the inexplicable will of the high god Zeus:

> That's how the gods spun life's thread for unhappy
>   mortals –
> to live amid sorrow, while they themselves are uncaring.
> There are two great jars, sunk down in the floor of
>   Zeus's abode,
> full of gifts he hands out, one of ills, the other of blessings;
> and the man who gets a mixed handout from thundering
>   Zeus
> will sometimes encounter trouble, and sometimes good
>   luck. (*Il.* 24.525–30)

There was honour in old age for Homeric men.

Even ageing Homeric women could exercise a kind of wisdom – though not always successfully. Foreseeing doom for her son, Priam's aged wife, Hecuba, added her own dramatic pleas to her husband's admonitions to their son: do not subject yourself to Achilles' pitiless spear. Reminding her boy that she had once nursed him, she 'opened her dress with one hand, in the other held out her breast,/ as, weeping, she addressed him' (*Il.* 22.80–81). Hector, however, did not listen to his parents.

Equally wise, Odysseus' old slave Eurycleia asserted her dignity and had better success. Purchased when a girl by Laertes, she had raised Odysseus and later Odysseus' son, Telemachus. She loved both devotedly. When Odysseus returned home and was disguised well enough to fool Eumaeus and his own wife, old Eurycleia alone recognized his identity as she gave him a stranger's welcome by bathing him:

> Both joy and grief
> took hold of her. Her eyes were filled with tears;
> her voice was choked. She touched his beard and said,
> 'You are Odysseus! My darling child!' (*Od.* 19.471–4)

But Odysseus, savagely unsentimental and anxious that his identity remain secret, grabbed her around the throat and threatened her with death should she let out a word. Eurycleia didn't miss a beat: 'What have you said! You know/ my mind is firm, unshakable;/ I will remain as strong as stone or iron' (*Od.* 19.493–4).

The words of the poet Sappho (*fl.* 600 BCE) were equally resolute, though not in response to a threatening master but rather to looming old age itself. In one of her poems, she presents the persona (likely herself) of a song and dance-mistress past her prime. Her body, once so lithe and graceful, is failing her. Graciously yielding the stage to her young acolytes, she accepts the inescapable fate of a human being:

> You, children, pursue the violet-laden Muses' lovely gifts,
> and the clear-toned lyre so dear to song;
>
> but for me – old age has now seized my once tender body,
> and my hair has become white instead of black;
>
> my heart has grown heavy, and knees do not support
> that once were fleet for the dance like little fawns.
>
> How often I lament these things. But what to do?
> Being Human, one cannot escape old age.
>
> For people used to say that rose-armed Dawn, overtaken by love,

> took Tithonus, handsome and young then, and carried
> him off to the world's end.
>
> Yet in time grey age still seized him,
> though husband of immortal wife.³

She laments, to be sure. Dance and song are the sacred gifts of the Muses. But old age cannot be avoided. Think of Tithonus, once so young, handsome and beloved by the goddess Aurora that she called on Zeus to grant him eternal life. Unfortunately, she forgot to ask as well for eternal youthfulness. Tithonus withered away until nothing was left of him but his babble.

Elder-Politics in the Polis

In the course of the sixth century, the leadership of the polis devolved from one-man rule to governance by many – and in some places by all. The authority of the Homeric hero (Odysseus, for example) gave way to the ascendancy of a community. Old men and women felt the consequences of these changes.

Let us concentrate on old age at Athens, a slave-owning democracy and the centre of Greek literature and culture in the fifth century. Free Athenian males gained political and social heft as they got older. At age eighteen they became citizens, began military training and became eligible for the ruling body, the Assembly. At twenty, they were liable for army service whenever the Assembly voted for a military campaign. For each campaign, a few generals were chosen from a group of ten, and they in turn conscripted male citizens. Theoretically, hoplites (infantry who fought in close formation) could be called up until age 58, but younger, more vigorous men were no doubt favoured.

At age thirty an Athenian citizen could become a juror and a magistrate. Most men married around that age and set up their own households, hoping for sons. When those sons had grown and were themselves married men, their fathers generally handed their property over to them. In that sense there were three ages of an Athenian man – youth, adulthood and old age – although Athenian poet, aristocrat, statesman and lawgiver Solon (d. *c.* 560 BCE) theorized ten such ages, and other writers proposed different numbers.

There were also three ages for 'respectable' women: maidenhood – which ended with marriage at around age fourteen – motherhood and old age. While their *domestic* power was greatest during their fertile years, those were also the years in which they were generally confined to the house. (To be sure, many wives found ways around that restriction, and nearly all participated in various religious festivals in the city, including some for women only.) Once they reached menopause, even married women were quite free to go out. Lower-class women were probably less cosseted throughout their lives.

Fragments from the laws of Solon suggest that he instituted a sort of family-financed social security for the old called *gerotrophia* ('elder care', we would say). His laws were based on charming analogies: 'When the father stork has brought up all his [offspring] and made them ready to fly, then must those young support the father in their turn.' And when the lion's offspring go off to the hunt, they let their father rest, but after 'they have captured enough for themselves and for their father . . . the young call the old'.[4] Adult children were expected to continue being solicitous even of their deceased parents, providing for their funerals and keeping their memories alive. Pleasing as were Solon's fables, they carried a punch because (at least by the fifth century) citizens convicted of neglecting their parents lost the rights of citizenship – a very severe punishment.[5]

In addition to laws, Solon wrote poems, some of which illuminate the ethical foundations of his legislation. The polis of Athens, he said, was not a conglomeration of disparate individuals but a moral community in which citizens were ultimately responsible for one another. Of course, they were unequal in wealth, birth and prestige. Nevertheless, all – no matter their riches – were governed by the same laws. Faction – rich against poor, powerful against weak – gnaws at a city and violates Justice. Intergeneration conflict – fathers who do not teach their sons, sons who do not attend to their fathers – flouts Nature.

Yet such conflict was imbedded in old traditions. Before Solon's time, Hesiod (*fl. c.* 700 BCE) predicted a dire fate for the elderly of his day, as the young will

> treat their parents with disdain as soon as they are old,
> Heartlessly finding fault with them in accents harsh
>   and cold;
> And ignorant of the punishment the gods mete, as
>   they are,
> They'll not be likely to repay parents for their care.[6]

And the problem of intra-city strife, including discord between young and old, grew greater in the course of the fifth century. As Athens democratized and Sophists began to tutor would-be leaders of the polis, persuasive orators displaced men of the traditional aristocracy. Trained to sway others to their point of view, Sophists were the 'influencers' of their day. Brash, glib and charismatic, they upset the Athenian Nestors – men who thought that the prestige of their long life and wide experience should trump cocksure upstarts.

That helps explain why conservative Athenians envied Sparta, where (or so they thought) the elderly were given the authority that they deserved. Writing after Solon's filial laws had lost much of their grip, Xenophon (d. before 350 BCE) asked rhetorically, 'When will Athenians show the ... Spartan respect for their elders seeing that they despise all their elders, beginning with their own fathers?'[7] In Sparta, he marvelled, old men ruled, and the young deferred to them.

Was that true? Sparta was a closed society, adept at spreading rumours about itself but keeping mum about what was really going on. Even today, most of the information we have about Sparta was written by non-Spartans. This is what some historians call the 'Spartan mirage', the image that it left behind, which either blames or praises but rarely analyses.

Yet even distortions may sometimes be sifted for realities. For example, it is quite certain that Spartan male citizens lived in army barracks until age fifty. It is also true that they could enter the *gerousia* (Council of Elders), a major deliberative body, only at the age of sixty.

However, there is another reality: that Council was restricted to 28 men plus Sparta's two kings. Obviously, not *all* old Spartan men past the age of sixty were admitted into it. In fact, membership was open only to the elite – and not every one of them. According to Plutarch (d. after 119 CE, but presumably drawing on earlier materials), when there were vacancies in the Council, the eligible men who wished to be elected presented themselves, one by one, to an assembly of citizens. Those receiving the loudest shouts (as determined by a select group of judges) were welcomed into the *gerousia* with tenure for life.

Afterward, Plutarch continued, the victor 'set a wreath upon his [own] head and visited in order the temples of the gods. He was followed by great numbers of young men, who praised and extolled him, as well as by many women, who celebrated his excellence in songs, and dwelt on the happiness of his life.'[8] Surely that experience fulfilled the victor's most delightful winter dreams. But how did the men who were *not* elected feel? And what were the feelings of the many old men who never presented themselves to the judges in the first place?

In the poetry of the Spartan Tyrtaeus (*fl.* mid-seventh century), the warrior who shows great bravery while young will find nothing but honour and joy in his old age. 'He stands out among the townsmen; no one seeks to deprive him of respect and his just rights, but all men at the benches yield their place to him, the young, those of his own age and the elders.'[9] But this passage also suggests that less battle-hardened old men might be disfavoured. And in another poem Tyrtaeus says that when a white-haired man falls to the enemy, he is a 'shameful sight', whereas a young man dead on the battlefield is beautiful.[10]

To be sure, the evidence suggests that elderly men held disproportionate power at Sparta, whether or not they were in the Council. Plutarch says that they decided which Spartan infant might live or die. They supervised the education of the young; they could stop boys on the street to interrogate them or order them about. They watched youths exercising at the gyms and critiqued them harshly.

The Spartans supposedly prided themselves on not revealing their emotions, although that too might be part of the Spartan mirage. But the topic is worth our brief consideration. Surely elderly men there 'felt powerful'. Feeling powerful has no place in most modern psychologist's list of emotions. Yet, like love and honour, it is pleasurable when gained and painful when lost. It can also be so intense that it may lead bosses to fire a good worker who does not pay them sufficient deference. That is why Solon wanted power to be tempered by his laws.

Within middle-class families in Europe and the Americas today, feeling powerful, with its concomitant pride and sense of entitlement, is rarely an experience of ageing. But it must have been a very important feeling for a segment of elderly male Spartans. As we shall see, first and foremost from plays written in Athens, there were plenty of powerful old men and women there as well. But their pleasurable feelings of power had to contend with youthful distrust and ridicule of elders. Indeed, Aristotle said that the pleasure gained from 'feeling superior' (*hubris*) was characteristic of *young* people! Since no source for Sparta admitted to any intergenerational tension there, outsiders looking in imagined that young Spartans felt reverent, obedient and worshipful towards their elders. Some concluded that that was why the Spartans remained disciplined and virtuous, while the Athenians 'grew careless of themselves, and have thus become degenerate' (Xenophon, §13). For such observers, talking about the old and young in Sparta was a way to critique Athens.

Eldercare in China

Had the Athenians known about Chinese society at around the same time, they would have found a more convincing and better-attested model of deference to the elderly. Confucius (551–479 BCE), much like his near-contemporary Solon, considered eldercare essential to social and political well-being. However, unlike Solon, he did not imagine it could be enforced through laws. The China of his day, while theoretically ruled by the Zhou dynasty (c. 1100–256 BCE), was in fact made up of a multitude of states where no one law held sway. If changes were to come, they would have to emanate from the men with influence and power at the dynastic courts. But such men were not interested in the good of all; they looked no further than to the welfare of their own noble class.

Confucius, who was not noble, taught that only men trained to serve the general good should be the counsellors of rulers. Grooming himself to become a gentleman bureaucrat, he gained the knowledge, skills and nobility of character that made his advice essential to every prince. And he taught his disciples to train themselves in the same way. They formed a new class of men nurtured on morality and ready to make China's leaders more just, ethical and responsive to the needs of their subjects. Eventually, Confucianism became central to the political foundations of the dynasties that followed the Zhou: the Qin (221–209 BCE) and the Han (206 BCE–220 CE). The Qin unified Chinese administration, while in the second half of the second century BCE, Han Emperor Wu made Confucianism the ideology of the state.

Already before Confucius' day, the legitimacy of a dynasty rested not only on right by conquest but on the approbation of its ancestors and the favour of the supreme deity from whom those ancestors sprang. The Zhou claimed the favour of a god who approved the perfection of their rituals. They sacrificed to their ancestral spirits, dressed in proper clothing and behaved in appropriate ways toward others while also excelling in the emotional sincerity and spontaneity with which they were supposed to carry out those duties. All this was summed up in the word *xiao*, piety toward the ancestors.

Confucius added to the meaning of *xiao* by emphasizing the importance of sustaining, obeying and respecting *parents* and, by extension, elders in general. The *Xiaojing*, the classic Confucian writing on family reverence, tells good – that is 'filial' – children to serve their parents daily. *That* is showing 'real respect'.[11] Their service is to be constant: children must tend to their parents' needs, strive to give them joy and care for them when they fall ill (illus. 12).

Soon filial piety was regarded as the pillar of good order not only within families but in societies and states. Almost from the start of the *Analects*, a canonical collection of Confucius' ideas, the tie between the personal and the public was made clear: 'A young person who is filial and respectful of his elders rarely becomes the kind of person who is inclined to defy his superiors, and there has never been a case of one who is disinclined to defy his superiors stirring up rebellion.'[12] Once Confucian thought became the ideology of the state under Emperor Wu, candidates for official offices competed not only to prove their loyalty to the ruler and his ancestors but to offer evidence of their exceptional filial piety.

The *Analects* pretended that there was no contradiction between the care sons owed to their parents and the loyalty, obedience and reverence that was required of them when they set out (often far from home) to serve the emperor. But how could they be good sons if they were many miles away from their parents, as was frequently required of government officials? Later sources record their guilt about abandoning their familial elders.

Thus, in ancient China *xiao* was a very complex emotion that pulled in two directions – one toward the domestic hearth, the other toward the imperial court. Brought up with the expectation of filial piety, children absorbed its emotional demands and felt the required feelings. And if they did not, simply going through the rituals of *xiao* would evoke the genuine sentiments, in a sort of feedback loop. One way or another, in ancient China young people felt respectful of and concerned about the elderly, and those feelings were tied to – but also in conflict with – their loyalty to the state.

In an autobiographical section of his *Analects* Confucius said, 'At fifteen, I set my mind upon learning; at thirty, I took my place in society [by mastering the rituals]; at fifty, I understood Heaven's Mandate; at sixty, my ear was attuned; and at seventy, I could follow my heart's desires without overstepping the bounds of propriety' (2.4). Ageing was empowering, the culmination of ethical training. It felt good to be old. It certainly felt better than to be young and constantly worried about one's parents. On the other hand, later sources suggest that the obligation that sons live near their elders backfired, for some young people insisted that their parents relocate with them as their state duties shifted. This was hard on old people with roots back home.[13]

Feeling Old in Athens

Athenian sons were not in service to an emperor and did not have to force their parents to move away from home. Solon's filial tenets were no doubt easily honoured when conservative traditions remained unchallenged and prosperity reigned in the city. That was the case in the first half of the fifth century, when many things Greek – grain, wine, money (above all money) – poured into Athens. By mid century, the city had gained an 'empire', dominating and collecting tribute from other nominally independent poleis. Most of them were coastal cities or islands in the Aegean, for the navy of Athens was the source of its power.

Sparta, the other major power in Greece, watched Athenian expansion with dismay. An inland polis, Sparta had its own sort of empire and a matchless land army. After minor skirmishes, the two cities fought the long and agonizing Peloponnesian war, which began in 431 and ended with the defeat of Athens in 404 BCE.[14] In the course of that conflict the whole idea of subservience to fathers and the old in general became less and less central to Athenian values. Conservative leaders – not always literally elderly, but advocating older traditions and policies – were increasingly outvoted in favour of audacious politicians who represented action, youth and victory. Near the end of the war the conservatives lashed back, establishing periods of oligarchic rule. Those experiences tore the city apart in bitter factionalism and reprisals. After the war, Athens slowly and painfully revived its democratic institutions, which persisted to some degree even when, in 338, Athens and its allies were defeated by King Philip II of Macedon. The subsequent conquests by Philip's son Alexander the Great ushered in the Hellenistic period (323–31 BCE), when poleis across the Aegean Sea were absorbed into separate post-Alexandrian monarchies even as they formed networks united by their largely common culture. It is telling that even in the 330s or so, one of the criteria for the appointment of an Athenian magistrate was 'whether he treats his parents well'.[15] The old values had eroded but were not defunct.

In the course of the Peloponnesian War, Athenian playwrights explored the feelings of the elderly as well as the feelings others had about them. Dramas were integral to the communal and religious life of the city. Each performance was attended by around 16,000 people, mainly men but perhaps some women too. Each work was performed only once at Athens itself (though possibly repeated elsewhere) during one of its many festivals dedicated to the god Dionysus. The playwrights, chosen by state officials, competed for prizes that were voted on after the performance by members of the audience. Often ordinary citizens (all men, since women were not citizens) joined the actors on stage, supplementing the two or at most three professional actors. The collectivity was further represented by the chorus, which commented on the stage action. That was made up entirely of amateurs drawn from the citizenry, accompanied by one professional musician playing the *aulos* – an oboe-like instrument consisting of two pipes of different pitch played simultaneously. Masks allowed the actors to communicate gender, status and age and, if necessary, to switch from one persona to another.

A seasoned actor knew how to use his mask as well as words, gestures and tones of voice to communicate feelings. And feelings were the main focus of the dramas. This was especially true in tragedies, which endowed the skeletons of well-known myths and stories with the words and emotions that brought them to life.

Euripides (d. 406 BCE), in particular, explored the feelings of the aged. Stressing the poignancy of their weaknesses, he also emphasized their special strengths precisely because they were *not* young. Three of his tragedies were particularly eloquent in this regard: *Alcestis*, *Hecuba* and *Heracles*. Let us concentrate on them.

The earliest, *Alcestis* (438 BCE), is based on a myth about the loving self-sacrifice of Alcestis, wife of Admetus. Because of a decree of the gods, Admetus, king of Thessaly, must die young unless he can find someone to take his place. He expects his parents to step forward. When they refuse, Alcestis volunteers. The elders' rebuff engenders bitter condemnation by all, even by the chorus of old men who represent public opinion. Alcestis, too, denounces the old couple for their treachery. Speaking to her husband, she says,

> your parents both betrayed you. They
> had reached the point where death was best for them –
> to save their child and their reputation
> would have been best.[16] (308–11)

The chorus sings its agreement; Admetus' parents are 'cowards'.

By now the Athenian audience is primed to despise the young king's father, Pheres. No doubt many watching this play and burdened by their ageing fathers sympathized with Admetus. How lucky the mythical Admetus was not to have to worry about Solon's laws! The play seems ready to defy Solon. But suddenly Euripides changes course. For when old Pheres arrives on stage, he does so to bring adornments for the dying woman and to share Admetus' sorrow at the loss of his wife.

He thinks that she, filled with filial piety, acted for *his* sake, so he would not be bereft of a son:

> [Alcestis] gave her very soul
> so you [Admetus] could live, my child.
> She would not leave me childless, let me waste away
> in miserable old age, deprived of you. (651–4)

Admetus is furious. Father and son have a heated argument during which the son disowns his old father, an almost unheard-of step in Athens at the time. Declaring that 'I don't consider myself your son,' Admetus imagines that he has been the best of sons and that his father has been ungrateful and unnatural:

> You cannot claim that I've dishonored you
> in your old age, and that's why you betrayed me
> and left me to die. I have been completely
> reverent toward you – and this is how
> you and my mother have repaid the favor.

Pheres is amazed and furious:

> This is an outrage! Where do you get off
> flinging these childish accusations at me?
> I gave you life, and raised you to be master
> of this estate; I'm not obliged to die to suit your whims.
> (720–22)

Pheres has properly carried out his own side of the familial bargain. To Admetus he has given part of his property and even the royal office that once was his. He intended for his son to inherit everything else. He asks his son, 'how have you been deprived?' (729). 'No ancestral custom ... no Greek law, either' says that parents must die in the place of their children (722–4). A requirement such as that would batter against human nature itself: 'You love to be alive, to see the daylight:/ what makes you think your father doesn't?' (731–2). Turning the tables, Pheres makes his son the coward:

> You . . . got out of dying, shamelessly stayed alive,
> avoided your due fate by killing her.
> *You're* calling *me* a coward? You're the worst!
> You've been outdone by your wife, who had the courage
> to give her own life for her fine young man. (735–40)

Pheres exits in high dudgeon while the old men of the chorus stay on to praise Admetus, bewail the death of Alcestis and rue the self-absorption and indifference of the aged.

In this play, Pheres, the old man, experiences a virtual kaleidoscope of feelings: grief, gratitude, admiration, outrage, anger and above all love of life. He's no different from a youth in any of that. But when the youths of the play (and the old chorus too) look at the old, they see only weakness, debility and exhaustion. To them, elderly people are as good as dead – so why don't they just die? And for a good cause, too. When Pheres refuses, Admetus, the chorus and Alcestis feel nothing but disdain. The Chinese inculcated respect and deference to parents starting in childhood, associating filial piety with a mother's milk. Just as parents nourished their children so children must feed their parents. That was Solon's point as well, though he knew it would be a hard sell. By presenting Pheres as a man of sound mind and keen self-insight, Euripides appealed to his audience to supplement Solon's laws with sentiment. Pheres is no hero. Rather, he models an 'everyman' at the twilight of his life. He's done his bit; he's lived a reasonably moral life (including doing much for his son). He may be 'shameless' in his love of life (that's what

Admetus says), but he is not foolish. He chooses to enjoy life while he has it. After Pheres exits, he is absent for the rest of the play, and the 'hero' Heracles (Hercules) rescues Alcestis from Hades. But the old man has made his point. The old are not expendable.

In a slightly later play, *Hecuba* (c. 424 BCE), Euripides explored the emotional range of an old woman.[17] Although the former queen of Troy is weak and hardly able to walk, she takes vengeance on Polymestor, the man entrusted to protect her youngest son, Polydorus. Greedy for the boy's money, Polymestor has murdered the child instead.

In Euripides' hands, Hecuba manages her revenge in the most challenging possible context: the Greek army camp where she and her entourage are held prisoners as spoils of war. Recall that Homer's Hecuba bared her breast to her son, as if the memory of nursing him would get him to abandon his resolve to fight Achilles. Now in Euripides' play, she has more tricks than motherhood up her sleeve. Her captor, Agamemnon, leader of the Greek army, laughs at her desire to avenge Polydorus.

> How?
> Poison? Or do you think your aged hand
> could lift a sword and kill? Who would help you?
> On whom could you count? (875–8)

He thinks she is unfit for action. Not only is she old, but she is a woman, essentially a baby-making machine, worth little after menopause (illus. 9). But in his play, Euripides overturns that fantasy. His Hecuba is clever, resourceful and devious.

Defying the expectations of the 'halting footsteps' with which she comes on stage, her lacerating sorrows and her very sex, Hecuba sends for Polymestor, the murderer of her child, along with his sons. She pretends to love him and plies him with honeyed words barbed with double meaning: 'You are my friend, a friend for whom I feel/ no less love than you have shown to me.' (1000–1003) She tells Polymestor that she will reveal to him and his sons the treasure she brought with her from Troy: it is in the tents of her attendants. The miscreant follows her there, and once inside, she and the other captive Trojan women blind him and slay his sons. Polymestor stumbles out, crying for vengeance.

Now Agamemnon sets himself up as judge and jury and has Hecuba and Polymestor litigate their cases before him. Hecuba, brilliantly persuasive, wins the debate and Polymestor is dragged away. Before he goes, he prophesies: Hecuba will turn into a dog, 'a bitch with blazing eyes'. Her tomb will be 'a landmark to sailors' (1265, 1272–3). What does she care?, she tosses back at him. She has had her revenge.

Hecuba's true metamorphosis has nothing to do with becoming a bitch. At the start of the play, she is a weak old woman, decrepit, a helpless (if eloquent) cry-baby. By the end she is a powerful orator, strategist and murderer. Once again Euripides overturns popular prejudices, this time about 'exhausted' old women. Different as Pheres and Hecuba are, both are similar in knowing exactly what they must do. When we first hear about these two old people, we are dismayed – by the weakness of Hecuba, by the selfishness of Pheres. By the time they exit, we appreciate and admire them.

In his even later drama *Heracles* (c. 415 BCE), Euripides makes old age an antidote to the madness of power.[18] At the start of the play, Amphitryon, Heracles' earthly father (his heavenly one is Zeus) is too old to wield a spear. The chorus, representing the old men of Thebes, consists of mere 'ghosts that walk . . . trembling with age' (111–12). Yet if someone doesn't quickly save Heracles' wife and young sons, a bloodthirsty tyrant who has just seized power in Thebes will kill them. What's keeping

Heracles from coming to the rescue? Everyone expects him to return home from one of his amazing labours to save his family.

To the horror of all, when he returns, he becomes the insane murderer of his wife and children, leaving only old Amphitryon to pick up the pieces:

CHORUS LEADER
Here the old man comes, moving along
with heavy steps, mourning in bitterness
like some bird whose unfledged covey is slain. (1039–41)

When the mad Heracles falls into a deep slumber, Amphitryon ties him up. Then, as the sleeper begins to awaken, the old man tells everyone to run away. He doesn't know if this hero-turned-familicide is still crazy. He alone has the courage to remain. When he sees that Heracles' spell of madness has ended, he explains to his son the bloody carnage surrounding them. Putting his finger on his son's mortal defect and its solution as well, he wails:

O my son, I implore you,
by your beard, your knees, your hand,
by an old man's tears:
tame that lion of your rage that roars you on to death,
yoking grief to grief. (1208–13)

Violent anger is the foundation of both Heracles' astounding virtue and horrific crimes. It is the characteristic mistake of a younger man. By contrast, Amphitryon's weakness gives him the strength of sanity and love. The illustration here (illus. 2) expresses a bit of what Euripides wants to show about old men, although it was sculpted after Greece had fallen to Macedon, some decades after the death of the playwright. It portrays an

2 Grave marker, 'Ilissos stele', 340–30 BCE, marble. The young man (a hunter) is sculpted as a classical hero, calm and unemotional. It is the old man who expresses brooding thoughts and feelings.

old man contemplating a dead youth, likely his son. The young man is depicted as a hero: all muscle and masculine beauty, his eyes look out impassively from his funeral stele. Below are a weeping child, perhaps the dead youth's servant, and a hunting dog whose head, too, is bowed in grief. By contrast, the old man, his hair and beard unkempt, is bent. Holding a staff to help him walk, he gazes thoughtfully at the image of the deceased. He is not so much a figure of sorrow as of deep reflection.

Euripides' plays demand that people who are weak and need help to walk be recognized even so for their wisdom and competence. Pheres refuses to be bullied; Hecuba avenges the death of her son; Amphitryon confronts the aftermath of a massacre. Their feelings are well ordered: Pheres cares for his son, honours his daughter-in-law and looks out for himself. Hecuba upends expectations about old women with her own good priorities: her love for her son and her determination to avenge him. Amphitryon is able to mourn his dead daughter-in-law and grandchildren and yet love their murderer at the same time. His emotional capaciousness makes him the true hero of *Heracles*.

There must have been at least a minority at Athens who admired these challenging dramas, for Euripides' plays were chosen again and again for the Dionysian festivals. On the other hand, they rarely won prizes.

THE COMIC PLAYWRIGHT Aristophanes (d. c. 385 BCE), some of whose works overlapped in time of composition with those of Euripides, did not make his old characters admirable. To the contrary, he made fun of the elderly and yet made ageing sound like a lot of fun. He did both by trading on growing tensions between the old and young. As we saw, Hesiod and Solon already worried about this, and Euripides' *Alcestis* featured a whole household itching for an old man's death. But the Peloponnesian War tore Athens apart politically, and the political opportunists who came to the fore during that time exacerbated the generation gap.

Already at the war's start in 425, Aristophanes saw the writing on the wall when, in the *Acharnians*, he orchestrated the lament of the 'tough old geezers' (180) from Acharnai, an Athenian subdivision:[19]

> We who are old, ancient, we blame the city.
> For we are not tended to by you in our old age,
>   in a manner worthy of the naval battles we fought, but
>   instead suffer terribly.

Some throw old men into indictments
and let them be ridiculed by youthful orators. (676–80)

A bit later, in the *Wasps* (422), the playwright highlighted generational tension in a play about a father and a son.[20] The great joy of old Procleon is to serve on an Athenian jury and to follow Cleon, a pitiless prosecutor, by imposing the most extreme penalty on everyone who comes to trial. Procleon is so addicted to this task that he daily foils every attempt by his son, Contracleon, to prevent him from attending court. The son tries to seal his house; the old father finds ingenious ways to escape, climbing through the water pipes, squeezing under the roof tiles, popping out of the chimney.

The names of these two scrappers (in the original Greek, *Philocleon*, lover of Cleon, and *Bdelycleon*, loather of Cleon) reveal the underlying source of their tension: the charisma of the vengeful orator Cleon. From the pens of Aristophanes and the historian Thucydides, we have a very negative view of that effective politician. In the *Wasps*, Cleon wows the jurors with fearful and specious arguments so that they will vote 'guilty'. For Thucydides and other conservative Athenians, Cleon is an upstart, the son of a tanner, who rises to power via his brash and effective oratory. He symbolizes the beginning of a sea-change in the political culture of Athens. The older generation of leaders had been well-born, cautious, thoughtful and deliberate. The younger vulgarians who arrive afterwards, men like Cleon, are keen to act. No long discussions, waffling or reconsidering! By the lights of the older generation, Cleon is a self-serving demagogue. He attacks the Athenians for being swayed by every seductive argument. Yet he himself is the pre-eminent master of the persuasive arts.

Cleon delights the old men – Procleon and his buddies, a chorus of aged jurors with large stingers on their behinds. They are the wasps. The courts are a great way for Procleon and other old-timers to exercise deadly political power. In other ways, too, Procleon entirely upsets the right order of things. While his son adheres to the laws of Solon and tries to take care of his father, Procleon acts out the implications of Cleon's brashness. The son is the true, sober, upright, conservative parent; the father is the child. Procleon cares nothing about manners or morals or what others think. Like a stereotypical Athenian youth, he gets drunk, tells dirty jokes and beats people up when they get in his way. He wants to take a flute girl home with him: 'I tell you what, my little honey-pot,/ you be nice to me, and as soon as my son dies, I'll buy your freedom, then we/ can be together forever' (1351–3).

He's all aflame for sex, and that's hilarious because, in the ancient Greek view (and long afterwards as well), sex was for young men. Fathers feel love; they don't *make* love. But in the *Wasps*, Procleon whips out the large phallus attached to the front of his leotard and asks the flute girl to pull on it and kiss it: 'You're making this very hard for me, my dear,' he quips (1350). She laughs, and no doubt the audience does too. An old man's sexuality is either non-existent or ludicrous.

We see the comedy of old women's sexuality too, in Aristophanes' *Women of the Assembly* (c. 392 BCE). When he wrote it, Athens had been defeated by Sparta and, although its democracy had been very recently restored, it was much enfeebled. In this comedy, women disguise themselves as men and take over the Athenian assembly. They are determined to save the state by declaring total equality, the abolition of private property, the eradication of marriage and free sex. Won't men take advantage of that freedom to choose only the pretty young girls? No, for the law declares that all the ugly ones must be made love to first! Now on the make, one old lady sings:

> Maturer women understand finesse
> better than girls do. No one knows the art of pleasuring
>   a love-boy
> so well as I. Mademoiselles
> fuck once and fly away to someone else.

But her young rival retorts:

> You, horrid crone,
> all trimmed and tweezed and plastered over with
> foundation, are the darling honeybun
> of Death.[21]

These are funny plays. But Aristophanes' the *Clouds*, written much earlier (423 BCE), casts a far darker shadow on the feelings of the old. Here old Strepsiades, a name meaning 'son of Twister', is badly in debt because his son, Pheidippides, meaning 'spare the horses', is constantly buying stallions and chariots for the races. True to his name, Strepsiades wants his son to learn the twisty, new-fangled arguments taught by the 'clever souls' at the Pondertorium. The teachers there are the orators, the sophists and – as we shall see – the 'Socrateses' of the time. They will teach Pheidippides how to 'twist justice' and get his father out from under the thumb of his creditors. Pheidippides is horrified: What? join 'that godforsaken bunch/ of pasty looking frauds, going around barefoot!/ You're talking about Socrates and Chaerephon!' (102–4).[22]

Since his son refuses, Strepsiades will have to go. He starts but then stops. He doesn't feel up to it. 'Oh, I'm just a stupid old fool. How on earth can I be expected/ to learn all those hair-splitting arguments at my age?/ I'm far too old and my mind's certainly not what it used to be' (128–30). Poor Strepsiades: he is too muddled to see through the tomfoolery that 'Socrates', the head teacher of the Pondertorium, tries to teach him, and he can't pick up enough of it to help him twist justice around.

At last, the old man convinces Pheidippides to go to the school in his stead. There the young man learns how to overcome the arguments of morality, justice and compassion with those of expediency and self-interest. Aristophanes offers two sparring characters, Superior Argument and Inferior Argument, who debate the value of the old forms of education against the new. Superior Argument asserts that Justice exists and resides with the gods, but he is quickly bested by Inferior Argument, who counters that the gods themselves never get punished for *their* injustices.

Quickly schooled, Pheidippides frees his father from his debts. But he also beats up the old man for preferring the plays of Aeschylus to those of Euripides. The son justifies his behaviour by arguing that since the old are now in their second childhood, they should be disciplined like children. When Strepsiades objects that 'there's not a place in the world where it is legitimate for a son to beat his father', Pheidippides points out that laws are made by men. He is now declaring his own law (1420). He has learned the sophists' arguments all too well.

Before they attended the Pondertorium, father and son had teased each other playfully, the elder for his son's constant need for money, the younger for his father's incessant worry. Once the son learns the tricks of Inferior Argument, he demeans his father. The two literally stage the growing alienation between generations that was happening all around them as the demagogues, masters of Inferior Argument, became the political darlings of Athens.

Socrates in and out of the Pondertorium

If Socrates (d. 399 BCE) didn't mind a 'roasting', he probably laughed during the performance of *Clouds*. After all, Athens was still a democracy when that play was performed, and Socrates had not been relegated to a Pondertorium except in a fantasy. In fact, he freely walked the streets of Athens and its environs, ready to talk to anyone who would not mind having a long discussion with him, and often trailing behind him a group of disciples and hangers-on.

We see him in this mode at the start of Plato's *Republic*. Socrates never wrote anything down, but his admirer Plato (d. 347 BCE) made up for that, often giving Socrates a starring role in his works. These took the form of dialogues, dramas and narratives, one of which was the *Republic*, where Socrates is the narrator.

The *Republic* begins with an old man, Cephalus, and the entire drama takes place at the house of Cephalus, a wealthy Syracusan who had settled in Athens and owned a shield factory there. The fact that Cephalus bows out of the discussion early is important, given that at bottom the *Republic* is about the gap between immutability (signified by Socrates' desire to understand the meaning of Justice) and mortality (symbolized by Cephalus).

When Socrates first enters the house, he sees the old man 'sitting on a sort of cushioned chair with a wreath on his head, as he had been offering a sacrifice'.[23] Socrates notices that Cephalus has aged. (Socrates was probably middle-aged when the *Republic* supposedly took place.) Cephalus greets the philosopher by bringing up his infirmities: 'You ought to come here more often, for you should know that as the physical pleasures wither away, my desire for conversation and its pleasures grows . . . Stay with these young men now, but come regularly to see us.' (328d) Indeed, many 'young men' – Cephalus' sons and their friends – are present, excited by the prospect of soon watching a festival for a new god that has just arrived in Athens' harbour.

But Socrates was at the moment more interested in the old man. 'Indeed, Cephalus, I replied, I enjoy talking with the very old, for we should ask them, as we might ask those who have traveled a road that we too will probably have to follow, what kind of road it is, whether rough and difficult or smooth and easy.' (328d–e) Cephalus is happy to answer. He says that most old people 'complain about the lost pleasures they remember from their youth ... Others moan about the abuse heaped on old people by their relatives.' (329a)

But Cephalus refuses to moan. He has loving sons around him, and apart from the 'mad master' of sexual desire, he had always lived moderately and contentedly. Now – with that randy despot no longer in charge – 'old age ... is only moderately onerous.' (328d) But neither the forgoing of sexual pleasures nor the abuse of the elderly is the point that intrigues Socrates. Rather, he fixes on Cephalus' relative contentment. Isn't his easy life due to his wealth? Not really, Cephalus replies: wealth is useful, but only because it 'does a lot to save us from having to cheat or deceive someone against our will and from having to depart for [Hades] in fear because we owe sacrifice to a god or money to a person'. (331b) He's been a good man; he isn't worried about punishment in the netherworld.

In denying that he fears death, Cephalus sets himself off from the general run of men. Normally, he avers, 'when someone thinks his end is near, he becomes frightened and concerned about things he didn't fear before. It's then that the stories we're told about Hades, about how people who've been unjust here must pay the penalty there – stories he used to make fun of – twist his soul this way and that for fear they're true.' (330d) In this recital, fear goes from mild concern to the intense pain of a soul twisted like a corkscrew. Cephalus (or, more precisely the persona of Cephalus presented by Plato) obviously has thought a good bit about this feeling. But Socrates doesn't focus on that point either. Rather he challenges Cephalus on the issue of justice, adding to the old man's words by pretending that they also included 'telling the whole truth'. (331c) He gives an example in which telling the truth would be a terrible mistake. One of Cephalus' sons jumps in, and the old man takes the occasion to excuse himself from the discussion in order to attend to a sacrifice.

It would be easy to fault Cephalus for bowing out and blame senility or stupidity for his lack of interest in a heady topic. After all, he said he missed the pleasures of conversation, and the one about to unfold promises to be long and productive. On the other hand, his own definition of being a just man included observing due sacrifices 'to a god'. Right when first seeing Socrates he had asked him to return 'another time', no doubt because he knew that this time he was responsible for an additional sacrifice. Readers of the whole *Republic* know that they must metaphorically take a 'thousand-year journey' to learn (in the final sentence) how to 'do well and be happy' (621d). Old Cephalus has made that journey in his own way.

We may say the same of Socrates when, as an old man, he was put on trial for his life. In 399 BCE, with Athens defeated and humiliated, he was tried as a sophist, someone who knew how to make 'the worse argument the stronger', who did not believe in the gods, and who undermined the old order that had once made Athens great (18c).[24]

Socrates was at that point seventy years old. At his court hearing, he pretended not to know the fancy oratory that others used to defend themselves. That strategy was part of the rhetor's trade – it was meant to capture the good will of his hearers. Thus (in Plato's account) Socrates begins his defence speech (his *Apology*) by saying that he will express himself 'in the first words that come to mind, for I put my trust in the justice of what I say' (17c). This was not only a dignified and politically astute move but a wise one given the way of life that Socrates had chosen. Although on one level he was like every other Athenian citizen, with a wife and three children, on another he was not like them at all. He had no 'job' but rather one constant and unpaid occupation – to question all 'those reputed wise' and see if their wisdom bore out their public esteem (21c). It never did. And yet, for Socrates, this work was a 'divine calling'. Its purpose was, in the first place, for him to understand why the Delphic oracle called him 'wise' when he knew he was not. In the second place, he was serving the polis, which *needed* his constant prodding and needling in order not to become indolent, lazy, weak and self-satisfied. He was the city's 'gadfly'.

The certainty that he had lived according to a salutary, just and divine calling buoyed Socrates even after he was condemned to death. If being dead was nothingness, then (he said) he had nothing to fear. If there *was* an afterlife, then he would spend it as he had spent his life in Athens: questioning and probing all who had passed out of this world. He would not flee his city to save his life, as some of his friends urged him to do. If he ran away from the consequences of the verdict against him, would it not be harming the polis and its laws simply because at that moment they wronged him? Would it not be forgetting that 'your country is to be honoured more than your mother, your father, and all your ancestors' (51)?[25]

As Socrates made clear to the friends who were with him to witness his death, his tranquillity was a privilege reserved for philosophers. All their lives they 'study nothing but dying and being dead'. Given that, they naturally are not 'troubled when that came for which they had all along been eagerly practicing' (63e).[26] The beauty of death is that it frees a person from his body, the enemy of philosophy because it 'fills us with passions and desires and fears and all sorts of fancies and foolishness, so that . . . it really and truly makes it impossible for us to think at all' (66c).

This almost rapturous account of the joy of giving up 'passions and desires' – emotions, in other words – makes Socrates a Stoic before the Stoics. But Xenophon offers another story. He says that he learned from Hermogenes, a Socratic disciple, that before his trial Socrates had explained to him why he would put up the sort of defence he subsequently made. He did not choose death because it would leave him free to pursue philosophy. Rather, he said, death is preferable to old age, which is 'the sink into which all distresses flow, unrelieved by any joy'.[27] He would rather be executed.

Aristotle's Wary Old Age

Aristotle (d. 322 BCE) did not think that philosophy was the study of death. To the contrary, he considered it the scrutiny of the here and now. He was interested in the causes of things, why they existed and, above all, what their purpose was – their 'final cause'. The final cause of human beings was happiness. Common people might think that happiness is pleasure. But that could not be right, for it did not take into account the human body in its matter, form and motivation. Aristotle considered all that and concluded that happiness is man's habitual 'activity in accord with virtue' (1199a25).[28] It must derive from the rational choice to practice virtue not just once but consistently throughout life. This is impossible for women and children unless they are under the tutelage of men. It is difficult for young men, too, because, like all living things, they consist of a mixture of hot, cold, dry and moist elements and in their case the hot and moist predominate, hindering their reason. Reason is most potent and clear-eyed when the mixture is well balanced – perhaps starting around age thirty. Aristotle never set an age for the end of that stage of life, but he knew that gradually men (and women and plants and animals) became cold and dry and thus again imbalanced.

That is the process of ageing. Old men no longer have the heat of youth, and their organs, being drier, are weaker. Their senses dry up: they see less clearly and they hear less acutely. Old men who have practised habitual virtue all their lives nevertheless still have the capacity to continue to do so. They may then have a 'happy old age', especially if their ageing is gradual and relatively painless. But even then, their happiness is difficult because their minds are not receiving all the sensory information that their reason needs to make proper choices.

Aristotle spent much time on old men in his *Rhetoric*, offering advice to orators and, more generally, anyone who wanted to persuade others with words.[29] Orators had to come up with winning arguments regarding public policy. Or move a crowd to rejoice or mourn. They might be hired to write the speech for a man who needed to defend himself before a court. The principles of rhetoric that Aristotle outlined needed to take old age into account because old men (think of Procleon) might be making judgments. Or they might need to be defended. Or they might need advice.

Aristotle knew that old people *want* to be happy, but their understanding of what that means is generally based on common beliefs rather than on philosophy. They think that people need wealth, dutiful children, beauty, health, friends and other benefits. They are not entirely wrong: such things are indeed helpful (if, strictly speaking, unnecessary), even for the habitually virtuous. But it's what one *does* with wealth that really matters: 'being wealthy consists more in the use involved than in the possession, for in fact the activity bound up with such things, and their use, is wealth' (1361a). If they don't use their riches for the right activities, old people will be unhappy.

Moreover, their very longevity and physical condition may lead them to be unhappy. They tend to be slow, hesitant, suspicious of others and vindictive because they have experienced enough of life to know how treacherous others may be. If they are tepid emotionally, it is because they are dry and cold. Nevertheless, they are prone to feel fear more intensely than younger men. This is partly because fear is a 'cold' emotion and partly because old people know how quickly good luck can turn bad. It is also why the elderly are miserly. Aristotle was not saying that *every* old man will have these characteristics; he simply wanted orators to know what they *might* have to deal with.

Personal Feelings in Ancient Greece?

Homer, Euripides, Plato and Aristotle knew a lot about the human heart. But they did not write about their own feelings. Perhaps Sappho was an exception. It seems that she wrote verses about her own old age, expressing wry humour and acceptance. Even so, that poem was a work of imagination and art. With that caveat in mind, let us glance at a few other apparent self-revelations.

The Athenian orator Isocrates (d. 338 BCE) was an old man when he composed 'model speeches' for his students to imitate. In one of these fictive orations, written when he was ninety years old, he addressed Philip of Macedon. Taking the part of an old man, he tried to convince Philip to lead a united Greek force against Persia.[30] He knew, he began, that making this argument to a king should by rights be left to a younger man who might actually go to war, but no young man had dared to do so. He would have to take up the verbal cudgels himself.

His speech was convincing, he claimed, precisely because 'I have not decorated it with any grace or adornment in its style. I used to employ such tools when I was younger . . . I am no longer able to accomplish such style because of my age, but I will be satisfied if I can simply set out only the actual situation' (5.27–8). As we have seen, Socrates had already made the same claim in 399 when he was seventy. To some extent, this was a rhetorical trick, comparable to a crack surgeon modestly introducing himself as a country doctor. But it was also an honest attempt to cut through excess verbiage.

The playwright Sophocles (d. 406/5) did not write about himself. But when he was in his mid-eighties he wrote about Oedipus as an old man in *Oedipus at Colonus* (c. 411). It was his only play to feature an elderly person, and it followed by many years his earlier tragedy about the young Oedipus, *Oedipus Tyrannus* (c. 425). The later sequel may tell us something about how Sophocles, not just Oedipus, felt as an old man, especially in the light of a tale told by Cicero (d. 43 BCE). According to this undocumented but intriguing story, Sophocles' children wanted to have him declared mentally incompetent. To prove the contrary, Sophocles read from his latest play, namely the one about old Oedipus. The judges acquitted him.

In his earlier play, Sophocles introduces Oedipus as the king of Thebes and an unmatched hero. In the course of the drama, however, Oedipus learns that he became king by unwittingly and unwillingly killing his father and marrying his mother. Once Oedipus knew what he had done, he undid his kingship by blinding himself. Then he insisted that he be exiled from Thebes as a polluted outcast.

Sophocles' first play about Oedipus leaves him more wretched than any other human being in all the world. His much later play picks up the story years later, in a sacred grove near Athens. Oedipus is a 'blind old man', accompanied by his loyal daughter Antigone (1).[31] Yet, in the course of this late Sophoclean play, Oedipus comes more and more to resemble the original, sighted hero. He now knows a different – a redeeming – fate for himself, determined by the same god who had decreed his miserable destiny at Thebes: he knows that his very presence will bring 'gains to those who'd take me in,/ but doom to those who cast me out and drove me away' (92–3).

He is determined that the lucky ones who take him in will not be Thebans, for (as he explains) they were the people who 'cast him out'. After his initial rage against himself had subsided, he had changed his mind and wished to stay in Thebes. But Creon, the person in power there, would hear none of it. Nor would Oedipus' two sons lift a finger to help him. Forced into exile, he had only his daughter, gentle Antigone, to support him. Later she was joined by her sister, Ismene.

Nothing will soothe his implacable anger against those who sent him from home. When Oedipus' older son, Polyneices, comes to express remorse, begging his father to bring his 'good luck' to Thebes, the old man is furious:

> I curse you again as I did before,
> repeat those curses and call them back to be my allies
> to teach you to honor your parents
> and not scorn the father who begat you
> because he is blind. (1375–9)

This is an old man's bitter diatribe against children who turned against him. He no longer blames himself for his patricide and incest. He had no guilty intent. Oedipus looks back on his life and pronounces it blameless. This is indeed a happy winter dream.

Oedipus' death at the end of this play is a triumph: blind though he is, he finds his own way to his 'sacred tomb'. Because its secret location is just outside of Athens, he will forever be the source of all of that city's blessings. Those blessings were in short supply at Athens after 401, as Sophocles well knew, but his play praises and celebrates the city, which 'believes in justice/ and decides nothing without the law' (913–14). The playwright might well have felt similarly about its decision to protect him from his unfilial children.

CHINESE RULERS THOUGHT about the rituals of deference they owed their ancestors even before Confucius, and Solon made care for parents a key duty of sons. In China the two ideas were fused by Emperor Wu into an ideology of reverence for the ruler and his family. It was so rooted in filial piety that patriotism began at home. Feeling like an old person there should have meant feeling like a king, but we know rather more about the guilt of Chinese sons who could not quite give their parents the ideal care the teachings mandated. We know even less about Spartan feelings, although its institutions should have made its old men feel powerful and its young men eager to get old.

Homer provided satisfying visions of elderly men settling into appropriate roles as husbandmen, counsellors and persuaders. They basked in the admiration of other men and looked back on their lifetime achievements with pride. Plato offered variants on this model. He had Cephalus living with loving sons and relishing his well-earned self-respect. He portrayed Socrates at his trial as the righteous follower of the god's oracle and, in his prison cell, as the wise man surrounded by disciples as he drank the deadly hemlock.

At Athens the winter dreams of the elderly showed that they were a lot more than father figures to whom reverence was due. They were people with emotions and concerns of their own. Pheres loved life; Hecuba had the last laugh; Procleon flirted with a pretty girl and gleefully upset the proper social order; and Socrates and Isocrates knew how to milk their age rhetorically. Aristotle's ideal old man retained enough of his senses and reason to remain virtuous. For citizens protected by the laws of Solon – albeit attenuated by the political effects of the Peloponnesian War – and the pocket money available to aged jurors, old age could be fairly enjoyable.

Two

Acceptance

In 2 BCE, Augustus was declared *pater patriae* – the 'father of his country'. Not long before, Rome had been a Republic, albeit one ruled by an elected elite. Augustus didn't declare the Republic dead; he simply absorbed its men and machinery into his personal 'fatherhood'. For Romans, fathers were potent and sentimental figures. 'Come, dear Father, onto my shoulders now', the Roman poet Virgil (d. 19 BCE) has the Trojan hero Aeneas say to his father as the victorious Greeks are reducing their city to ashes: 'You will not weigh me down, and come what may/ We will face it together, peril or salvation' (2, ll. 833–5).[1] They escape together with Aeneas' son, Ascanius, or rather Julus, to make their way to Italy.

This was propaganda tailor-made for Augustus, for when Virgil wrote his poem the future *pater patriae* was consolidating all governmental power under himself to become the first Roman emperor. His rulership came from the victories of his armies, but it gained legitimacy through his illustrious ancestry. He was the adopted son of Julius Caesar, who belonged to the ancient family of the Julii. That was why Virgil changed Ascanius' name to Julus and why he had Aeneas' father take with him the ancestral gods of their household – the *Penates* – 'the sacred gods of our fathers' (2, l. 844).

Fathers, and sons who became fathers, were the people with power and prestige at Rome. Their authority expressed itself in many ways – legal, emotional, religious, political. Old men had power at Rome, far more than in Athens or China and perhaps Sparta as well. But they were also the objects of far harsher resentments.

Roots

Like a turtle, Aeneas carried his house on his back. In illustration 10, his father rides on his shoulders, carrying in turn a box containing the ashes of the family's ancestors. At his side, Aeneas holds his son's hands. In other representations of the fleeing Aeneas, the household gods sit atop the box. Those gods rooted all the generations in traditions and customs long ratified by time. The statesman Cicero (d. 43 BCE) once asked, 'What is more sacred than each citizen's home? It houses his altars, his hearths, his Penates, his sacrifices.'[2] But he could equally well have said simply that a man's home is the place of the household gods. For the 'hearth' did double duty: it was a source of warmth and it served as the family's altar to the Penates. They were acknowledged at mealtimes and given token offerings – the 'sacrifices' Cicero mentioned. The symbolism of the meal was direct, for the Penates were above all gods of the food stored at home. (The Romans said that the name was derived from *penus*, food, and *penitus*, within.)

The Penates and other household gods anchored the family to its basic needs. At the same time, they linked present generations to their past, since they had been worshipped from time immemorial by the family's ancestors. To Romans – at least the elite Romans about whom we have some information – the ways of the elders (*mos maiorum*) guaranteed morality, prosperity and success. The elders most worthy of honour (those who had been elected to high office during the Roman Republic) continued to 'occupy' the house in the form of wax masks. Melted wax was applied to their faces while they were alive, then peeled off to form a mask. These were kept by future generations as precious relics of their honoured ancestors. At funerals, the masks were taken out and worn, functioning as status symbols; at other times they were kept in a cupboard in the family's reception hall, the most important room in the house.

But the elders *most* present in the household, presiding over it, making its decisions, controlling its wealth, were fathers. Or, perhaps, grandfathers. For the man who held the *patria potestas* – the paternal power – in each family was its oldest living male member. Theoretically he had the power of life and death over his dependents. He had the right to be a despot and to treat his children almost as slaves.

Theoretically, but probably not often in reality. For those paternal rights contended with an equally potent obligation, *pietas*. This was the sentiment of respect, compassion and even affection that fathers were expected to feel toward their sons. Conversely, it was the obligation of sons, much as in China, to love and care about (and for) their fathers. Nor was pietas only a male preserve. Romans explained that their temple to Pietas was built in honour of the love shown by a daughter who kept her condemned mother alive in prison by breast-feeding her every day. This was 'pious devotion' indeed. There were other potent myths of pietas in action: a husband dying in place of his wife, a brother falling ill when his brother lost an election. Many Romans thought that family affection was natural. Pietas was far more than an obligatory duty.

Old Age Appreciated

There were many good reasons, then, for Romans to love and appreciate their fathers and all their elders. Cicero, who insisted on the importance of a man's house, was an especially eloquent spokesman for the benefits and excellence of being old. Yet we should be wary. He emphasized the importance of a house because he was trying to recover his own. It had been confiscated when he was forced into exile. Later he wrote about an ideal old man, Cato. But he probably did not so much believe his own argument as he was trying to cheer himself up.

Cicero lived in tumultuous times. He was a staunch republican, believing in the prerogatives of the Roman Senate and other elected officials. The very word 'Senate' derived from *senex*, meaning 'young old' and wise, not 'old old', as was the *senium* or *senilis*. But in Cicero's day republican government was, at best, on life support. This was the result of protracted historical processes. As Roman armies waged wars and racked up conquests beyond Italy, the state turned its new appropriations into colonial outposts to be exploited for their wealth. Some Romans grew fabulously rich. They paid private armies and wielded them to compete for power at Rome itself. Republican institutions, once sustained by a silent gentleman's agreement within a hereditary elite, crumbled. The senators had depended on 'clients' to vote for them and keep them in power. Now the clients who counted were armed to the teeth by a few moneyed generals – Caesar, Pompey, Antony, Octavian (later to become Augustus). They paid for their 'clients' – their soldiers. Sometimes the generals joined in alliances of two or three (for example, the triumvirate of Caesar, Pompey and Crassus), then split as they found new opportunities. Men who wanted to get ahead – among them Cicero – had to choose sides. Unfortunately, he backed the wrong man.

When I began to write this book, almost everyone to whom I mentioned the topic of old age knew that Cicero had written a treatise on it. It turns out, however, that the astonishing fame of that dialogue began only during the Renaissance. Before that, it was mildly popular for a time, then declined in importance during the Middle Ages.[3]

Cicero's treatise is an extraordinarily upbeat account of old age. Its spokesman is the severe Censor Cato, supposedly expounding on his views in his 84th year. He tells his two young listeners how contented he is to be old. Indeed, every old man worth anything should feel similarly. The dialogue, the full title of which is *Cato the Elder: On Old Age*, is set in 150 BCE, a year before the historical Cato's death and a century before Cicero was writing.[4] *On Old Age* is thus not a dialogue that reflected Cato's feelings but rather, obliquely, those of Cicero.

Cato declares that he is still active mentally, intellectually and politically. He describes approvingly another old man, Appius Claudius, who didn't let his blindness prevent him from going to the Senate to deliver a brilliant speech. Everyone can be like that if they have lived honourably and well and have not expended their youthful energies on useless things, says Cato. If they no longer have the strength they once had, they make up for that with their wisdom. If the pleasures of sex elude them, they now have more time for other joys, such as partaking in moderate eating, drinking and conversation (Cicero was here cribbing from Plato's account of Cephalus). But an old man's greatest joy comes from seeing 'the productivity and nature of the Earth herself'. He marvels at the wonders of the seed, out of which spring mature 'rows of grain' (234–5). He rejoices in knowing how to graft vines and manure the earth. A well-ordered farm – one that provides food, shade, water and warmth – is the foundation of an old man's true happiness. It brings joy far beyond gold and silver and all other material possessions.

People say old men become senile, but that happens only when they stop exercising their memories with daily practice. It's their fault. All the sorrows of the elderly are their fault. If old people are avoided by the young, it's because they are not proffering the advice that the young want and need. If the elderly tend to be 'morose, and petulant, and ill-tempered', it's because they are weak-minded: they need better habits and a better education (234). If they do not gain the respect (*auctoritas*) that is their due – the Latin word suggests both authority and honour – it's because they hadn't prepared the ground for it earlier in life.

A man is 'old' only when he stops meeting his obligations, stops carrying out his public and private duties, and starts obsessing about death. Then he is useless, and his life is over. As for death: don't worry about it, says Cato. Death means either that the soul is liberated from the body and is happy, or that one feels nothing at all. It's all good.

We have already seen Socrates make the same point about death, and after him the philosophical school of Epicurus argued still more forcefully that we lose all feeling when we die. Thus, after eulogizing Epicurus, his 'illustrious master', the Roman poet Lucretius (*fl.* first century BCE) turned to proving that 'death is nothing to us' (89), for when we die, we no longer think or have emotions.[5] Those things must be enjoyed while we are alive. We have a beginning and an end, like everything else, even rocks and mountains. Our mortality is natural and we are stupid if we don't recognize that. As Nature herself says to the fearful man, 'Stop sniveling you dolt!' (93).

Cicero was not an Epicurean. He was, however, strongly attracted to Stoicism, which also preached calm in the face of death. And so his Cato was perfectly tranquil. But why did he write in the persona of a man long dead? Cicero claimed that he used the Censor as his spokesman because his own *auctoritas* was inadequate. Under normal circumstances, that would have been another rhetorical gesture, another trick that ancient writers used to capture their reader's sympathy. But Cicero was not writing in normal circumstances. In the civil war between Caesar and Pompey for control of Rome (49–45 BCE), Cicero had tried to support whichever man who would restore the Republic. At one point he pinned his hopes on Caesar, but so unenthusiastically that Caesar's assassins even imagined that he might join them. He declined their invitation, but it is clear that, around the time when he wrote the *Cato*, Cicero had no role at all in politics. He had indeed lost his *auctoritas*.

Even after the assassination of Caesar on 15 March 44 BCE, Cicero's hopes for his own resurrection were tepid, and in that he was correct. Octavian, Caesar's 'adopted son' and the man who would become Augustus and the first Roman emperor, put Cicero on a hit list. He was soon murdered, and his severed head and hands were displayed in the centre of the city. Of course, Cicero could not have predicted that terrible outcome. But he felt defeated after the assassination of Caesar. As he wrote to his friend Atticus, to whom he had dedicated the *Cato*, 'I need to read *Cato the Elder* [i.e. his own book!] more often . . . For old age [*senectus*] is making me more ill-natured. Everything makes me boil with rage. But I'm done with life; let the young see to it.'[6] The *Cato* was his 'consolation', his winter dream, and writing it had indeed cheered him up. He hoped it would console Atticus as well.

Long before Cicero wrote *Cato*, the Greeks had pioneered a literature of consolation. Most of it survives only in fragments but, as we have seen, Homer's Achilles offered one to Priam, helping the bereaved old man to ease his grieving. Cicero imported the tradition when he wrote a *Consolatio* (now lost) to help him overcome his grief when his beloved daughter, Tullia, died. If *Cato*, too, began as his own *consolatio*, as Cicero wrote, then evidently the feelings of *his* old age were miserable, as if the loss of his public importance were a real death.

That is the conclusion of one of the dialogue's modern editors: 'it is probable enough that Cicero felt the exact opposite of all the favourable sentiments about old age which he makes Cato utter in the dialogue'.[7] But it seems to me more likely that Cicero was of *two* minds. Yes, he was an unhappy, enraged and peevish old man, his life as good as over. But he also was planning a comeback: even as he wrote *Cato* he was composing speeches that were intended to influence public policy and restore his reputation. He could hope that one day he would feel as he imagined Cato had felt. He could not know that events were against him.

In *Cato* Cicero was speaking to men like Atticus and himself – men of wealth, superior education and high intelligence. You are never too old, he was saying to those of his ilk, to be involved in anything to which you are dedicated. Later Plutarch (d. after 119 CE), an educated Greek living in the Roman Empire's eastern regions, limited that argument to public affairs, declaring that retiring from them was tantamount to retreating to the domestic sphere. Disgraceful! For him, the idea of the self-governing polis remained. But much later, when Renaissance scholars read Cicero's *Cato*, its political implications were reduced to serving a prince.

Today, although many of my acquaintances recalled reading *Cato* in college, they remembered it not as an argument for continued political participation but rather an essay on the pleasures of old age. When one of them developed physical debilities, she moved to a new-style home for the elderly that boasted a pool, a library, book clubs, a friendly staff and caring residents. The facility took care of all her meals, household chores and medical needs. While Cato was surrounded by slaves ready to do his bidding and young people to hang on his every word, my friend had a corps of maids, nurses, therapists and doctors to do more or less the same for her. 'This is where I belong,' she told me. She had long been a political activist, but now she gave up all that. Not so differently, President Joe Biden (b. 1942) was obliged to withdraw from the race for a second term in office at the age of 81. Contrast that with the fate of the old and blind Appius Claudius. Not only did he attend the Senate but he gave a speech that carried the day. In the Roman Republic old (elite) men had prestige; in the United States today, feelings about them are more ambivalent. They may inspire our love, but perhaps not our votes.

Old Age Maligned

Cicero's treatise was a man's text. There was nothing like it for women, no model of graceful or pleasant ageing. When Romans wrote about old women, they vilified them as ugly, sexually voracious, wine-bibbers and whoremongers. No wonder that Claudia Toreuma, a young woman who died at the age of nineteen in the early first century CE, wanted inscribed on her tomb the words, 'O, interminable old age: I, Claudia Toreuma, spent the short space of my life happily and escaped your abomination.' She had once been a popular entertainer and the slave of an emperor. Now she was a freedwoman and glad to die young. Her tomb was decorated with vegetation, suggesting her paradisal afterlife.

Had Toreuma lived long, she might have ended up like the old women in the *Epodes* of Horace (d. 8 BCE). Initially an opponent of Octavian/Augustus, Horace eventually became one of the emperor's apologists. His *Epodes* were invective poems written to insult and abuse, even as their metrical perfection and unexpected imagery were meant to dazzle. They featured three old women, all probably one and the same witch, Canidia (her name recalled *canities*, grey hair). In Epode 5, Canidia, wanting to win back the love of Varus (possibly her husband, since she accuses him of adultery), plans to make a love potion to reclaim him. She certainly needs one: she looks like Medusa (Horace says) with 'one purple tooth', claws in the place of fingernails and 'vipers bound around her messy hair'. Too bad (for her) that her magic, which she orchestrates with the help of other crones, doesn't work. That is less true in Epode 17, where the poet himself is presented as the victim of Canidia's torments. She is riding him like a horse, burning him, flailing him and working him to the bone day and night. Because of her, he has become an old man, his hair white as snow. Ostensibly she is punishing him for revealing her magic tricks in Epode 5. But the metaphors make clear that what she is *really* doing is running him ragged with her sexual demands.

Horace's Epodes 8 and 12 feature unnamed old women who are doing just that without the metaphors. In the first, the hag demands that her poet-lover satisfy her lusts. She is sucking him dry. He complains:

> Do you, half-rotten from extreme old age,
>   dare ask what saps my potency?
> When your one tooth is black, and elderly
>   old age ploughs up your brow with wrinkles.
> (Epode 8, ll. 1–4)

But something surprising happens in Epode 12: the old woman argues back. She taunts her lover. Can't he have even one erection for her? She complains of his ingratitude; after all, she sent him a 'woolen fleece twice dipped in Tyrian purple' – an expensive gift. At the end of her tirade, she bewails her wretchedness as he flees her. Her feelings, fictional as they are, may not be entirely off the mark. Certainly, some Roman men of the time threw over their old wives in favour of younger women. Cicero himself did so, divorcing his wife to marry his very young ward.

Had Horace's old women been men, they would have had it all. We know that they were wealthy, since Canidia had witch-slaves to do her bidding, and the harridan in Epode 12 sent her lover rich gifts. They were also well educated: the old battle-axe in Epode 8 reads Stoic philosophy, and the one in Epode 12 demonstrates the same brilliant metrical mastery as the poet. But they are not men, and they are given (by Horace) only one vocation, one purpose in life – sex. When they can no longer have that – when their lovers will no longer oblige – then they are in a situation parallel to that of an old man unable to carry out his public duties. If such men are as good as dead, then Horace's old women are already corpses.

It's not enough to say that Horace's *Epodes* insulted young women too. That is true; slander was the essence of that sort of poem. But Horace's *young* lovers, both 'soft boys and girls', possessed him, rendered him indolent, made him burn and stew. We might say, then, that Horace (as poet) thought rather little of women in general. But at least he awarded those still in the blush of youth not only some hold on his love but satisfying lives of their own. To old ladies, however, he allotted only unbridled sexual desire, cruelty and misery.

Despite their advantageous social position, old men did not normally fare particularly well in Roman writings, either. *Cato* was an exception. That is clear from the comedies written in the early Republican period, before Rome's conquests transformed its society. In those plays, aged fathers were satirized mercilessly. Tight-fisted and uncomprehending, they held on to their money without caring about the lives and loves of their sons and daughters. The Romans borrowed this portrayal from the Greeks of the Hellenistic age; we saw it already in Aristotle, who characterized old men as misers.

Above all, it was the Hellenistic playwrights who created this penny-pinching father. In their New Comedy plays, writers of this time rejected the political barbs implicit in the works of Aristophanes. They *knew* Aristophanes – and they, too, wrote in Greek. But they chose to produce comedies of manners that focused on true love misunderstood, thwarted and (at last!) fulfilled.

Roman playwrights brought New Comedy to Rome toward the end of the Hellenistic heyday. Although writing in Latin, they kept much else the same: the settings were generally in Athens or Attica; the costumes consisted of the Greek short cloak instead of the Roman toga; and the characters were drawn from the old Greek stock, including miserly old men.

Even so, the more nuanced sensibilities of old people in Greek New Comedy did *not* carry over into early Roman plays. For example, the very funny *Pot of Gold* by Latin writer Plautus (d. 184 BCE) follows the plot of *The Arbitration* by the Greek playwright Menander (d. c. 291 BCE). Both plays are about a rocky new marriage. In both an old miser is the major barrier to the young couple's happiness. In both he is so hilarious and absurd and uncomprehending that the audience surely roars with laughter. But the similarities end where the *feelings* of the elderly begin.

In Menander's *Arbitration*, the father is not a miser at first. Indeed, he has paid a generous dowry for his daughter's marriage. Furthermore, he has a strong sense of justice; he is the fair 'arbitrator' of the title. But when his daughter's marriage founders, the old man misunderstands the reasons for the couple's falling out. In Menander's play, the old man is clearly clueless and insensitive, but he is not dismaying.

Now fast-forward about a century and turn from Menander to Plautus. Like other playwrights at Rome, he had a hard time making his voice heard. Whereas in Greece the plays were the centre of attention at the festivals of Dionysus, in Rome athletes and entertainers competed with comedies for the public eye. And while in Greece the audience was largely composed of elite males, the ones at Rome and other cities in Italy were rowdier. They welcomed anyone who wanted to attend – men and women, rich and poor, slaves and their owners.

Further handicapping playwrights such as Plautus, most stages in Rome's Republican period were ad hoc affairs made of wood. Stone theatres were a Greek invention slow to come to Rome, although a few Italian cities outside the capital were better furnished. In effect, the plays of Plautus' day were the poor foster children of their Greek prototypes. They didn't even have a chorus to comment on the action, although sometimes an actor turned to the audience and addressed it as if it were part of the drama. Instead of using a chorus to highlight the emotions and poetic meter of the moment, a musician played the *tibia*, the Roman equivalent of the *aulos*.

What sort of emotions might the *tibia* have tried to evoke when an old man came on the stage? Pure mirth, it seems. In Plautus' *Pot of Gold* (his rewrite of Menander's *The Arbitration*) the old father, Euclio, is a skinflint without redeeming qualities. He has found a pot of gold, and it has taken over his life. He is precisely what Aristotle said of old men: suspicious of everyone, vindictive, shameless, grasping and selfish. He doesn't want to provide a dowry for his daughter, Phaedria, because he'll then be known as rich and his pot will be discovered. He checks it ten times a day, imagining at every moment that it has been stolen. He takes to carrying it around under his cloak – a hilarious solution because the 'Greek cloaks' worn by the actors were short.

Euclio is clueless: he doesn't know that his daughter, Phaedria, has been raped and is pregnant. He wants to marry her off to an old man who won't ask for a dowry. Plautus solves the dilemma thus: a clever slave robs Euclio of his pot of gold; the young man who raped Phaedria marries her, declaring himself the father of the baby. As that young man is also the thieving slave's owner, he orders the stolen gold to be returned to Euclio. No doubt at the end of the play (missing today), Euclio sees the error of his ways and presents the pot as his daughter's dowry.

Acceptance

It is not hard to see in Plautus' Euclio a critique of *patria potestas* and a rebellion against elders. It's the young people who are the heroes of the *Pot of Gold*, offering cathartic relief for an hour or two to an audience otherwise morally bound to the 'ways of the elders'. To appeal to a Roman audience, a comic writer had to exaggerate the defects of old men precisely because in reality their power was nothing to laugh at.

Thus, even when Plautus himself became old, he did not change his portrayal of the elderly. In his *Pseudolus* (191 BCE), written when he was about 63, he presented his elderly character Simo with the same flagrant disrespect as he did all his earlier old men. Simo was nothing more than a typical miser unwilling to help his son secure his true love. In this case she is Phoenicium, a courtesan who has just been sold to a soldier by her pimp. The last payment is due today. Pseudolus, the slave of Simo and Simo's son, comes to the young man's rescue. He bamboozles Simo and runs rings around the old pimp, too.

While the wives and courtesans in Plautus' comedies are frequently not only smart but wise, the women identified as 'old' are slaves. Did the plays pay attention to their feelings? In a way, yes. The old slaves were perplexed by the behaviour of their owners and – above all – they feared whippings. That too was part of *patria potestas*, for the household head's absolute authority extended to his enslaved dependents, and pietas played no role in their relationship. Comedies were a way for Romans to recognize the power of their fathers even as they ridiculed and humiliated them.

How far did the resentment of the elderly go? It is one thing to dislike a father who will not permit you to marry your girl; it is quite another to kill him. Yet some historians see evidence of patricide at Rome. During the reign of Emperor Vespasian (d. 79), the Senate passed a law declaring that it was illegal for a creditor to lend money to a son who stood to inherit his father's wealth. Claiming that such a loan 'often provides evil dispositions with means of ill-doing', the senators possibly feared that sons in debt would kill their fathers to get their inheritance.[8] But the senatorial decree was against the *creditor*, not the young borrower. Since many senators hated usury, their law may have been meant to harm creditors rather than protect fathers. Certainly Cicero, when defending a man accused of parricide, argued that such a crime was 'so immense, so terrible, and so extraordinary, and committed so rarely that, if it is ever heard of, it is thought to be a portent or prodigy'.[9]

That senicide was an *impulse* in the ancient world is undeniable. We saw it already, in Euripides' *Alcestis*. Such urges exist in our own society as well.[10] Working out – cautiously – that only between 6 to 8 per cent of the Roman population was over sixty years of age at any one time, Richard Saller argued that many young males must have reached adulthood without a father.[11] However, this view has been vigorously disputed, partly by calling into question Saller's methodology, partly by citing evidence from Roman law (such as the one drawn up under Vespasian), and partly by generalizing from the practice of patricide and matricide within imperial families.[12]

But there is little evidence that senicide was normative within the general population unless neglect of the aged poor is considered one of its forms. For at Rome there were no rest homes to care for the elderly, no charitable institutions to help those unable to care for themselves, no 'old age pensions' such as the one that Procleon could draw as a juror in an Athenian law court.

Ah Youth!

In 27 BCE, five years after Octavian's defeat of Antony, the Senate (already in Octavian's back pocket) awarded him the title of Augustus. Ruling with an iron fist even before he was declared

Father of his Country, Augustus encouraged marriages, prohibited divorces and criminalized adultery. He was expanding the role of pietas and at the same time trying to control domestic morality.

Those new regulations did not sit well with everyone. We may glimpse that emotional community – the one that slept around and enjoyed it – by considering the sly and witty Ovid (d. c. 17 BCE), an author of love poetry whom Augustus exiled for his freewheeling exuberance. Ovid mainly wrote about young people and their amours, but he also devoted a few poems to old women, whom he grudgingly admired. They knew what life was about and had their priorities straight. Indeed, sometimes they were all *too* wise for the poet's own good. Consider his depiction of the old witch Dipsas, who offered her young protégées clever advice about how to treat lovers – so clever that the lover-poet despairs.

In perhaps his earliest work, his *Loves* (*Amores*), Ovid calls Dipsas an ugly old woman and a madam (*lena*; 1.8, l. 2).[13] The very name Dipsas means 'thirsty'; she's an old drunk. But if hung over, she is nevertheless exceptionally capable. She is no sad and powerless Canidia wild for love. Rather, she is a tough and independent woman. Her magic is potent; she has an 'eloquent tongue'; and she supports herself by grooming young ladies to make money for her and themselves, as the poet learns as he hides behind her door:

> Do you not know, my sweet, [says Dipsas to one of her
>   pretty novices] that you caught a young man's eye, last
>   night – and not just any young man. He's rich!
> He was held fast and could not take his eyes from your face.
> All that's fine. You're beautiful, after all.
> Second to none, I say. The only thing you need is the
>   training to match, and this we shall have to work on.

If you are wealthy, I will share in your good fortune. Our interests coincide. (1.8, ll. 23–8, trans. Slavitt, p. 24)[14]

Her 'training' consists in time-tested techniques to snag a wealthy man. The general principle is easily stated; control your emotions and pretend. Or, as Dipsas puts it, 'Let your tongue be your helper and hide your feelings' (1.8, l. 103; illus. 11). Some specific instances: don't blush from modesty but rather when it suits your purposes. Take many lovers, and all at once: 'beauty, unless exercised, gets old' (1.8, l. 53). Shun poets! (Does she suspect that Ovid is eavesdropping?) Don't be taken in by rank, since even a former slave may be rich. Is your lover woeful in bed? Never mind. You can always lie and say that he is great – if that loosens his gift spigot. Are you feeling contrite? Turn it into anger – but not too much. Learn how to shed tears on demand. Sometimes you can teach your clever slaves to wheedle on your behalf: you'll get big gifts and you'll tip them well. In fact, most of the women in your household can collaborate with you: 'And your sister and mother, and your nurse too, can fleece your lover' (1.8, l. 91).

With Dipsas, Ovid builds on old prejudices and then overturns them. His old lady is certainly an inveterate wine-bibber and a witch as well. That's the standard fantasy. Yet she has formidable strengths as a survivor. She may be a tippler – why not, if she likes wine? – but she also knows how to make a living.

The poet wants to beat her up, but he can hardly do that in front of his sweetheart. Instead, he prays that the gods will give her an impoverished old age, 'long winters and perpetual thirst' (1.8, l. 114). He ought to recognize that the advice that she gives to her girls, which treats love as a flirtatious game, is exactly the same as the good counsel Ovid gives when (in a different poem) he tells his mistress how to behave at a dinner party with her husband. She must make clear that she does not *really* love that spouse of hers. Otherwise, the poet (who will also be there) will be beyond jealous. And when she goes home together with her husband, to whom (Ovid realizes) she 'owes' sexual availability, she should only *pretend* to enjoy it. Or, at least, she should not say otherwise when she sees the poet the next day. In a different poem (2.19), Ovid talks about all the ploys used by his mistress to string him along and keep him guessing; she's following his own advice (which is also that of Dipsas) to keep love alive. Twenty or so years later, Ovid published an entire book, The Art of Love (*Ars Amatoria*), to add to the repertory of womanly wiles he had already provided (via Dipsas and his own musings) as well as to offer men parallel instruction.

It is easy enough to see how Ovid felt about Dipsas, that eloquent and crafty creation of his: grudging admiration. But how did *she* feel about being the old witch? It is not an inappropriate question. Yes, Dipsas is a fiction. Moreover, she probably represented a 'type' of old woman rather than a particular person. But Ovid's education in the Romans schools of rhetoric and declamation taught him to inhabit his character's inner life and to present his subject as if she were a fully rounded human being. A typical example of this rhetorical practice is in Cicero's treatise On Oratory (*De oratore*) where he cites with approval the laments of Medea in a play by Ennius (d. 169 BCE): 'Where can I turn now? And what path must I choose to go?/ To the house of my father? Or perhaps to the daughters of Pelias?'[15] Medea, a witch who has just avenged herself against her wayward husband by killing their children, is a detestable character. But Ennius endows her with real pathos: abandoned by her husband, rejected by her father, hated by the daughters of Pelias (whom she tricked), Medea truly has nowhere to turn.

We know that Ovid too wrote a *Medea*, though it is now lost. But Dipsas is her quasi-double, with 'magic powers to charm, such as Medea had' (1.8, ll. 5–6, trans. McKeown 1.2, p. 305).

Unlike Medea, she is a *happy* doppelganger with no need to lament. To the contrary, much like the elderly Cato, Dipsas takes advantage of her wrinkles to play the sage to the younger set. Taking the part of the girl she is 'training', she sympathizes: the young innocent is beautiful but, 'oh, dear me!' (*me miseram!*) she badly needs some good advice (1.8, l. 25). The two will get rich together. Self-confident and self-admiring, Dipsas ends her speech by predicting that the well-trained girl will remember and think fondly of her:

> If you remember this advice and use it,
> not letting my words float away on the winds,
>   you will think well of me as long as I live,
>   and after I'm dead, you'll pray that the earth lie light
>   on my bones. (1.8, ll. 107–8, trans. Slavitt)

Romans wanted to be remembered after they died; we saw this already with Claudia Toreuma, who must have spent a lot of money to have her tomb carved and engraved. The purpose of such memorials was to remind passers-by of the deceased and to mark the place to which family members should bring offerings. The formula 'may the earth sit lightly upon you' was so common on epitaphs that it was often abbreviated, much as *requiescat in pace* (may he/she rest in peace) has become R.I.P. today. Dipsas awarded the equivalent wish to herself. She was an independent woman to the end.

Looking Old

Dipsas was not sorry to be considered old. Nor were many others – mainly men, however – who 'decorated' the streets of Italy in Cicero's and Ovid's day. I refer to the portrait statues and busts that were put up in their honour. Earlier depictions of

3 Bust of Cicero, 1st century CE, after a Greek original of 45–3 BCE, around the time of Cicero's death. The clear marks of old age were meant to remind viewers of the Republican ideals with which Cicero was associated.

Roman citizens tended to idealize their subject, and that always remained the case for respectable women. Chastity (meaning fidelity to one's spouse) was portrayed as a mature – but not particularly elderly – woman. She was always fully draped and touched her face in a gesture meant to fend off the male gaze.

But something new happened in the age of Cicero. As if his admiration of Cato wafted into the sculptor's studio, male portraits made in and around the time of Cicero and Ovid

4 Grave relief of Publius Aiedius Amphio and his wife Aiedia, c. 30 BCE. Carved of marble, this grave marker shows Aiedius as a hard-toiling servant of the state, advertising his seriousness, wisdom and self-discipline.

seemed to praise old age. The jowly portrait head of Cicero shown here (illus. 3) makes no apologies for the years it represents. That was particularly true of the funerary portraiture of newly freed slaves. With the wealth of Rome's colonies pouring into the city, some former slaves became rich enough to put up fine monuments to themselves. One example is shown above, the grave relief of Publius Aiedius and his wife Aiedia (illus. 4). (Their names echo that of their former owner.) It was once displayed on Rome's Via Appia alongside numerous other such burial markers. More than 90 centimetres (3 ft) tall, it virtually begs passers-by to peek through its 'window' and take note of the people shown there. Aiedius' portrait shows bags under his eyes, sagging jaws, warts at the mouth, deeply incised laugh lines, a receding hairline and a furrowed brow. He wears a toga, testifying to his hard-won status as a free citizen. His wife, however, does not advertise her age, though she is clearly not young. Instead, she displays her status as Aiedius' wife by showing her wedding ring. Slaves could not wed, but now that she was a freedwoman, she could wear a woman's equivalent of the toga of a citizen.

The origins of this new verism have been – and continue to be – much discussed. Did it derive from Etruscan, Egyptian or Late Hellenistic Greek portraiture? Was it, perhaps, homegrown from the Roman elite's practice of making and displaying ancestor masks? Whatever its lineage, there is no denying that it represented late-republican tastes. Indeed, in the transitional period from Republican to Imperial Rome (*c.* first century BCE), unsparing portraits of old men often signalled republican, rather than imperial, sympathies.

It follows that, by contrast, Roman *imperial* art celebrated everlasting youth. A nearly 2-metre-high (7 ft) statue of Augustus himself (illus. 5) was the model. Although the date of its commission is highly disputed, without question the emperor was already in middle age when it was made. Even so, it shows the emperor as a beautiful youth. This image, widely copied throughout the Roman Empire, tended to drive out the verism of Cicero's time. The Roman elites wanted to follow the model of this young Augustus (and that of the equally idealized image of his wife, Livia).

The non-elites were not necessarily so inclined. A funerary portrait of Lucius Vibius and his family, sculpted around the same time as Augustus was advertising a youthful image, depicts Lucius as a very wizened old man (illus. 6).[16] The toga that he wears suggests that he was a citizen active in public life. That was unlikely: only the emperor and his favourites had a role in government at the time. The inscription on the tombstone tells passers-by that Lucius' wife is a freedwoman, and she, like Aiedia, proudly displays her wedding ring. As befits a Roman *matrona*, she also touches her cheek in the gesture of chastity.

Sculpted portraits, however, can tell us only so much. The *feelings* of the elderly in the post-Augustan world may be fruitfully seen in the first place via the works of Seneca. Born in or around 1 BCE, he was sickly all his life but never let that get in his way. Politically ambitious and a brilliant orator, by his late thirties he had joined the dangerous circle that lived and died at the whim of the early Julio-Claudian emperors. He survived Caligula; was exiled by Claudius; and remained at Nero's court until he lost all influence there. He evidently tried to be a moderating force on the emperor, yet it was he who wrote Nero's speech justifying the emperor's matricide. Twice, in 62 and 64, according to the historian Tacitus (d. *c.* 120), Seneca tried to resign from court, but Nero refused. Then, in 65 the emperor was all too willing to let him go, accusing Seneca of treason and ordering him to take his own life.

In his admiring account of Seneca's suicide, Tacitus wrote that even 'at the peak of his prosperity and power, Seneca had been paying heed to his final moments'.[17] Indeed he had. Throughout his life Seneca had studied philosophy and was especially attracted to Stoic teachings. He did not consider old age worse than any other. Terrible things may happen to people at any time of life, and death is constantly around the corner. Yet the end always strikes at the right time: 'No one dies too soon, because he was not going to live any longer than he actually lived.'[18] We should face all of life's evils and our inevitable fate with tranquillity. In that sense, Claudia Toreuma was right to be happy to die when she died.

Seneca's feelings as an old man are sketched out in several letters written two or three years before his death to a younger friend, Lucilius. There he considers the foibles and challenges of his senectitude (he was in his early sixties). Thus, when he visits his country estate and notices how its main edifice is falling apart and its grounds deteriorating, he laughingly

5 Augustus wears the cuirass of a war hero as richly carved as the divinely-wrought shield of Achilles. It has been dated as early as 27 BCE, when Octavian was declared Augustus, and as late as the reign of his successor Emperor Tiberius (r. 14–36).

realizes that the villa mirrors himself: 'My suburban villa has done me a service; it has brought my age before me at every turn. Let us embrace old age and love it. It is full of pleasure if you know what use to make of it' (Sen. Let. 12, §4).[19] What use ought to be made of it? 'You should keep learning how to live for as long as you live' (Sen. Let. 76, §2). Seneca wants to keep meditating how to face trials (including the final one, death) with courage, honour and boldness. He admires his contemporary Aufidius Bassus, 'who has had a stroke and is wrestling with the advance of years . . . Yet our friend Bassus is as lively as ever in his mind. Philosophy does this: it enables a person to be cheerful within sight of death . . . Bassus looks on his own end with such a calm expression that

6 On this marble tombstone carved between 13 BCE and 5 CE, Lucius Vibius and his family proclaim the honour of free citizens, a dignity valued at any age. However, *verismo* portraits of mature people remained out of favour within the upper classes until the mid-first century and beyond.

if he looked so on another's, you would think him uncaring'
(Sen. Let. 30, §3).

Emphasizing the life of the mind signals a change from the attention to public service in the time of Cicero's *Cato*. Seneca's active life is within him. He no longer thinks that a man who cannot carry out his public duties is as good as dead. Quite the contrary. He himself experienced the fullest possible public life that a man could have under an absolute ruler, and, even before Nero ordered him to take his own life, Seneca knew how fatal power could be. He had no illusions.

What *was* fatal for Seneca was to be unable to read or think. When he recognizes that he has reached not just 'old age' but the next step, 'the age of disintegration', he becomes anxious. He is glad that his mind remains vigorous, but when reason tells him that 'old age is its time of flourishing', he has his doubts. Has that lifelong study of philosophy he has dedicated himself to really led to the calm fortitude that he admires? Or has he been fooling himself?

> I scrutinize myself as if the time of trial were drawing near . . . I say to myself, 'My words and actions up to this point do not prove anything. Those are slight and deceptive pledges of courage, wrapped up in a great lot of blarney. Death will disclose to me what progress I have made.' . . . Is it just brave talk, or do I mean what I say? Were they for real, those defiant words I spoke against fortune, or were they just theater – just acting a part? (Sen. Let. 26, §§1-5)

His anxiety weighs on him. It is not that dismay about the end of life had no earlier antecedents: Cephalus' friends worried about Hades, and Socrates' friends needed the reassuring calm of his unanswerable arguments. However, such misgivings came and went. Cato, for one, was not concerned. As imagined by Cicero, he was confident that he had done and was doing everything required of him. He belittled any who could not follow his footsteps. They mustn't have lived properly in the first place; they mustn't have kept their mind active as they aged.

Seneca, a rarity in this company, was not so sure. Living with Nero for so long, he well knew what it meant to 'act a part', for Nero prided himself (scandalously so) on his thespian and musical talents. He loved to go on the stage. Seneca himself was a playwright as well as a philosopher. He could imagine eventually losing his mental acumen, becoming weak-minded, and suffering dementia. He was hard-bitten enough to face the possibilities: 'I will not abandon old age as long as it allows me to keep my whole self – that is, the whole of my better part. But if it begins to attack my mind and lop off parts of it – if it keeps me alive without allowing me a life, then I will fling myself from the decayed and collapsing edifice' (*Sen. Let.* 58, §35). His rejection of senility seems to fly in the face of his conviction that a man must accept his fate gladly. But perhaps he means that one can help fate along when he sees the writing on the wall.

One of Seneca's tragedies is relevant here. Like the playwrights of ancient Greece, he took up the great myths and infused them with dialogue and feeling. In his *Oedipus*, the hero explicitly welcomes – indeed wishes for – a fate worse than that of Tithonus, the ever-shrivelling lover of Dawn. As Oedipus blinds himself, he asks Nature – always rational and just, however arbitrary it might seem – to revisit its punishment on him over and over, even to the point of disrupting the normal sequence of birth, decay and death by recycling him forever:

> Let Nature not be annulled, whose fixed laws
> Change only for Oedipus. Let that inventor
> Of new births find new punishments for me.

Acceptance

You must live again, you must die again
And be eternally reborn – to be punished
Each time anew.[20] (*Oed.* ll. 942–7)

He realizes that he has brought his fate on himself. Now he welcomes his punishment. Its horror means that he will never have a final death nor a final old age either. That ever-repeating cycle is the worst fate of all. How lucky most mortals are to simply get old and die!

Seneca accepts his old age, makes the best of it and advises Lucilius to do the same. When he writes lines for Oedipus, he makes clear that never getting old is the most terrifying punishment of all. So read, study, and when the time comes, face death with the wisdom that you worked toward all your life.

The orator Marcus Cornelius Fronto (d. 166) is not as famous as Seneca. But a letter that he wrote to Emperor Marcus Aurelius (d. 180) yields precious evidence of the feelings of an old man in imperial Rome. For many years, Fronto was one of the tutors of Marcus Aurelius and his brother Lucius Verus, and after they no longer needed schooling, Fronto remained a friend of both emperors and (to some extent) an adviser. They exchanged regular visits and carried on a lively correspondence.

About a year before his death, Fronto wrote a long letter to Marcus Aurelius that plumbed his feelings as a man nearing the end of his life. Its occasion was the death of Fronto's little grandchild, but it ranged far beyond that, trying to make sense of his experiences, the apparent irrationality of Fate, and the meaning of death. Scholars have criticized the letter because most of its sentiments were derivative. Of course they were! Fronto taught Latin literature, the books that the well-educated Roman had to master; their sentences and sentiments came readily to mind. And if his letter was filled with commonplaces, that is all the better for our purposes. His platitudes hint at the general emotional expectations and norms of (at least) the Roman elite. After all, if we are honest, lack of originality comprises most emotional expression. We have only to think of how happily and freely we use emojis.

'Fortune has tested me throughout my whole life with many sorrows of this kind', Fronto's letter begins.[21] He had lost five children – an almost unbearable experience each time. *Almost* unbearable because he prided himself on his ability to meet the pain with Senecan calm and fortitude. However, this time he could not hold back his tears: 'Now, with my grandson lost, my grief is compounded by the anguish of my daughter and by the anguish of my son-in-law [Victorinus] . . . I melt away beside him.' Note his emphasis on the boy's father here, even though the mother was his own daughter. How could the gods allow a man so good, honest and blameless as Victorinus be 'crushed by the bitterest blow that was the death of his son?' And why are the sons of *evil* men allowed to outlive their fathers?

He tried to comfort himself and his reader. We need to recognize that everything happens for a higher reason. This, too, was Senecan. Then perhaps death is a good thing; perhaps it 'brings an end to our labours and worries and troubles and carries [us] who have been freed from the bonds of a wretched body to a tranquil and beautiful place'. That was both Socratic and Senecan. It was even a popular idea; Claudia Toreuma strongly hinted at it with her beautiful tomb evoking paradise. Even so, as Fronto lamented, we who are left behind still feel bitter grief. 'We long for the presence, voice, beauty, and spirit of our children.' The once-glowing child is now drained of colour, a lifeless corpse, horrible to look upon.

Fronto mused that he should have died before the boy did. At any rate, he surely had not much longer to grieve, and that gave him consolation. Like Seneca, he considered his life to have been a test. Unlike Seneca, he gave himself a passing grade, noting, as he looked back on it, that

> I have done nothing shameful, or disgraceful, or scandalous... On the contrary, I have always done many things graciously, out of friendship, faithfully, and loyally... I have lived in complete harmony with an excellent brother ... As for the [public offices] which I myself obtained, I never desired to acquire them by inappropriate means. I have devoted myself to cultivating my mind rather than my body... I have never been lavish in my spending, and any profit I made was only what was necessary.

Were those things true? For us, it hardly matters. Fronto tells us how old men of a particular class felt – or thought they ought to feel – about themselves. His boast about keeping only fair profits should remind us of Cephalus; that about cultivating his mind rather than his body harks back to Seneca; and his pride in obtaining public offices without chicanery recalls Cicero's Cato. Fronto had been honest, affectionate and caring, someone who felt his losses deeply and meditated on their meaning. These were satisfying winter dreams.

It is just possible that Fronto read the poems of the dyspeptic satirist Juvenal (d. shortly after 130). If so, Juvenal's fierce diatribes against the immorality of the imperial court would not have pleased him. He might have lent a more sympathetic ear, however, to the poet's observations about ageing, which began with invective and ended in pathos. For Juvenal, old age was the ultimate betrayal of humanity:

> First and foremost, look at the face –
> misshapen and hideous beyond recognition; instead of skin,

you see a misshapen hide, baggy cheeks, and the kind of wrinkles that are etched on the aged jowls of an African ape.[22] (10.191–4)

Old men are repellent to themselves and disgusting to their wives and children. They can't have sex and have forgotten its pleasures. They don't go to the theatre because they can no longer hear. They are assailed by illnesses and debilities: 'Here it's a shoulder crippled, there a pelvis or hip;/ *this* man has lost both eyes, and envies the fellow with one;/ *that* man takes food with bloodless lips from another's fingers' (10.228–30). To describe the horrible, animal-like and frightening bodies of old men, Juvenal has imported the savage portrayals of old *women* (as for example in Ovid and Horace) but without their sexual rapaciousness.

Yet as his satire continues, Juvenal's tone shifts. He asks his readers to imagine a perfectly healthy, perfectly sane old man. His prayers for a long life have been answered. What then? He is condemned to see his loved ones die, to be left alone to grieve and hope for his own quick demise:

> Suppose his mind retains its vigor, he still must walk in front of his children's coffins, and bear to gaze on the pyre of his beloved wife or brother and on urns full of his sisters. This is the price of longevity. As people age, the disasters within their homes forever recur; grief follows grief; their sorrows never cease, and their dress is the black of mourning. (10.440–45)

This final thrust surely hit home. Fronto certainly felt it. Modern social historian Tim Parkin estimates that around 30 per cent of infants born alive in the Empire died before the age of one. If they survived to age five, however, over 80 per cent might 'reach age 20 and over 30 percent age 60.'[23] Since a woman who

7 Described as orphaned by her loved ones (*orba meis*) and lonely in her old age (*deserta senectus*), Papiria Tertia is torn between her desire for more children and her envy of barren women spared forever the grief of losing a child.

reached the average maternity age bore five or six children, Parkin suggests that estimates of female deaths due to childbirth itself may be exaggerated. It is more likely that they had died beforehand, joining the ranks of the 50 per cent or so of Roman girls and boys who died before the age of ten.

A glimpse of some telling inscriptions on Roman tombstones adds to this picture. From the city of Rome itself comes a father's lament that his nine-year-old son's untimely death means that he had to do 'what the son should have done',[24] namely bury a loved one. Another memorial, this time from Umbria (Italy), 'scolds' two-year-old Flavius Hermes for 'mocking' his grandmother, 'for he used to say that he would feed and support her in extreme old age'.[25] The words evoke the image of a dear little boy on his grandmother's knee promising to be her staff and support when he grows up.

The grief of a wife and mother is expressed in an inscription from Ferrara (Italy), where Papiria Tertia mourns the death of her husband and their son. All three are represented on the tombstone that she had erected, the busts of the parents above and larger than that of their son (illus. 7). While Papiria does not *look* particularly old, she says that she *feels* both old and deserted:

> You behold how I, bereft of my loved ones, erected their memorials.
> And sad, quite old, and pitiable, I long for offspring.
> My lonely old age should be included among the evidence
> Supporting the view that barren wives may truly rejoice.[26]

Why should they rejoice? Surely because barren wives will never have to mourn their lost children.

In ancient Rome it was emotionally tolerable to be old, but not to outlive your little children and grandchildren.

The Aged Patient

The physician Galen (d. 216), Fronto's younger contemporary, granted that ageing was inevitable, but, like Cato, he knew many practical ways to cope with it. Born in Pergamum (then Greek; now part of Turkey), educated in philosophy as a youth, Galen spent some time in Rome in his early thirties to continue his medical training before returning home. In 168 Emperor Marcus Aurelius brought him back to Rome as his personal physician, and there he remained for much – perhaps all – of the rest of his life.

He had not been particularly healthy as a youth, but as a middle-aged adult he could boast that the only disease he had experienced for many years was fatigue. He attributed his good health to his theory of hygiene. The word meant to him (as it does to physicians today) 'preserving health'. For Galen, elaborating on the ideas of earlier physicians, hygiene involved not sanitation (for germs had not yet been discovered) but rather diet and nutrition, exercise, massage, bathing, evacuation and sleep. Galen boasted that people who adhered to his precepts and did not burden themselves with overwork could preserve themselves entirely from diseases throughout their lives.

Of course, everyone will die. That is natural. As Aristotle and others had already noted, every living thing must grow, come into flower, and eventually weaken, dry out and die. Galen added the idea that there is a hygiene proper to each of those stages. For 'health' is not one thing. There is the faultless health of young people, and there is the geriatric health of the old. And even old age itself has stages, each of which needs its own sort of hygiene. In the first old age, men (Galen sometimes had women in mind too, though not here) are 'still able to carry out civic duties' (379K).[27] In that case they need only to continue the practices of their younger years while keeping in mind that they are not – and never will be – as strong as they once were. In the second stage they must lead a quieter life of bathing, eating, sleeping, exercising and getting suitable massages to maintain their bodily warmth and to remain 'sound in all parts', free of pain and disease (311K). In the third phase, in which (following all these good precepts) they will have staved death off as long as possible, they will die.

Galen admitted that some people had bad luck. They had accidents, or fell prey to heatstroke or cold or fatigue and other such things. What annoyed him was the old man who could have been in perfect health if he had followed the proper hygiene. Now that man had to be 'carried around by others due to gout, or to be brought undone by the pains of [kidney] stones, or pains in the colon'. He needed others to feed him and could not clean himself up 'after defecation'. How shameful! It would be 'a thousand times better for him to choose to die before enduring such a life' (311K). Such a man had only himself to blame for living unhealthily before he got old. Recall that Cato, as Cicero pictured him, had blamed unwise practices for the *mental* deficiencies of old age. He thought one might as well die if he could no longer fulfil his public duties. Galen considered that dream unrealistic in the second phase of ageing. At that point responsibilities *had* to be shed. Even so, a man at that stage could continue to live pleasantly and pain free, enjoying his meals and baths and gentle exercises. Old age was not an abomination as Claudia Toreuma claimed – not, at least, if a person and his doctor were willing to work at it! Be vigilant, correct any hygienic practices that do not work for your particular body, and make sure that nothing is done or taken to excess.

Galen's medical theory was based on balances among the four humours: hot, cold, wet and dry. These qualities are contained (always in mixtures) within the physical substances of the body – the four humours of blood, phlegm, black bile and yellow bile. A skilled physician can often tell which bodily mixture prevails by touching the skin on the palm of the patient's hand. Old people are by nature cold and dry. Some doctors (noted Galen) have been misled by the quantity of the bodily secretions of the elderly, confusing external with internal features, for 'old men are dry . . . in the actual solid parts of the body: bone ligament, membrane, artery, vein, nerve, coat and flesh; and Aristotle's parallel between old age and a plant drying out is an apt one. For plants, too, are soft and wet when young, but can be observed to become increasingly dry as they grow older, finally drying out completely, at which point they are dead.' As for being cold, 'old men are evidently cold to the touch: they easily become chilled, turn black or livid, and are easily seized by cold diseases.'[28] By 'turning black', Galen may have been referring to what are called 'age spots' today. Given their condition, the elderly should eat warm foods, exercise moderately and take warm baths. Sexual relations (which should never be excessive) become positively contrary to good hygiene as one ages, for sex depletes moistness and warmth.

Galen's theory thus explains why an old man of the ancient world did not need to be like the ridiculous Procleon of Aristophanes but instead could end up like the wise Cato of Cicero. But recall that Procleon had a lot of fun, while Galen's patient must be so preoccupied with his food, bathing and massage – with righting this imbalance and maintaining the other – that the pleasure is hard to see. Galen's old age was not abominable, but it was truly a full-time job.

WHEN AENEAS HOISTED his father on his back and his father in turn took the Penates of the family in his hands, both were demonstrating the reverence due to Roman elders. By the same token, fathers, ancestors and gods functioned as the disciplinary and moral backbones of the Roman family. But the counterpart to the respect due the elderly was the delight Romans took in laughing at old misers and deriding wrinkled old ladies.

The Romans didn't have law courts that paid the sort of old-age pension that Procleon got in Athens. They did not offer a retirement package even for Senators. Nor did they obligate children to care for their parents by law. They made no provision for the mentally or physically unfit old person, and Cicero and Galen faulted the person rather than the ageing process for all elderly debilities. We know next to nothing about how poor old men and women managed to live, but there must have been beggars in antiquity, and someone must have given them alms. It is likely that such help came from non-elites, although it is true that Seneca once remarked that 'the wise man' need not recoil 'because of someone's withered leg or their ragged emaciation or their old age supported by a stick'.[29] But did he therefore offer them alms?

The wealthy knew that their senectitude would come, and for the most part they accepted it. Their own lives would be absorbed into the immemorial generations of the past. They put up tombstones to remind the living to think of them. Sometimes philosophy helped. For Seneca getting old offered the time to prepare productively for the ethical tests – to face all that happens and will happen calmly; to put little stock in ephemeral things; to see the irrationality of our petty passions; and to recognize that, while much may seem unjust and inexplicable, all are part of the wise plans of the cosmos. Again, one senses a sort of good-humoured acceptance here. We find the same in Fronto, grieving for those he had lost even as he assesses his life's course as virtuous and just. And we see it in the fictional Dipsas and the grieving Papiria Tertia.

In ancient Athens, Sparta and China, filial piety was a key emotion, both for the elderly and for those who cared for them. In ancient Rome the power of the old over the young was added to that mix. Had Priam, the old father of Hector, lived under Rome's laws, he could have *ordered* rather than begged his son not to fight Achilles. In ancient Athens, fathers had to persuade their sons to go to the Pondertorium, just as orators had to convince citizens in the assembly. In ancient Rome, the power of the father in the family eventually turned into the *pater patriae* of the emperor.

But there were other emotional communities at the time, though hard to glimpse. Already the tomb of the young Claudia hinted at a 'life to come'. Perhaps the idea consoled her. An inscription from Cirta (then in Roman North Africa, today in Algeria) makes the hint explicit:

> Here I am, silent. I show my life by my verses.
> Having enjoyed the light of day as long as possible,
> I, Praecilius of Cirta, practiced the art of banking.
> My honesty was always admired, and I was truthful.
> Obliging to all, to whom did I not show compassion?
> Everywhere and always, I enjoyed laughs and pleasures with my friends.
> But after the death of my virtuous wife, Valeria, I have not found another like her.
> I led as happy a life as I could with my saintly wife [and] celebrated a hundred happy birthdays.
> But the last day has come as my spirit leaves my useless limbs.
> I had the inscription that you are reading prepared while I lived for the day of my death,
> Fortune, as it willed, never abandoned me.
> Follow my footsteps; come: I expect you here.[30]

Praecilius may well have been concerned about his *patria potestas* and the *pietas* owed to him (and he to others). But his inscription shows that other things were more important to him. He had been wealthy (a banker), honest and compassionate. He had been happy, and his wife saintly. He was a sociable man and looked forward to the next life, where he would welcome new friends and greet his old ones.

Scholars date the inscription of Praecilius to the first half of the third century. By then, a small tsunami of groups and individuals – among them the Gnostics and the worshippers of Mithras – were awaiting the life after death with serenity. So too were a growing number of Christians. In the next chapter we shall look more closely at their winter dreams.

Three

Reciprocity

The Roman Empire could have given voice to its vast mosaic of traditions, peoples, styles and languages. It did little of that. True, in some instances, it borrowed from its conquests (such as Greece), but it quickly assimilated that culture to itself in a Romanized form. We saw how that happened with comedies: the Romans based their stories on Hellenistic Greek models but changed them to suit Roman tastes. In other places Roman institutions were copied by provincial elites, creating (as it were) numerous miniatures of Rome, complete with forums, baths and Roman-style mosaics. The Empire also allowed for a third solution: when native traditions asserted themselves, the Romans renamed them to make them 'Roman'. Thus, once the god Baal of North Africa was given the name of the Roman god Saturn, the cult was allowed to flourish alongside the rest of the Roman pantheon.

There were Jews in the Empire even before 70 CE, when the Romans conquered Judaea, and thereafter even more of them scattered to cities around the Mediterranean, where they constituted small minorities. Their integration within the wider society could only be partial, however, because they clung to their one God, Yahweh, and rejected all others. Moreover, their observance of the Laws of Moses required them to follow certain customs strange or even distasteful to the pagan majority around them, such as observing the Sabbath and practising the circumcision of males. When their numbers were sufficient, they set up synagogues to serve as community centres as well as houses of worship. True, many of those living in the eastern half of the Empire spoke and wrote in Latin and Greek, gave their children assimilated names, and attended the same entertainments as did other urbanites. Those living in the west got their 'Romanization' by living as slaves in the houses of gentiles. Yet, despite their quasi-incorporation, the Jews were always suspect within the Empire, and, like unwanted bits of DNA in the larger body politic, they were attacked from time to time by its immune system.

The Hebrew Bible suggests a world largely apart from Greco-Roman culture. Its single God requires not only worship but love. It recognizes an afterlife even less well-defined than the one that the ancient pagans envisaged. While it features wars, its heroes are religious leaders. Perhaps oddest of all, it teems with old people – especially old men – who live to unheard-of ages. A revered 'Ancient One (or Ancient of Days)' appears in a dream-vision of Daniel: 'As I watched, thrones were set in place,/ and an Ancient One took his throne,/ His clothing was white as snow/ and the hair of his head like pure wool./ . . . A thousand thousands served him,/ and ten thousand times ten thousand stood attending him' (Dan 7:9–10). In the Greek world, Sappho's white hair was sad, but in the book of Daniel it is an attribute of the highest purity and authority. Around the time that Claudia Toreuma was calling old age an 'abomination', Jewish communities, and perhaps some fledgling Christian ones as well, were chanting Psalm 93 in their religious services:

> The righteous flourish like the palm tree,
>   and grow like a cedar in Lebanon.
> They are planted in the house of the Lord;

> they flourish in the courts of our God.
> In old age they still produce fruit;
> they are always green and full of sap.

Being green and full of sap did not preclude Isaac from going blind in his old age (Gen 27:1) nor did it prevent the elderly King David from becoming so cold that his servants had to find a young girl to lie with him and warm him up (1 Kings 1–4). Yet those old men, like many others, had special prestige in Hebrew Scriptures. When Solomon's son rejected the advice of 'the older men who had attended his father' and turned instead to his own youthful companions, Israel fell apart (1 Kings 12:6–8; 14:15). When the suffering Job lost patience and disputed with God, his friend Eliphaz rebuked him for thinking that he understood righteousness; 'the gray-haired and the aged are on our side, those older than your father', said Eliphaz; they know that God has his reasons (Job 15:10).

When Christianity was adopted as the official religion of the Roman Empire at the end of the fourth century, it overturned the traditional definitions: an old person 'reborn in Christ' was young; a young unbeliever was 'old'. It was a blessing to be advanced in years if you believed in Christ. Christians adopted the Hebrew Bible as prophetic of their own teachings, but they called it the 'Old' Testament. Their Gospels and other writings about Jesus were incorporated into a 'New' Testament. The birth of Isaac to old Sarah and Abraham in the Old Testament was understood as the precursor of the conception of John the Baptist by the elderly Elizabeth and Zechariah. Christian commentators transformed the Ancient of Days of Daniel's dream-vision into the 'One' of John's book of Revelation. Not only was *he* ancient, but he was surrounded by 24 old men: 'I looked,' said John, 'and there in heaven a door stood open! ... and there in heaven stood a throne, with One seated on the throne! . . . Around the throne are twenty-four thrones, and seated on the thrones are twenty-four elders, dressed in white robes, with golden crowns on their heads.' Soon a Lamb (interpreted as Christ) arrives and the elders worship it, each old man 'holding a harp and golden bowls full of incense, which are the prayers of the saints' (Rev 4:1–5:8).

That imagery was irresistible to medieval artists and sculptors. Illustration 14 is from the abbey church of St Peter at Moissac, one of many churches along the popular pilgrimage route to Compostela in northern Spain. Here the elders, some playing harps, fill every level of the tympanum (the semicircular space above the church portal). Even if we did not know about the visions of Daniel and John, we would know that these men *must* be old: their long beards give it away. Those in the bottom tier crane their necks to gaze at the One (here Christ). Twisting and turning like youngsters, they peer through the clouds on which He rests his feet, basking in the dazzling vision of the divinity.

Eyes on the Prize

Those old men were doing what all Christians were supposed to do. They had turned away from sin, the temptations of the flesh and the desire for earthly pleasures. In the Garden of Eden, Adam and Eve had savoured every joy virtuously. But as soon as they were tempted by the rebel Satan and had bitten into the one fruit forbidden to them, they lost all bliss. That was their Fall, a terrible fate, and with it God condemned them to labour and suffering, to old age and death. Only the birth of the sinless Christ offered humankind a way – a chance – to overcome the Fall and gain Paradise.

But that would happen only after the world came to an end. St Augustine (d. 430), an eloquent spokesman for this idea, explained that the purpose of life on earth was to make the right use of its blessings and hardships. Are you old and crippled? Suffer those conditions willingly and use your cane to walk to church. Virtuous old people knew that life after the Fall was not meant to be happy. Yet it was necessary, for it offered at least a taste of God's good order and peace in its social and political life. Its schools, churches and other institutions were necessary for people to learn about God, discover the salvation offered by Christ and obtain the promise of Paradise offered to the righteous. Earthly life also gave Christians the opportunity to *feel* rightly – to direct their love to God, not towards impermanent things; to exercise their anger on behalf of God, not to express their personal peeves. Heaven is always the goal. The believer on earth is like a pilgrim, pulled as if by a magnet to the place she longs for. Yet she is obliged to stop along the way to eat and sleep and perhaps (but just to keep the human race from dying out) to procreate and raise children. She makes use of earthly things while keeping her eyes on the prize.

The here and now is a perilous testing ground, weeding out the bad from the good. The aged pilgrim might come across a Fountain of Youth and, forgetful of her true goal, imagine she can blithely gambol in the waves, indulge in wanton sex and remain young forever (illus. 19). God forbid! For her there will be no salvation but punishment in the end.

More than three centuries before Augustine, Seneca had already suggested that life was a test, and both he and Augustine thought that its pains and sorrows should be endured with tranquillity. For Seneca, calm was achieved by seeing oneself as a cog in an intelligent (if indecipherable) universe. For Augustine, it was gained by clinging to God and his promise of eternal beatitude. He argued that everything on earth is impermanent. Only God is unchanging and eternal. The pleasures of the Fountain of Youth are temporary. Even peace, health and love (apart from the love of God) are temporary.

The true pilgrim understands why she must suffer: the pains of this world exist to punish her sins. If she has a long life, that is a blessing (no matter how abominable her old age may be) because it gives her a chance to be 'brought to penance . . . and amend'. The evil, the impure, the unbeliever, by contrast, does not understand the purpose of pain. She will persist in her hardness of heart. She will lay up 'a store of wrath in the day of God's anger and of the revelation of the just judgement of God'.[1]

Suffering on earth is necessary in order to gain eternal beatitude. This was a brand new idea, foreign to Jewish and Greco-Roman traditions. New models of behaviour, attitudes and feelings were needed to teach people how to face the sorrows of this life rightly. Such models were offered in written compositions called *Lives* and in sermons preached by priests and bishops. At first the *Lives* were about the martyrs, who endured deadly torture for their beliefs. Later, when no more martyrs were to be found, these texts told of the saints.

Other models abounded as well. Monks spent their whole lives in lengthy prayer and other ascetic practices. By the twelfth and thirteenth centuries there were numerous variants of monasticism. Consider Robert of Arbrissel, the founder in 1101 of Fontevraud, a monastery for both men and women. As he got old, 'he was ever more passionate in love of God, ever fresh, ever more devoted' (185).[2] When he became weak and knew that he was about to die, he made, according to one biographer, a 'praiseworthy end' by visiting his monks and nuns to strengthen their resolve to stay the course (187). Another biographer compared Robert to Job, since both died 'old and full of days' (Gen 42:17). Both were righteous men, but Job belonged to the old dispensation that promised only life on earth, while Robert belonged to the new that promised the eternal life to come.

Fighters

The monks and nuns of Fontevraud followed the *Rule* written by the sixth-century Italian abbot Saint Benedict. Somewhere between a set of laws and guidelines, it told those who wished to practise the religious life to cease following their own will and instead to take up 'the all-powerful and excellent arms of obedience to fight under the Lord Christ, the true king'.[3] Monks and nuns were expected to adhere to that Rule and continue its metaphorical battle until they died.

On grislier battlefields as well, the warrior for life was the prevailing ideal. The elderly medieval knight did not ordinarily have the option of sleeping near his weapons by night and doling out good counsel by day, as old Nestor had done. Rather, like Macbeth, he should remain 'bloody, bold, and resolute'. Let us listen to the testimony of two poems. The Old English *Beowulf* was probably originally composed in the eighth century, but the earliest exemplar left to us was written in the early eleventh century and reflects the ideals of its time. The Middle High German epic *Willehalm* was written by the German poet Wolfram von Eschenbach (d. after 1217).[4]

Beowulf features two very old kings: Hrothgar first.[5] King of the Danes for fifty years, he had once been 'the disperser of rings, gray-haired and vigorous in battle' (127).[6] But now, in his dotage, he sits as if paralysed on his throne, letting a monster come by night to eat his brave warriors. Rescue comes in the form of Beowulf, hero of Geatland (today's southern Sweden). Young, strong, resolute and enraged, he offers to help Hrothgar. The ogre arrives that very night, and Beowulf kills him.

Next he must face the monster's mother, bent on revenge. In her we see in medieval garb an old woman who, much like Hecuba, will stop at nothing. Beowulf is forced to pursue her to her lair at the bottom of an endless pool. The young hero defeats her at last, but only when he grabs her by the hair, throws her to the ground and kills her with her own sword.

Beowulf returns to Geatland and eventually becomes king there. Like Hrothgar, he rules for fifty years as 'an aged guardian of the homeland' (231). Then, repeating the Danish experience, a monster spewing flames now comes to his kingdom. Unlike Hrothgar, however, the aged Beowulf is ready to pick up his weapons. He seeks the serpent out, accompanied by twelve companions – like Christ and his Apostles. When they see the monster setting Beowulf afire, all (like multiple St Peters) deny their leader and run off in terror. Only one returns to help him. Together he and Beowulf slay the dragon.

Beowulf is mortally wounded, but before he dies, he speaks his feelings. Much like Cephalus, Cato and Fronto, he looks back and is pleased. Like them, he declares himself to have been a just man: 'I lived out at home my allotment of time, managed well what was mine, did not go looking for unwarranted aggression, did not swear multitudes of oaths in injustice . . . I can take satisfaction in all that.' He is gratified by the 'golden objects' that he has won from the dragon and asks to gaze on them as he dies so that 'in view of those costly things I will be able to give up more gently my life and my nation' (267).

The feelings of the warriors in *Beowulf* entail anger against the enemy, the joy of winning and the honour symbolized by rich booty.

In the thirteenth-century poem *Willehalm* there is still great joy and honour in winning, but now all combative anger derives from love. Here there are *three* old warriors, one of them female. There is Terramer, an infidel who loves his daughter, Giburc, even though she has married a Christian and converted from her father's religion. And on the other side of the war are old Heimrich and his fierce elderly wife Irmschart, the Christian parents of Willehalm, who is the loving husband of Terramer's daughter Giburc. The young people adore each other; the old people dote on their children. It is as if Wolfram, well-known for his love poetry, wanted to comment on how it felt to get old in the context of a Europe besotted with crusading spirit and romance.

Old Terramer and his troops win the first battle and surround Giburc in her castle. (Her husband, Willehalm, has left her alone to recruit more warriors.) In the upper tier of illustration 15, Terramer comes with Giburc's former, infidel husband to plead with his daughter: 'Alas, unhappy man that I am . . . that I ever had such a child . . . Whatever has happened, or will yet happen to you because of me, is my very own misery. Indeed, I would lay down my life for you' (4:115). He sounds like a chivalrous lover even though, at the same time, he is honour-bound to fight this recalcitrant daughter of his. Thus, when Giburc is unmoved, Terramer must authorize the assault, as he does in the bottom tier. (On the next page, top tier, not pictured here, Willehalm arrives home with reinforcements to save Giburc in the nick of time.)

The entire story of *Willehalm* is activated by love. Love makes old Terramer brave and a leader of his beloved men. It inspires his anguish when he sees that he has lost 23 of his finest. It leads him to tell Giburc that he would lay down his life for her. It also explains why young Willehalm and his elderly father, Heimrich, support each other. It is behind the delicate courtesies Heimrich shows to Giburc as they eat and drink with their warriors before the final battle. And it accounts for the fervour with which Willehalm's mother, the aged Irmschart, rallies dithering knights to fight for her son: 'Is this the way you show your bravery? . . . You must offer loans and gifts and help him who has come to us' (3:84). She offers 'an army at my own expense . . . to help you, dear son, [and] . . . I shall wear armour myself. I am a woman strong enough to bear arms at your side' (3:88).

Reciprocity

Old women warriors? Old men on the battlefield? Yes. Let us turn from these poems to assess other evidence. The Islamicate world sustained a warrior culture, much like Europe at the same time, and we are lucky to have the eyewitness testimony of Muslim writer Usama ibn Munqidh (d. 1188).[7] Usama reports that Hamadat, an 'old and feeble' retainer of his uncle Sultan in Syria, agreed to retire on a stipend of 'two dinars every month and a load of flour'. A bit later, he 'came to my uncle and said, "Sir, by God, I can't get used to just sitting around the house. I would rather be killed on my horse than die in my bed."' A few days later, when Sultan's army was attacked by crusaders, Hamadat 'was among the most courageous group' of defenders (60).

It was also sometimes the case that old women fought in Muslim armies. During an unexpected attack on Shayzar, the castle belonging to Usama's family, one very old woman, a former servant of Usama's grandfather, picked up a sword and 'went out into battle. And she kept at it until we [men] were able to climb up and overpower the enemy. So no one can deny that noble women possess disdain for danger, courage for the sake of honour and sound judgment' (137). Usama had great admiration for the old women that he knew, and he contrasted Muslim respect with the insolence of the crusaders, who did such unseemly things as set two 'decrepit old women' at one end of a field and have them race to win a roasted pig: 'At every step, the old women would fall down but then get up again as the audience laughed' (151). No doubt this was anti-crusader propaganda.

But we know from other sources that there were indeed women – even old women – in crusader camps. They usually worked as servants, such as the laundresses who kept linens clean for Richard I of England (d. 1199). Old women in crusader armies sometimes found their calling in making prophetic-like pronouncements, warning the fighters to repent or urging them into battle. At the other end of the social scale, female rulers and noblewomen sometimes put on war gear, and a few led expeditions and joined the men on the battlefield.

But many medieval battles, including those of the crusades, were fought by hired soldiers. Knights had many things to do in wars other than picking up arms: they prepared the crossbows and munitions, herded the livestock out of the way, determined strategies and raised troops, as Willehalm's mother promised to do. Old people could and did do all that.

There was no retirement age for warriors. Where vassalage was prevalent, it was a lifelong commitment, a quasi-marriage in which the lord (the army leader) and vassal (the lord's subordinate) pledged lifelong fidelity. It should not be surprising, therefore, that medieval histories and chronicles mentioned many old men who remained in the field. The most famous was the doge of Venice, Enrico Dandolo (d. 1205). Although in his nineties and blind, he led the assault of the crusaders on Constantinople during the Fourth Crusade.

It is true that here and there in Western Europe a few laws exempted the elderly from knightly service or excused old vassals from having to travel to do homage (pledge fidelity) to their lords. Some date as early as the twelfth century, but they are sparse. By contrast, archaeological, pictorial and literary evidence suggest the sheer normalcy of white-bearded men going to war.

Ageism

Didn't medieval poets, monks and warriors know that old age often brought crippled knees, strokes, dementia, blindness and other maladies? Of course they did! But those weaknesses were tolerable. There was one disability, however, that they considered outrageous and risible: old men and women who were still sexually active or who wanted to be. That was a legacy of the ancient world, which (as we have seen) featured impotent old men and rapacious old hags. In the Middle Ages, those ancient attitudes were reinforced by the ascetic values of the most prestigious of Christians – monks, hermits and recluses. Some saints, in youthful folly, might have been tempted by a beautiful woman, but none yielded, and all led blameless lives thereafter. It would be useless to ask about the sexual feelings of *old* saints: by definition, saints had conquered such feelings (if they ever had them) in their youth. Saints' lives were written (mainly by churchmen) for many reasons, but one of the most important was to offer them as models of feeling and comportment. That did not include sexual passion, which was labelled lust.

These models worked, especially when they were reinforced by social institutions. In the eleventh century, along with defining love as a sin if it was not directed to God, the Church newly emphasized clerical celibacy. This effectively forced churchmen into the saintly mould. Thus Peter Abelard (d. 1142), the most famous philosopher of his day and the passionate lover of Heloise in his youth, later condemned his once powerful feelings for her as pure lust. He conformed to that saintly model under extraordinary pressure – his clerical career required him to be celibate, and Heloise's furious uncle had him castrated. Heloise (d. 1163), unlike Abelard, never bought into it. Influenced by Ovid and troubadour love poetry, and shored up by her own keen intelligence, she maintained that unmarried love and sex together were the freest and least forced form of love. But she did not have a chance to test out her argument for very long, since Abelard became a monk and insisted that Heloise take vows as a nun.

Had she not entered a monastery, would she have maintained her opinion as she aged? She certainly would have been hard put to find sympathetic models of elderly passion to bolster it. Medieval writers followed the stereotypes of antiquity reinforced by a whiff of Christian asceticism. In his *Confession of the Lover* (*Confessio Amantis*), John Gower (d. 1408) presents himself as an old man sick with love. He appeals to various allegorical figures to cure him of his pain and suffering. At last, Venus decides to give him relief by telling him some hard truths. Old men try to make love but always 'fail in the attempt' (2415). The moral: Don't even bother. Was there no remedy? In a swoon Gower sees a parliament of all the great lovers of history. They are young; they dance, drink, feast and rejoice. Then he sees Old Age with *his* followers. No one smiles, and young girls dump their elderly swains as fast as they can: they take as their guide the seductress Delilah, who cut off Samson's hair and with it his masculinity. At last Venus takes pity on the poet. She takes out a mirror 'in which she bade me behold myself/ and take heed of what I see' (2822-3). He looks at a face without colour, eyes without sparkle, cheeks gaunt, wrinkles everywhere, hair turned grey (illus. 17). In short, he sees a man in the winter of his life. That cures him.[8]

Ludovico Ariosto (d. 1533) treated the issue succinctly. In *Orlando Furioso*, the beautiful Angelica is pursued by every man who meets her. When rescued by an old hermit, she imagines that she has found safe refuge at last. But no: he starts to hug, caress and touch her everywhere. She faints; he has her all to himself. But the joke is on him: 'He is limp as a rope. His aged body betrays him now.'[9]

If that hermit was stupid and ridiculous – and evil to boot – old women around the same time were utterly disgusting. Florentine poet Rustico Filippi (d. *c.* 1295/99), while dedicating many poems to young love, cultivated a satirical, vituperative register with which to berate political enemies, unfaithful wives and, most repellent of all, old ladies: 'Wherever you go, you bring the stench of the cesspit, you stinky old woman'.[10] Her odour reeks 'of a thousand tombs'. In the same vein, the English poet Geoffrey Chaucer (d. 1400), a good friend of John Gower, tells the tale of a knight forced by promise and obligation to wed and then go to bed with an old crone.

> For privately he wed her in the morning,
> And all day afterward he hid himself like an owl,
> So woeful was he, his wife looked so foul.
>   Great was the woe the knight had in his thought
> When to bed with his wife he was brought;
> He wallows and turns writhing,
> His old wife lay forever smiling,
> And said, 'O dear husband, bless me,
> Does every knight act with his wife as ye?'[11] (1080–88)

The old woman argues, with all the wisdom of a scholar, why her husband is wrong to reject her, concluding, 'Now where you say that I am foul and old/ Then do not fear to be a cuckold' (1213–14). The knight sees her point. Happily for all, she turns into a young and beautiful bride and a faithful wife to boot, the perfect mate for a knight driven by obligation.

Dissenting Voices

If ageism and misogyny were the norm, they were also contested. The poet Bertran de Born (d. 1215) argued that 'old age' is only 'in the mind'. A man is old only, he wrote, 'when one day flirting doesn't appeal to him'. In effect, when a man behaves like Ariosto's hermit, he is not yet old. And a woman is old only when 'she satiates herself with two lovers', suggesting that the more lovers she has, the younger she will be.[12]

Chaucer's crone, with her learned arguments about the benefits of marrying an old woman, in effect bucked the tradition.

So did Giovanni Boccaccio (d. 1375) in his *Decameron*, a collection of lively stories. One of them was about Master Alberto da Bologna, a wise yet amorous old man. His story offered a strong and poignant exception to the ageism of the day.[13]

Alberto, Boccaccio recounts, was a famed doctor nearly seventy years old. Even so, 'the nobility of his spirit was so great that it could still receive amorous flames even when almost all of the natural heat of his body had departed'. In due course, Alberto fell in love with 'a stunningly beautiful widow, Malgherida dei Ghisolieri'. Unable to rest unless he caught a glimpse of her each day, he haunted her neighbourhood. But she, gossiping with her friends and neighbours, knew exactly what was going on and made fun of him behind his back: 'It was as if they believed that the very delightful passion of love could enter and dwell only in the foolish hearts of the young and not anywhere else.'

The ladies continued to laugh at him and worse: one day they invited him over and plied him with sweets. Then, courteously but firmly, they upbraided him for thinking he might have a chance with a young beauty whom many eligible young men were courting at the same time. The good doctor was not at all embarrassed: 'My lady, the fact that I am in love should not be astonishing to any wise person, and especially not to you, since you deserve to be loved. And although the strength needed to make love has been taken from old men by Nature, it does not follow that they lack the feeling or understanding of what should be loved.'

In this story, Boccaccio adopted the famous dictum of a half-century or so before his day by the poet Guido Guinizelli: 'Love always finds its home in the gentle heart'.[14] In that poem, Guinizelli makes love and nobility synonymous; it nestles in the heart of those who are virtuous. Nobility does not consist in family bloodlines but rather in the worth of a man, indeed, in the worth of his very heart. With Master Alberto, Boccaccio declares that all 'gentle' men, old ones too, may feel love as strongly as the young. Indeed, perhaps they may feel it even more truly and fiercely because they have had more experience in such matters. Even if, perhaps, they cannot act on it.

The literary culture known as *adab* in the Islamic world had its own gentle way to deal with the erotic sorrows of the old man. Drawing on pre-Islamic Arab poetry, Jewish traditions, Islamic religious writings and Persian, Greek and Christian literature, the poetry of adab complained that women turned away from old lovers. But its moans were soft and tinged with hope: 'Don't be put off by the first few streaks of white:/ That's the smile of thought and refinement'.[15] And when it despaired, the sentiment was voiced lightly, expressing sweet nostalgia for lost beauty and days of merriment. Adab poetry never descended to the disgust of a Gower, the mockery of an Ariosto, viciousness of a Filippi or dogged earnestness of a Master Alberto.

Care for the Body and Soul

As a teacher at the University of Bologna, Master Alberto would have known a lot about the physical ailments of old age. No doubt he commented on the latest medical texts to his students, and very possibly he treated the sick and elderly. We know quite a bit about a different university master, Bartholomew (d. mid-1160s), who not only published many major medical commentaries that were widely known and copied, but treated the ailments of the aristocrats of his day. One of his patients was Louis VII (d. 1180), king of France; another was Peter the Venerable (d. 1156), abbot of the monastery of Cluny. Cluny was an institution of renown at the time. Beloved of donors rich and poor eager to give it gold and land in return for its spiritual benefits, Cluny also led an entire 'order' of monasteries that followed its customs, were subject to its regulations and benefited from its privileges.

When, about six years before his death, Cluny's Abbot Peter could not get rid of a persistent head cold and debilitating laryngitis, he wrote a desperate letter to Master Bartholomew. The usual remedy for illness was to purge diseased blood through bloodletting, but Peter had tried that. Bartholomew put his finger directly on Peter's problem: 'an excess of phlegm'. He advised the abbot to stop letting blood and instead to use 'medications [such as myrrh] that dry by purging [the] humor [of phlegm] and also soften [it] by moistening'. It is not odd that the doctor would prescribe this, since he knew, as he noted in one of his commentaries, that old age (*senium*; which started, he said, in one's fifties or sixties) was characterized 'by an accumulation of phlegmatic humour'.[16] A younger man might need bleeding but, as Galen had stated long before, each stage of life had its own remedies.

In an early fourteenth-century illustration of the Wheel of Life (illus. 16), God is at the centre of ten radiating spokes, each topped by a roundel. As in the scheme of the closely related Wheel of Fortune, life's high point is at the top. There, in the fifth roundel, is a richly dressed man seated on a throne. He wears a crown and holds a golden sceptre. Encircling him are the words, 'I am the king. I rule the world. The whole world is mine.' Thereafter, however, his fall is extremely rapid: in the sixth roundel, he uses a cane, in the seventh he must be led by a child; and in the eighth he is on his deathbed, attended by a doctor. (Stages nine and ten show his funeral and his tomb.) That the 'king' is fooling himself is clear from his quick fall into decrepitude and from the inscription circling Christ in the centre of the wheel, which says, 'I determine all simultaneously. I govern everything by my law [*ratione*].' There is no way any man or woman may escape the swift decline that God decrees.

Reciprocity

One churchman, friar Roger Bacon (d. *c.* 1292), thought he had discovered the secret recipe for the food that slowed down the wheel's speed and kept Adam alive to age 912 (Gen 5:5). But most clergymen advocated spiritual remedies – intercession and penitential charity – to delay death and secure salvation. Intercession was provided by exemplary religious figures – paragons of virtue who reconciled ordinary, sinful Christians with God. The penances that these saints imposed on themselves – prayers, humiliations, deprivations, obedience, fasts – gave them special purity and power. Christians who did not devote their whole lives to Christ thus gained vicarious spiritual benefit from those who did. They associated themselves with monks, hermits and other ascetics by donating land and alms to them. As they got older and closer to the day of reckoning, they often redoubled their charity.

As Lothario di Segni, the man who would become Pope Innocent III (d. 1216), wrote at the end of the twelfth century, rare are those who reach old age.[17] But the ones who do suffer in double measure. Physically, they are beset by weak hearts, tremors, loss of energy and reeking breath. That was an old refrain, borrowed from Aristotle and Roman satirical poets. But now, consider their spiritual suffering: they are terrified that they have not done enough to repent for their sins.

That was the dread that seized the young monk Egbert (d. 729). While studying in Ireland, he became very ill. Feeling himself at death's door, he 'began earnestly to consider his past life. He was so stricken with remorse at the memory of his sins that he wept bitterly, and prayed God with all his heart that he might not die until he had had time to make amends for all the thoughtless offences of which he had been guilty during infancy and boyhood and to practice good works more abundantly.' God granted his prayer. He remained as an exile in Ireland, fasted long and often, chanted the entire Psalter (150 psalms) every day along with the usual portion sung by all the monks, preached and gave away 'whatever he received from the rich'. Never flagging in his good works, he died 'beloved of God' at the age of ninety.[18]

Knights, too, sometimes heeded the call to do penance. Bertran de Born (d. 1215), the poet who thought old age was in the mind, was a wealthy lord in southern France. He loved war as much as he loved bedding down: 'War pleases me, though love and my lady make war on me all year long, for I see courts and gifts and pleasure all enhanced by war.'[19] Nevertheless, as a relatively old man, Bertran repudiated his erotic and warlike life to become a monk, retiring to a nearby Cistercian monastery at Dalon and endowing it with much of his property. (The Cistercians were Cluny's most important competitor for prestige and support.) He was soon prohibited from writing poetry but at least he, like all monks, chanted the poetry in the Bible every day, including the psalm that told them that old people were 'always green and full of sap'.

Why did Bertran hand over his land to a monastery? Indeed, why did he enter one himself? Those acts were part of a great round of reciprocation. Monasteries were great devourers of wealth. At the same time, they redistributed much of what they took in. Or they kept it in order to expand, build and sustain the monks within their walls in their never-ending lives of virtue, in which all Christians were thought to participate. Recall that wealthy people gave gifts to Egbert but then he, in turn, gave everything away. He was 'rich' yet voluntarily poor, a microcosm of the ideal monastic model.

So Bertran gave his property and himself to the house at Dalon, and some of those gifts were turned into aid to the 'poor', for whom he, even when a knight and poet, had shown particular solicitude. Swept into this category were the aged, who generally were indeed poor. People with weakened hearts, shaking heads,

8 Priam claims his son's dead body, scene from an amphora, c. 520–510 BCE. White of hair and beard, Priam confronts Achilles, under whose couch lies the corpse of his son. We know how the father and younger man must feel – Priam desperate to save Hector, Achilles contentedly drinking wine from a bowl – because we know the story. Otherwise, we might imagine a father reaching out to hug his son.

9 Marble head of an old woman, Roman copy of a Hellenistic original from the 3rd or 2nd century BCE. This head owes little to the classical ideal of beauty and may have been meant to evoke disgust or even derision in the Hellenistic viewer. Nevertheless, as she holds her head up high and even sports a slight smile, she may also have expressed the dignity of a woman who had laboured long and hard, possibly as a nurse.

10 Aeneas carries his father Anchises and leads his son Julus by the hand as they escape Troy, 1st century CE, terracotta. The image of Aeneas carrying his father as they escaped the ravaging of Troy was iconic in both ancient Greece and Rome.

11 Three actors playing female roles, 2nd century to early 1st century BCE. This scene from a Greek or Roman comedy on a floor mosaic features an old lady who, much like Dipsas, is giving advice to two young women. Her frontal position suggests that she is advising her audience as well.

12 Li Gonglin, *The Classic of Filial Piety*, c. 1085, detail, ink and colour on silk. The artist has created a visual ideal of family reverence. The elderly parents sit on a raised dais as their son and his wife provide them with food. Entertainers, along with the seated grandchildren, add to the old couple's pleasure.

13 Angelo Morbelli, *Feast Day at the Trivulzio Hospice*, Milan, 1892, oil on canvas. Wintry sun illuminates a sad scene: it is a holiday, but these old men sit lonely and apart in a large, bare room at their hospice, Pio Albergo Trivulzio. An act of piety when founded in 1766, at the end of the 19th century, when this painting was made, the hospice symbolized not good deeds but rather the neglect of the poor, old and sick.

14 Detail of the tympanum in the south portal, Abbaye Saint-Pierre de Moissac, c. 1125, which depicts much of John's vision of heaven in Revelation 4:1–5:8. John's vision makes elderly men major players in a drama of praise and worship.

15 At the top of this carefully organized and illustrated manuscript of *Willehalm* (1270–75), Terramer is fitted out like every other warrior, in chain mail and helmet. But in the lowest tier, his age is telegraphed by his white hair and beard.

16 Wheel of the ten ages of man, from the Psalter of Robert de Lisle, *c.* 1310. Here the ages of man include not only infancy, youth and adulthood but the various stages of decline and demise. Even death constitutes an age, integrated through prayer into the world of the living.

17 An artist nearly contemporary with John Gower (early 15th century) presents him in this manuscript illumination as an old man making his confession to a priest.

18 Aert Pietersz, *Rich Children, Poor Parents*, 1599, oil on panel. The impoverished parents virtually beg from their richly dressed progeny, who hold out empty hands. Their explanation is written on a plaque at the right, 'O father see,/ I have nothing,/ being married now,/ to give to you.'

19 Giacomo Jaquerio, *Fountain of Life*, 1418–30, detail, fresco. Medieval fountains usually evoked Paradise, but this one, painted on a wall of the baronial hall at the Castello della Manta, is a fraud, a place of lustful coupling and dissolute behaviour.

20 Giorgione, *The Old Woman*, c. 1506–7, oil on canvas. The woman points to her chest as she holds a banderole with the inscription *col tempo* (with time). She depicts both a particular person and an allegory about the fate of us all.

21 Bartolomé Esteban Murillo, *An Old Woman Holding a Distaff and a Spindle*, c. 1650–60, oil on canvas. The new capitalist work ethic demanded all to work unless they were utterly incapable of doing so. Spinning was a typical job for old women. It could be done at home amid other domestic chores.

22 Françoise Duparc, *The Old Woman*, before 1778, oil on canvas. This old woman crosses her reddened arms, evidence of the hard work she has done. But unlike the old woman in illustration 21, she is not hard at her distaff, nor is her face lined with wrinkles. Indeed, she is gently beautiful, and her expression frank, kind and benign. She expresses the sort of tranquillity about ageing that hitherto had been communicated almost exclusively by men.

23 Jean-Baptiste Greuze, *Filial Piety* (*The Paralytic and His Family*; *The Benefits of a Good Education*), 1763, oil on canvas. It was Diderot, guiding spirit of the *Encyclopédie*, who advocated the subtitle *The Benefits of a Good Education*. The entire family gathers around the old grandfather as he is being fed. Even the dog (bottom-right corner) is looking on.

24 The Ostermeyers, Iowa homesteaders who had lost their land, 1936. Hired to chronicle the poverty of tenant farmers in the north, Russell Lee (d. 1986) produced six photographs of the elderly Ostermeyers, Andrew (age 81) and his wife (age 76). The couple lost their own farm to a loan company and at the time of this photograph worked on the land of their son.

waning vigour and reeking breath might invite scorn, but they also inspired charity. A miracle story from the late thirteenth century tells of Gilbert of Sens, sixty years old, who suffered from a debilitating palsy.[20] Because his head and hands shook so violently, 'he could not bring his cup to his mouth.' He survived by begging. But in order to eat, he depended 'many times on his neighbours or the people who lodged him' to spoon-feed him. Happily, he found a richer and more powerful patron to care for him: Saint Louis. Hearing of the wonders at the saint's tomb, Gilbert went there and remained there 'day and night for many days in order to be cured'. A miracle took place: his shaking ended, he was rejuvenated, he no longer needed to beg, and he could feed himself.

It was Christianity, not the ancient world, that institutionalized almsgiving. Guilds helped out those within their ranks who were too old to work, and monasteries such as Cluny and Dolan regularly offered food to the poor in rituals of caregiving at particular times of the year. The monks and nuns at Fontevraud 'took in the poor and did not reject the frail. Nor did they refuse unchaste women, concubines, lepers, or the powerless' (176–7). The feelings that motivated these gestures very likely included pity and compassion for the sick and aged, but they also involved self-regarding feelings: the hope that such acts would be judged as pious and worthy of heavenly salvation. Monks and nuns practised the reciprocal economy of salvation: the laity gave alms to them (or rather to God through them); they in turn helped Christ's poor. All were saved. That was the theory, at any rate.

Getting By

Thanks to the research of Lucie Laumonier, we know a good deal about some key charitable institutions at late medieval

Montpellier, one of a number of precocious commercial centres along the Mediterranean littoral.[21] Although called 'hospitals', their first calling was not medical. Rather, their major vocation was to protect the weak, the abandoned, the defenceless and the poor. The elderly figured among all of these. Montpellier's four large hospitals were capacious enough to accommodate most of its needy citizens, and some smaller hospitals took in most of the rest. Administered by the municipal government, these institutions attracted support from all quarters of the city, endowing them with land and property as well as alms. It was a good thing, too, for in the course of the wars, famines and plagues of the thirteenth through fifteenth centuries, numerous Montpelliérains fell into miserable circumstances.

Some people dedicated themselves to a hospital, their testaments making clear the connection between their self-sacrifice and their piety. A document drawn up by a notary for Béatrice Gavandarie in 1347 at Montpellier reads in part, 'considering that to serve God is to reign [with him] and wanting to dedicate myself to the service of God and the Blessed Virgin Mary, I sell, give, and dedicate myself to [them] to serve the poor and the beggars that flock to [the hospital].' She promised to give the hospital a sum of money, bedding and two chests. In return, she would be assured of a roof over her head as well as food and drink for the rest of her life (330).

At any one time a bit less than 8 per cent of the population of Montpellier was counted as elderly. That is not a large number; in Florence around the same time, those aged sixty and older made up a bit more than 14 per cent of the population. It is likely that the difference is due to documentation; Florence kept meticulous records that still survive. What is absolutely clear, despite its sparse documents, is that old age in Montpellier often meant poverty. Most of the elderly who lived with others were poor, and those who lived alone were poorest of all (299).

That was a bitter pill. When tax officials there described impoverished old women, they omitted the honourable term 'widow', identifying them simply as 'old, penniless and very poor' (300). And when they met with men too old, weak and debilitated to work, these nevertheless often declared a profession to avoid shame. As the people of Montpellier became old and sometimes descended from wealth to poverty, they did not – could not – shed the status assumptions of their day.

Families were expected by both law and custom to care for those members who could no longer care for themselves, and emotions could run high over this. In 1433, for example, a woman named Astruga disinherited her married daughter because the younger woman had not visited her for two months even though she knew her mother had been ill. But a reconciliation was still possible, and Astruga's move in 1433 was probably part of a longer story of mother–daughter estrangement and reconciliation (304). No wonder many elderly people preferred to turn to surrogate families. Thus, when the widow Bartholoméa ceded her property to the farmer Peyre Bérenguier, she did so 'on account of the close and true and cordial affection that I have toward you' – the 'you' referring to her adoptive family. In return Peyre promised to maintain her until her death with food, clothing, shoes and a roof over her head, 'just as a good son ought and is expected to do for his mother'.[22]

Landowners at Montpellier sometimes turned their families into corporations of a sort. Thus, Peyre Marsan and his wife arranged and generously provided for the marriages of their daughters but stipulated that everyone live together under the same roof; patriarch and matriarch keeping the profits from the land while the young adults worked it. While a practical arrangement, it no doubt had emotional ramifications ranging from familial affection to resentment and conflict. But the latter probably was kept under wraps by filial piety and the fact that the parents held the purse strings. In due course the younger set would inherit the property (310–11).

In Florence and its environs, gerontocracies such as Peyre Marsan's were the ideal though not always the reality. In the fictional dialogue *On the Family* by Renaissance polymath Leon Battista Alberti (d. 1472), the familial model included a large and fine house 'in a good neighborhood . . . where honorable citizens lived'. Within, everyone in the family was happy to 'live under one roof, to warm themselves at one hearth, and to seat themselves at one table'.[23]

The wise speaker in Alberti's dialogue was the aged Giannozzo, a real person recently deceased but distantly related to Alberti. Alberti portrayed him as the happiest of all men. Like Cato in Cicero's dialogue, Giannozzo is in admirably good health, though he complains a bit about his flagging energy. Yet consider: he is the centre of the common table, telling everyone what to do, demanding and getting the reverence of all, doling out advice to the youngsters. An old man may be weak, but he has many compensatory privileges.

Alberti, an artist and architect as well as a writer, might well have painted the familial dinner scene something like Leonardo da Vinci's *Last Supper* (1494/8), where the disciples occupy the space that normally would be filled by the family gathered around its patriarch.[24] Court cases show how tyrannical and manipulative Florentine fathers might be and how unhappy and resentful they could make their sons. A father's death often spelled their liberation – and that of their wives as well.

Patriarchal models had less influence in the north of Europe. In the English countryside, old peasants found ways to ensure a decent retirement as long as they had some property to exchange for their care. Manorial courts drew up legal contracts on behalf of the elderly, imposing obligations on all sides. If agreements were broken, the courts imposed penalties. So, for example, in

1322 Estrilda Nenour, a widow living on a manor in Essex, drew up a contract with her daughter Agnes. She transferred to her a *messuage* (a house, outbuildings, some land) and another fifteen acres of land; in return Agnes promised to provide for her with food, clothing and shelter. Five years later, Estrilda brought a claim against Agnes for defaulting. The manorial court judged in her favour and returned her original holdings to her. That same year she entered into a similar agreement with Robert Levekyn and his wife, probably unrelated to her though living on the same manor. This time the contract stipulated that if the arrangement did not work out, then Robert and Alice were to give her an annual cash payment instead. Not long afterwards, Robert and Alice set up a similar arrangement with younger people on the same manor. Not a pension system, for it had to be initiated by old people rather than come to them as their due, it nevertheless suggested – along with urban hospitals and guilds – that family support for the elderly could be supplemented by other institutions.

Retiring on a Pension

The weavers' guild at Ghent (in Flanders) founded a hospital (*godshuis* in the Low Countries; *maison Dieu* in northern France; almshouse in England) for its elderly members before 1336, but space was limited, and some beds were reserved for masters and the sick. At nearby Bruges, seafaring skippers supported a hospital for their elderly guild members to save them from begging. The families of the old men went with them, and sometimes their widows stayed on. This was a twist on the patriarchal model: the former 'breadwinner', once an active member of the guild, continued to provide for his family – and not only because his earlier status entitled him to share in the fruits of the labour of his younger 'brethren' but because, unless he were utterly decrepit, he could continue to work at light tasks, such as gardening, cleaning and nursing.

Guilds treated the language of brotherhood seriously. Not only were all Christians brothers in Christ, but guildmembers were brothers affectively as well. They cared for their own – provided that their needy members were deserving of aid and were of upright morals. In the fourteenth and fifteenth centuries, the major London guilds established or were entrusted with almshouses for their sick and elderly guildsmen and -women. A portion of the income for these guilds – from rents, entry fees and alms collected from guildmembers – was generally placed in a strongbox and distributed once a week in the form of small pensions. Between 1400 and 1409, the number of mercers (dealers in fine fabrics) who received guild alms each year averaged around four, while the number of tailors hovered at fifteen. In the next decade the tailors were joined by a few drapers and brewers.[25] Clearly the numbers cared for were symbolic. Such hospitals did not solve the problems of the majority of destitute men and women, even those who laboured all their lives. And it may be that many former urban workers resisted entering almshouses, which required them to pray a lot. Indeed, the denizens of almshouses were sometimes called 'bedesmen and -women' – 'men and women who prayed'. In that sense, they had the same social role as monks.

Richard Whittington's bequest to create an almshouse for the mercers' guild in London helps us see some of the emotional norms and expectations of the wealthy merchant class of the fifteenth century. Whittington (d. 1423), by the way, inspired the rags-to-riches tale of Dick Whittington and his cat. He explained why he endowed the almshouse: 'The fervent desire and best intention as a prudent, wise, and devout man should be . . . to make secure the state and the end of his short life with deeds of mercy and pity . . . Whereby on the day of the Last Judgment he may take his place with those that shall be saved.'[26] Desire, devotion, mercy and pity – all to save Whittington's soul. It is sometimes thought that such wills reflected fear of Judgement Day, and surely that was the hope of fire-and-brimstone preachers. But two things modify this view: first, such deeds *secured* a happy outcome; Whittington had no need to be afraid. Second, largesse on the scale of Dick Whittington's tended to be the case mainly for the childless rich. Without heirs, he could freely give away his money.

Let us turn southwards. Florentine guilds were unlike others in serving the wider urban community as well as their impoverished and elderly guild members. Evidently the image of patriarchs who never gave up their power (reinforced by Alberti's picture of the family and Florentine tax documents) told only part of the story. The great guild of cloth finishers annually distributed grain to the urban poor as well as to their own guild members fallen on hard times. An annual receipt of grain was not, however, equivalent to a pension.

Further south, though, in Islamic Syria and Egypt, the elites continued the public service tradition of Cicero's Cato. We see that most clearly in the thirteenth to fifteenth centuries, when well-educated men – those with positions in law, government and higher education – tried to serve until they expired. Some lived into their sixties, nearly as many into their seventies and a few reached their eighties. True, a few were unable to continue. Some of these retired to the equivalent of monasteries. Others may have silently let their sons take over their jobs without fanfare.

Those men had desk jobs. The story was different for the professional soldiers who worked for the Egyptian sultans of the time, the Mamluks. While their ideal was still to die in the saddle (as it was for warriors in Europe, as we have seen), some swordbearers became too feeble to ride and fight.

In such instances, the sultans granted a special privilege: the good old soldier was permitted 'to settle down as [a] *tarhan* and ... no longer be demanded for service neither by day nor by night, neither to use the javelin nor the horse'. Moreover, he was given 'benefactions and abundant favors'. In short, the *tarhan* received an old age pension. Allowed to retire from service, he could 'stay where he wants and ... travel whenever he likes'.[27] The practice seems to have become more common over time. Given that the Mamluks were organized as a militia with state power, the *tarhan* might well have mourned his loss of status as a warrior. Indeed, there is some evidence of this. But having the privilege of a *tarhan* in hand did accord him a kind of dignity in his old age.

It would not be until the twentieth century that states instituted quasi-automatic pension systems for people (men and women) who, after a lifetime of working, reached a certain age, generally in their sixties. Mamluk pensions were different: they were unsystematic, limited to male soldiers only and dependent not on age but debility. Nevertheless, Mamluk state support was in other ways very modern. It acknowledged that a man's working life could properly come to an end without shame. It divorced financial help from religious charity and moral behaviour. And it recognized that old age involved both neediness and dignity. All this was an exceptional historical development.

The Voices of the Old

The soldiers of the Islamicate world celebrated both war and love, but they did not put the two together as Bertran and Wolfram and other Western writers did. This we can see in the *Book of Contemplation* by the old Arab soldier, Usama ibn Munqidh, whom we have met briefly before reporting on old women knocking themselves out for a pig. Like all first-person accounts, his *Contemplation* invites both delight and scepticism – delight because at last we hear a real voice; scepticism because people may misremember, make things up and put a self-interested spin on things. And that same point holds for the other voices I will take up here: a very personal treatise on old age written by Boncompagno da Signa, and the letters written by the Italian humanist Francis Petrarch.

In 1095, the year in which Pope Urban II preached the First Crusade in Europe, Usama ibn Munqidh was born in Syria. We saw that his family held the castle at Shayzar, impregnable against the attacks of the various Muslim factions, the Byzantines and the crusaders of the time. But Usama, exiled as a possible rival by his uncle, left home in 1137. Twenty years later, an earthquake shattered Shayzar and the remainder of Usama's family was wiped out. Constantly on the move, Usama served as a warrior and adviser to several important Muslim commanders and was also renowned as a poet and accomplished practitioner of adab.

The conflictual political situation in Syria and Egypt during his lifetime required him to spend much of his life as a warrior – whether against (or on occasion with) the crusaders or against factions of the Islamic community. But at the age of 69, he more or less retired from the battlefield and moved to Diyar Bakr, far to the north of his usual haunts. It was then that he turned to putting together anthologies on particular topics and composing books of poetry. He probably also began working on his *Book of Contemplation*, a compendium of exemplary anecdotes, reminiscences, reflections on Fate (God determines all, down to the very second) and his own feelings as an old man.

He was miserable being old, nor did he see anything redemptive or admirable in his pains. He was no Galen, no Bacon, thinking that he could stave off the pains of old age with diet and exercise or secret remedies. He mourned the loss of his physical strength, stamina and agility: 'Bent with weakness to the ground I nearly touch, my limbs twist into each other ... My present self I do not recognize, my past I smother with dismal sighs.' Where now was the 'firebrand in war' he once was? 'I fanned the flames with the striking of swords on our enemies' heads./ My concern has ever been personal combat with my rivals, whom I considered/ But simple prey, such that they shook in terror of me.' Unlike Western knights such as Bertran, love of a woman had nothing to do with Usama's fighting spirit. If anything, he belittled women and, as an old man, ruefully declared himself 'like some sort of young girl'. Once glorious in armour, he was now wrapped in rich silks – 'shame on me, shame on this cloth'. The life of ease made him feel 'rotted through'; at night he tossed and turned on his 'downy pillows' as if they were 'sharpened stones'.[28]

Most personally painful was the loss of Shayzar Castle, now a fallen ruin, and the greater part of his family dead in the rubble. In the preface to an anthology of poetry (some his own) that he compiled in his mid seventies, he wrote that after the earthquake, 'disaster followed after disaster from that time and henceforth. And so I sought solace in compiling this book, and fashioned it as a keening for my homeland and beloved ones ... [From God] I beg recompense from what I have encountered in my life, my separation from my household and my kin, and my estrangement from hearth and homeland.'[29]

To some extent, he got that recompense before he died. The new sultan, Saladin, invited him to live out his final days in Damascus, offered him every honour and plied him with gifts. In prose bordering on poetry, Usama reflected on this unexpected change. 'In his mercy [Saladin] sought me out across the land ... in a forsaken corner of the world [Diyar Bakr], having no kith, no kin ... The parts of me Time had broken, he put them in splints to hold, and in his generosity he found a market for that which others had deemed unsaleable, too old.'³⁰ What Usama left out of this encomium is that he had greased Fortune's wheel himself by showering Saladin with poems of praise even before the conqueror became sultan.

In Damascus, Usama got a new lease on life at first: the presence of his own son, Murhaf, who served Saladin; the favour of the sultan himself; the company of other masters of adab at court. But when Saladin went off on campaigns or moved his court to Egypt, he was once again overcome with loneliness. He fought against that feeling by continuing his *Book of Contemplation*.

Loneliness has come up in this history before now, but only rarely. The Greeks did not talk about it much. Juvenal imagined how it would feel to lose beloved children in one of his poems, and at least one tombstone bewailed it. In medieval Europe, most warriors did not move around from one commander to another – they had incomes from their castles, neighbourhood support, families to depend on and monasteries to retire to. Usama reveals the emotional suffering of the peripatetic Muslim warrior grown old, especially one who no longer had an extended family. No doubt Usama was particularly gregarious; nevertheless, we may see from his example why some Mamluk retirees might not have been happy even with a nice pension.

At least Usama was well-off, unlike Boncompagno da Signa (d. after 1240), author of *On the Evil of Old Age and Senility*.³¹ He spent the first part of his life as a master of rhetoric at the University of Bologna (around the time that Boccaccio's Master Alberto was teaching there) penning no less than ten books and receiving the city's highest honour. But with stardom came envy and enemies, and he was forced to leave Bologna to seek his fortune in other cities. For a while he got a job as papal legate, but his connections at the papal curia did not last. By the time he wrote *On Old Age*, he was an old man himself and down on his luck. It was his last book and his final attempt to find a patron to support him. It did not succeed, and Boncompagno died penniless in a hospital in Florence which, as we have seen, was open to the larger urban community.

Boncompagno meant his book to be a companion and comfort to the old, since it was written by someone himself subject to their deterioration and humiliation. He had read Cicero's *Cato* but was unimpressed. How could Cicero's book be useful to the elderly when it didn't tell them how to cleanse their sins with 'laments and penitence' and to protect themselves from the 'contagion of the vices' (5)? How could they understand what was happening to them if they didn't know the ordinary course of ageing and its physical effects? Boncompagno would give them the guidance they needed. That he would supersede Cicero was quite a claim coming, as it did, from a professor of rhetoric. Cicero was in his day the model rhetorician par excellence.

For Boncompagno, Cicero not only was useless for old people but missed the main point: Cato's contentment derived from his wealth. He may have claimed that he enjoyed old age because he had always lived temperately, but Boncompagno knew better. 'The punishment [of the old] is physical pain aggravated by poverty. Their misery is a painful torment of spirit and body pressed down by the weight of illness and indigence' (11). If some people of the same age seemed older than others, continued Boncompagno, that was because their health was better, and that was the case when they were better off economically. People get old fast when they lack the means to sustain themselves. They work beyond their limit; they are poor; they are sick; they live in a substandard environment. The people of Venice live longer than others because they have healthy air, sea, and sky (16–17).

There is no way to count the punishments and miseries of the old, 'because everything they do and everything that they think are a sort of chastisement' (11). Even so, Boncompagno enumerates some of the sorrows and points out that all lead to shame, humiliation and rejection. Boncompagno lived in an honour society, much like the one that the Florentine tax records described, where the old paterfamilias should theoretically bask in his prestige and dominate the entire household. But, Boncompagno says, the emotional reality for the old man – even the rich old man – is very different. He expels fluids that offend those around him; he is ashamed when he compares himself to those in their prime; he is humiliated as others – above all the young – avoid him, repelled by his very looks.

And he *is* repulsive: his teeth are falling out, his gums are decaying, his eyes are rheumy. His backbone is curved so that head touches his knees. He wants to speak but his tongue can't form the words. Here Boncompagno has employed the old tropes about the aged for a new use: to show not only that the old are repugnant but to make clear the emotional consequences of *being* repugnant. He is explaining how the old (himself included) feel about being objects of scorn and about thinking of *themselves* that way. Much later John Gower will allow Venus to tell him the same hard truth, but that fact is couched in an allegory and is meant for laughs: Ha, ha: how could the old poet imagine he might be a lover? Even he laughs at himself. Gower says nothing about how poverty exacerbates the scorn. Boncompagno is a realist before realism. He recognizes that feelings are social; that a poor man will get less respect than a rich one, and that when the family (even a wealthy one) doesn't care to spend time with 'old grandpa', the old man will not laugh at himself (as Gower supposes) but rather will feel rejected, weeping at his inability to control his bowels.

Aristotle had criticized old men because they were suspicious of others. Boncompagno explains why: 'the old – particularly the deaf and the blind – mistrust the actions and words of others because they suspect that all of them nurse malevolence in their heart in whatever they do or say' (13). Perhaps that was the case in Aristotle's time as well: although care for elderly parents was the law, children did not necessarily enjoy doing so. Admetus wanted his parents to die in his place; Procleon's son was dismayed by his father's wanderlust; Sophocles' son reportedly wanted his father to be declared mentally incompetent by a jury so that he would no longer control his money, although the old man outsmarted him by reading his final play aloud in court.

Boncompagno speaks particularly of the deaf and blind because they have the disabilities that make the elderly even more suspicious than usual. But another disability is suffered by most old men: the double torment (as he puts it) of their sexual impotence. 'While they expend their energies on their ridiculous love ... they find neither the spirit that urges, nor the heat that melts, nor the humour that rushes forward.' Their wives are repelled by them, and they live in the intolerable fear that someone else is 'planting a gourd in their garden' (15). Here the author touches upon the usual derision of the aged lover. But he does so to make a new point. Old men haven't a chance: either they are laughed at or they are despised. It's one thing to laugh when they do or say something stupid. But when their wives deprecate them, their sons vilify them, their friends abandon them – when, in short, no one wants to talk with them – then they are not ridiculed but abominated, deigned unworthy of human company.

How far we are from Socrates who 'delighted' to talk with the old (it was Cephalus who retreated from the conversation) and from Cato, who boasted that young men sat entranced at his feet. Boncompagno lived in the era of the palsied beggar Gilbert of Sens, and because his own age and need for charity demanded it, he was sensitive to their plight. He was exceptionally aware, too, of the gap between rich and poor – a social fact that north Italian city-states made clear on every street.

Given that there was no 'third way' between being abominated and ridiculed, Boncompagno observed, it was no surprise that everyone over fifty, men and women both, tried to hide their ageing with dyes and make-up.

Francesco Petrarca, or Petrarch (d. 1374), however, found a third way: he was one of the pioneers of humanism and highly regarded throughout his life. Living about a century after Boncompagno, Petrarch belonged to a new movement. The son of a notary, his calling was classical Latin literature. He collected and read old manuscripts from monastery and church libraries, considering both activities part of a sort of rescue mission. What he saved from oblivion (he thought) were the ideas and eloquence of the ancient Romans. Unlike Boncompagno, he had the money and leisure to spend his life this way by taking clerical orders, obtaining various church stipends and serving as an ambassador for various wealthy high office-holders of the Church. His patrons were not necessarily scholars themselves, but they were always exceptionally interested in what the humanists were discovering, much as wealthy CEOs today are excited by AI, deep sea exploration and space travel.

The old manuscripts represented the writings of the great Roman authors, masters of elegant Latin and ancient thought. But Petrarch was almost equally enamoured of the verses of vernacular poets such as Guinizelli. Indeed, Amor (Love personified, as it had been for Guinizelli) found its 'refuge' in Petrarch's heart via a young woman named Laura, the sight of whom shattered the barricades that guarded his feelings. Scholars are not sure that Laura was a real person, but she certainly lived for Petrarch, who so fully embodied her in his mind's eye that she existed for him not only as his young and beautiful Lady (the usual fantasy) but as an old woman, with 'the light of your beautiful eyes dimmed and your hair of fine gold turn to silver'.[32] Now that her face has lost its rosy hue and her presence no longer dazzles him like a spring day, does he, like Rustico Filippi, make fun of the stinky hag? Not at all! He had never dared to declare his love to Laura, for her marvellous beauty overcame his senses, her virtue paralysed him and her eyes offered him nothing but scorn. But now that she is no longer ravishing, he will have the courage to reveal to her 'the years, and the days, and the hours' of his torment. 'And if time is hostile to my sweet desires, at least it will not prevent my sorrow from receiving some little help of tardy sighs.' As an old woman she will know how much he loved her, and she will regret her youthful disdain. More than a century had to pass before an artist painted an old woman who similarly evoked both the bitterness and pathos of her lost youth (illus. 20).

Petrarch involved himself in politics, hobnobbed with the great rulers of church and state, and gained fame for his poetry and prose in both Latin and Italian. He never wed but had two children whose mothers are not known. Throughout his long and varied life, he made his feelings the constant focus of his thought, considering them from every angle and in every context, as one might examine a highly faceted jewel under different lights. Inspired by Cicero's letter collections, Petrarch gathered his own missives together (in the process discarding many, making some up, revising others and changing some dates). When that compilation became too large, he assembled the remaining letters for another book and, at about the same time, started a new miscellany that he called the *Seniles* (*Letters of Old Age*). He began it in 1361, when he was around 57 years old, and continued it until he died.

The first letter in *Seniles* (carefully chosen as such by the author) is full of laments about old age. The plague of 1348, the so-called Black Death, had long before made off with many of his dearest friends as well as his beloved Laura. Now, in 1361, a new wave of the pandemic has hit. Two of the people closest to his heart have succumbed: his 24-year-old son, Giovanni; and his very best friend, Socrates (Petrarch's admiring nickname for Lodewijk Heyligen, a Flemish monk). Taking on the persona of a Roman such as Cicero and Seneca, Petrarch confesses his sorrow while at the same time declaring his fortitude. He wants to cry and moan, but that would be unseemly for a man of his years, education and virtue: 'A groan is more shameful than a fall' (1.1).[33] Turning to a related issue, Petrarch reconciles his vaulting ambition and desire for fame with the futility of seeking glory in the grand scheme of things: 'O treacherous life of man! Never do we cease embarking toward distant hopes that cannot be realized in such a brief period. Yet we keep on, toiling away, and even – how insane! – we find pleasures and exult in honours' (1.3).

Yes, it is insane. Yet Petrarch understands very well why he continues to toil and exult: his writings are his 'little children', the progeny that will keep him alive and speak to posterity when he is dead and gone. They are unlike human children, so sweet, so beloved – and so terribly mortal (10.4). The brilliant Latin writers of the past – Cicero, Seneca, Ovid and the others – are vividly 'present' for Petrarch through their deathless offspring. His friends are reincarnations not of the flesh but of the voices and thoughts of the ancients. Petrarch's children will be immortal for future generations too – you and me!

He has not forgotten the models of Christian saints and ascetics nor repudiated the existence of heaven and hell. Rather, he folds them into God's good plan, which includes secular affairs. Writing to the priest Francesco Nelli, to whom he dedicated his *Seniles*, he observes that the deaths of his dear ones – and his own demise one day – mean that 'we must cease our groaning and useless complaints and turn to holy offerings and prayers for their salvation' (1.3). Yet even as he says that, he is not praying but rather planning to travel northwards, whence he has been summoned by Emperor Charles IV. Wars frustrate his plan, but at least he may retreat to his study, and he begs Nelli to send him a book, 'the promised ornament of this library, in which dwells all my repose and my mind's delight, and now the sole solace of my life' (1.3).

He knew that old age meant losing your beloved friends and anticipating your own death down the road. Yet at one point in his sixties, he wrote to unnamed friends about how fully he rejoiced at being old. He was, as he admitted, 'not yet bent over, looking at the ground', but he imagined that even when that happened, he would, like Seneca, remain tranquil (8.2). And, at least in his public persona, that turned out to be true. Even when, at the age of 66, he became very ill, he wrote long, joking letters to one of his doctors, making light of the prescribed remedies.

Petrarch bypassed Boncompagno's terrible alternatives for the old, which hovered between abomination and ridicule, because he was a humanist, part of a new and hugely prestigious calling in the war-torn and plague-ridden Italy of his day. Humanists sought balm for the wounds of the present in the solutions of the ancient past. Creating an informal community of like-minded men (and a very few women), they built networks of friends that crossed boundaries and included (through their reading) the dead as well as the living. They scorned what Petrarch scorned – false prophets, astrologers, quack doctors (the majority) and hasty, foolish people – and valued what he valued: communing with the ancients, learning from them, creating poetry and books inspired by them and mingling his thoughts with theirs by writing to or visiting with humanist friends.

Thus, as an old man, Petrarch continued to do what he had always done. He even intended 'to double my pace, especially now, and hasten to the goal at sunset' (17.2). When his friend and disciple Boccaccio worried about his own humanistic studies because a so-called prophet told him that he had little time left and that he had better repent, Petrarch declared the idea nonsense. We all know from the moment of our birth that we will die. Just because a man is old does not mean he must 'concentrate on the things of the soul'. That would mean depriving a humanist of his one source of happiness – the classical muses. 'I see nothing in this but taking away solace and comfort from your old age,' he wrote to Boccaccio (1.5). To abandon what has always given you joy from your earliest youth is a terrible idea. Petrarch recognized that Saint Augustine had said that the purpose of life is to spend it in tears and penance. But he also knew that Augustine had spent most of his life studying knotty Latin texts. Had that great Church Father given those up for a life of ascetism, he never would have created the decisive theology of the Western Church. The study of the ancients 'can contribute to general knowledge, character building, eloquence, and, finally, the defense of our religion' (1.5).

That was the humanists' justification. By writing for a large reading public, they put their enormous 'general knowledge' to use. They 'cultivated character' by absorbing Roman notions of virtue – temperance, fortitude and magnanimity – which, in their view, were entirely in accord with Christian teachings. They 'defended Christianity' with the eloquence they learned from the ancient pagans.

Like Boncompagno, Petrarch garnered fame and glory, and like that earlier compatriot, he was hounded by the 'envious'. But Petrarch knew how to insult and humiliate his enemies right back, and he was not driven from his city nor left to die alone in a hospice. He had the support of many friends, church benefices (providing land and income) and wealthy patrons who highly valued humanists (some even identifying themselves as such). They made sure that his enemies could not harm him. It was his good fortune to be alive a century after Boncompagno, else he too might have ended his life in an almshouse.

WINTER DREAMS

IT WAS EASY to be old if you were rich and convinced you had spent most of your life doing what was best. That was Plato's point when he painted the portrait of Cephalus at the start of his *Republic*. His other point was that it was all *too* easy, and this he demonstrated when Socrates tried unsuccessfully to query the old man about justice.

But Plato didn't ask what it was like to be old if you were poor. Most Greeks who wrote didn't bother with it either. Nor did most literate Romans. Cicero's Cato was essentially a more talkative Cephalus, ready to elaborate on how good things could be if you had lived a sober and temperate life. He dismissed the issue of wealth.

Christians could not so easily dispose of the matter. They had the damning words of Christ himself: 'It will be hard for a rich man to enter the kingdom of heaven' (Matt 19:23). They heard sermons that told them to use their wealth to help them get to the next world, the one that counted: give alms to the helpless, the sick and the poor. By the 'poor', sermonizers meant churches, monasteries and the masses of the indigent, some of them old. The unintended consequence of emphasizing the 'poor' was to create what Peter Brown has called a 'binary tunnel vision' that divided society between the wealthy and the impoverished, without groups in between.[34] The poor were not only recognized; they were created as a category suitable for receiving alms. As for the old: in this bipartite scheme they were the 'thrice blessed' in that, like Gilbert of Sens, they were not only old but often helpless and sick.

In the thirteenth century we hear for the first time of institutions to care for the elderly apart from their biological family. Hospices took in old people who had nowhere else to go. The Mamluk state awarded old warriors with pensions. Enterprising peasants went to manorial courts to draw up documents to ensure that their private arrangements for their care would stick. Elderly people in Montpellier consulted notaries to do the same.

Competing ideologically with this concern for the elderly were some strains of Christianity that justified the pains of old age as punishments due to the sinful. Disability, weakness, poverty, fatigue: these were righteous judgments meant to be borne cheerfully.

Some people resisted. The elderly Boncompagno knew the theological justifications for his hardships, but he was anything but cheerful about them and did not know anyone who would be. The writers of *Beowulf* and *Willehalm* avoided considering the debility of the old by pretending it didn't exist. Indeed, only a few people faced it straight on. In the eleventh century we saw Usama talk about his loneliness; in the thirteenth century, Boncompagno. Petrarch found a remedy in his humanistic studies.

Most consoling of all was the prevailing ideal of reciprocity – the circle of give and take. God gave, people took, and then they gave back via prayers, virtuous living and donations to churches, monasteries, mosques (in the case of Muslims), hospices and other worthy entities. That charity ensured (they hoped) that they would return to God in the end.

Four
Work

Shakespeare's *King Lear* was not only a meditation on ageing for all time but a poignant reflection on the importance of work, of the constant and unremitting productivity demanded in much of Europe in the early modern era. When Lear divided his kingdom among his daughters, he said that he meant 'To shake all cares and business from our age,/ Conferring them on younger strengths, while we/ Unburdened crawl toward death' (1.1.39–40).[1] Yet he did not intend to give up his *power*. He kept his crown on his head. He wanted to stop working, give up his land and his revenues, and yet keep his status, his followers and his prestige. He even imagined that he could order his daughters, hitherto dependent on his favours, to reveal to him the contents of their innermost hearts. When Cordelia – his favourite, youngest daughter – was unable to 'heave/ My heart into my mouth', he became so furious that he declared her 'a stranger to my heart and me' (1.1.91–2; 116). His anger against her was implacable. No matter. Surely his two other (older) daughters, Goneril and Regan, would offer him and his followers the hospitality that he needed now that he had given up his throne. After all, they had been willing to speak the words of love that he had wanted to hear. Vain hope. When, to his fury, he and his entourage were refused by both, he realized his folly and fled into a storm. Under the pelting rain, he philosophized with his Fool and other poor souls about the frailty of humankind.

As we have seen, caring for parents was an obligation in ancient Athens and China. In Rome such care was part of the sentiment of pietas. In the Middle Ages, it largely fell to mechanisms of charity. Always it appealed to family feeling – often something of a mirage. Had Lear taken care of *his* parents? He was under an illusion to think that his two older daughters would care for him. Why should they? They hadn't been his favourites, and they knew it.

The fantasy that he could depend on the young was not Lear's alone. More than a century after *King Lear* was written, for example, Daniel Defoe (d. 1731) acted under the influence of the same delusion. Author, merchant and political pamphleteer, Defoe had at some point toward the end of his life turned all his assets over to one of his sons to escape the hounding of a creditor. In a letter written a few months before his death, Defoe described his anguish

> [because of] the injustice, unkindness, and, I must say, inhuman dealings of my own son, which has both ruined my family and, in a word, has broken my heart . . . I depended on him; I trusted him. I gave up my two dear unprovided children into his hands. [Defoe's daughters, Hannah and Henrietta, were still unmarried and needed dowries.] But he has no compassion and suffers them and their poor, dying mother to beg their bread at his door and to crave, as if it were alms, what he is bound [to do] under [contract] . . . He himself, at the same time, lives in a profusion of plenty.[2] (see illus. 18)

Defoe grieves, he regrets, he worries. However, he does not rage in fury as Lear had done.

Indeed, even Lear stopped seething and felt only disillusion and grief once he recognized the extent of his abandonment and ran into the storm. There he met yet another old man, the Earl of Gloucester. As depicted in the drama, Gloucester's last years were, like Lear's, a variant on the theme of banking on the wrong child. He erroneously believed that his dear son Edgar wished to kill him, and he fatally credited the deceitful words of his bastard son, Edmund, who told him lies. All that Edmund wanted were his father's estates.

Both Lear and Gloucester should have known from long experience which of their offspring was true to them. But they had lost perspective. Recall that when Seneca thought of the possibility that he might lose his mind, he planned to do away with himself. Shakespeare was not so hopeful; in his view, muddled old men do not notice their own decay. Lear and Gloucester recognized their senile folly only when, as with Defoe, brutal reality broke their hearts. But why had they nourished their foolishness in the first place when, as historian Pat Thane observed, 'the line of material obligation [in early modern England] was downward not upward through the generations,' that is, from parents to children?[3] In that context, it was fine for Lear to give away his kingdom and absolutely wrong of him to expect much from his daughters.

Goneril and Regan salved any guilty feelings they may have had by claiming that the old man was decrepit: "Tis the infirmity of his age'. That was a good way to deny him the capability and competence generally acknowledged for a man in his 'green' old age. 'Green' was the Elizabethan term for the modern label 'young old'. Just before Shakespeare wrote *Lear* (in 1605-6), Henry Cuffe (d. 1601) made painfully clear what was involved in being 'old old': '[When we are decrepit], our strength and heat is so far decayed that not only all ability is taken away, but even all willingness to the least strength and motion of our body.'[4] By that definition, however, Lear was *not* old old, for even at the very end of the play he had the physical strength to carry the dead Cordelia in his arms and the presence of mind to understand how wrong he had been. Goneril and Regan found it convenient to label their father 'infirm' to disempower him.

'Infirmity' was the criterion that the English state used when, in the Act for the Relief of the Poor (1601), it determined who was eligible for gratuitous relief: only people – including old people – who were too poor to support themselves and too disabled to work. (We have already seen this idea aborning in late medieval commercial centres such as Montpellier.) Lear had divested himself of his wealth, but he was not too disabled to work. In that case, the Act had ways to employ him. It taxed the householders of each parish so that the local Justices of the Peace (JPs), churchwardens, and two to four 'substantial householders' would have the resources to provide a stock of 'flax, hemp, wool, thread, iron, and other necessary ware and stuff to set the poor on work' (illus. 21).[5] The 'able-bodied' included children whose parents could not care for them and anyone else, 'married or unmarried', who had no trade.

Lear, however, did not wait around to do make-work but, as we know, preferred to rush out into a violent storm. There he found, over time, several companions – his Fool, Kent (Lear's faithful follower, now disguised) and Edgar (Gloucester's loyal son, now disguised as 'poor Tom' – a wounded and impoverished madman). They took shelter in a hovel, soon joined by Gloucester, now blinded by the connivance of his bastard son. Eventually Lear's dear daughter Cordelia arrived as well, bringing with her an army from France. Lucky Lear, not to have been abandoned by those faithful followers.

But suppose that he *had* been physically and mentally so weak that he could not work. Then the whole family – even available grandparents – would have been required to assist and maintain him. If they did not do so, then the JPs were empowered to enforce the law by charging those recalcitrant family members twenty shillings per month. In reality, however, the penalty was implemented only rarely. Instead, the parishes tried to negotiate in good faith with families and neighbours to find some way to support the elderly indigent. In the end, the parish usually took on most of the burden. Indeed, 'the confidence with which the elderly poor approached their parish officers for assistance indicates that these individuals felt that their parish was obligated to support them.'[6]

But the support was generally inadequate. Disabled and poor, Lear would have received from his parish an outright pension of a few pennies (or, later in the century, a bit more) to buy food and fuel and eventually to pay for his funeral. Since he was homeless to boot, he might have been consigned to one of the cottages for the old that (the Act said) were to be constructed on waste or common land. Or he could have gone to an existing hospital or almshouse. Despite these provisions, no doubt many ended their days in hovels, like Lear, asking the question, 'Is man no more than this?' (3.4.101).

We know a bit about some *real* elderly poor in early modern England, although their conditions differed from place to place. It seems that the general pattern was for poor old people to start with a small pension (supplemented by other sources, such as alms and a bit of work if they could get it) in their fifties or sixties. The pension increased as they aged and was at its highest point when they died, perhaps some ten to fifteen years later. 'Once on relief, the only way off it for most was by death.'[7] Even just before they died, though, their pensions were rarely adequate. In the large city of Norwich, which began to care for its indigent already in the mid-sixteenth century, a census of the poor in 1570 declared that Margaret Fen (a typical example) was sixty years old, lame and she 'doesn't work but goes about and is an unruly woman and dwelt here always'.[8] She was supported by the city, probably at one of its hospitals, on two pennies a week. That would not have been enough for her to live on; she would have had to find funds from other sources. Fen's age was not unusual; according to the Norwich census, fully a fifth of the poor men and a quarter of the women living in that city were age sixty and above. A few were over eighty.

Those were the facts. But how did it *feel* to be old and poor? A petition for relief to the JPs of Norfolk in 1647/8 in the name of Edward Messenger was straightforward about that:

> Your said poor petitioner, being [eighty years of age], almost blind and very lame [because of] his ankles, by which infirmities he is made unable to sustain himself by labour any longer or to travel abroad to gather relief from charitable people [by begging], and is allowed but six pennies per week [in relief] from the town he [inhabits], which in these hard times of dearth and scarcity will not buy any considerable or competent maintenance for his relief. Also, for lack of repair (which he is utterly unable to bestow upon it) the house in which he dwells will not shelter and defend him from wind and rain.[9]

Wind and rain beset Lear, too, and Messenger was as blind as Gloucester. It is as if Shakespeare wanted to channel all the lived experiences of old age into one play.

Messenger's petition continues:

> So that he perceives such distress coming upon him in his decrepit old age that he is likely to perish by hunger and cold, and sees no means left to him whence to escape that imminent misery which otherwise will inevitably come upon him, but only by making known this, his pitiful, distressed conditions to your Worships . . . hoping that you will not turn away your eyes and ears from the cry

of the poor but rather cause those responsible to allow some more competent relief and provision.

Unlike Lear, Messenger did not express anger or outrage. He had never been a king. But he was hungry and miserable and, like Lear, had nowhere to sleep but a leaky hovel in poor repair. And then, again like Lear (who reconciled with Cordelia before he died), Messenger found a bit of respite before his demise, for the JPs who heard Messenger's petition ordered his parish to pay him twelve pennies a week.

As Messenger's appeal made clear, the times in which he was living were exceptionally difficult. During the 1640s, England suffered great scarcity. Its harvests were meagre and its wealthy elites hoarded grain in order to inflate prices. Men were pressed into the armies of the warring royalists and Parliamentarians, and their wives and widows were left behind to fend for themselves. Some people banded together to demand redress. Others petitioned local magistrates to regulate the grain market; still others resorted to outright stealing. Messenger, old, blind and lame, was particularly vulnerable. He could not even drag himself out to a place where he might beg. That was probably just as well, for there was both official and unofficial hostility to beggars.

Work and Charity Transformed

Recall the old and palsied Gilbert of Sens in the previous chapter. He had to beg until a miracle at the tomb of Saint Louis healed him. Begging was not exactly a laudable occupation in the Middle Ages, but that era boasted enough stories about Christ appearing in the form of a beggar, or about saints gladly sharing their food with paupers, to endow alms-seekers with legitimacy. Furthermore, the voluntary poor – mendicant friars such as the Franciscans, who begged for their daily bread – lent a luminous halo to destitution. The friars had enormous prestige because they gave up everything to 'follow Christ', imitating his preaching and poverty.

Little of that sort of charity remained in the early modern period, as newly strong rulers sought to put their own stamp on social policies. The population across Western Europe doubled in size, while the decline of manorialism meant that more people were on the move in search of work. Freshly hatched post-Reformation denominations found good reasons to stress the virtues of labour. Protestants considered toil to be God's righteous punishment of Adam and Eve's transgression and of all their sinful inheritors. Catholics argued that employment was a 'charitable medicine', however unpalatable it might be, for both the involuntary jobless and the obstinately idle poor.[10] The failures of mercantilism (which focused on accumulating bullion) led to innovative thinking about the importance of *productivity* as the measure of the wealth of nations.

Participation in work, trade and industry became the measure of man, woman and child. The man was defined by his tools: maps, ploughs, pen and paper. The woman by hers: womb, distaff and spindle. According to a memorandum proposed by philosopher John Locke (d. 1704) in his capacity as Commissioner on the English Board of Trade, poor children should be sent to school between the ages of three and fourteen to learn wool-spinning, knitting or the like. *Their* implements would be needles and wheels.[11] Europeans considered themselves more civilized than the Indigenous peoples they encountered in the Americas and Africa in part because they had better instruments. All of these factors together formed the context for new attitudes and feelings about poverty, work and the place of the elderly in both.

The changes were first evident in northwestern Europe, especially in the Netherlands and England. The very old man

WINTER DREAMS

25 Ralphael Sadeler I, *Sorrow*, 1591, engraving after Maarten de Vos. The old man awaits death. On his wall is a painting of the Last Judgement. Outside a woman is burying his riches, looking over her shoulder to see if he notices. In the distance are various elderly and disabled figures, and at the church labourers are preparing for a burial. The legend beneath the picture speaks in the old man's voice: 'Now I am preoccupied by doctors and with the Judge on high. I lead a miserable life as one half-entombed.'

in the last of a series called the *Four Ages* by Flemish engraver Raphael Sadeler I (d. 1628/32) has no energy (illus. 25). He slumps in his chair, dejected and waiting for death. As a youth (shown in the first engraving of the series), he had been a lover; as an adult an expert craftsman. In middle age, he enjoyed the honour and riches that his industry had earned him. But as an old man, he became the picture of Sorrow (*Dolor*), which forms the very title of Sadeler's engraving. He's nothing but a burden to himself and others.

This attitude was quite new. No one expected Cephalus to work, nor did his self-esteem depend on it; the same must be said of Socrates, Seneca and even Gilbert of Sens. We have seen a number of unhappy elderly men and women in earlier periods of history, but their misery had nothing to do with their idleness. It was due to their losses: of loved ones, of authority, of self-reliance or sexual potency.

By contrast, in Voltaire's *Candide* (1759), the unhappy and unfulfilled lives of the eponymous hero and his assorted companions are put right only when they meet a wise old man who knows that happiness lies in labour. Work keeps at bay the 'three great evils: boredom, vice and need'.[12] Candide takes the lesson to heart, and he and the others roll up their sleeves, each exercising his or her particular talents.. Candide's ugly wife turns out to be an excellent pastry chef, the prostitute embroiders, the friar is a very good carpenter and the old woman takes care of the linens. Here is a microcosm of the ideal society – the virtuous and the vice-ridden, the young and the old. All become amiable, productive and contented through work.

By the end of the eighteenth century, industry and its tools were of such great prestige that the exhaustive, multi-volume *Encyclopédie* produced over the years 1751–72 focused on the mechanical arts. A monument of the French Enlightenment, it treated even old age as a technological issue, 'the breakdown of our entire machine'.[13] The idea was influenced by William Harvey's discovery (published in 1628) that the heart is, in essence, a mechanical pump. Once even the smallest blood vessels were observed, ageing was understood by the most forward-looking physicians of the day to be due to the hardening of the body's fibres and the consequent difficulty for blood to get through. But most physicians combined this with some remnants of Galenic thought. Louis de Jaucourt (a prolific contributor to the *Encyclopédie*) described old age as the product of two automatic processes: drying out (the Galenic idea) and ossification. Vital sap fills out the young man, expanding his bones and making him hefty and strong, but (writes Jaucourt) it has no place to go once a man is fully grown. Then his bones get hard, preventing the sap from circulating freely. By age seventy he is desiccated and stiff – like wood. This applied to women as well, since medical writers of the time believed that men and women became more alike as they aged.[14] In both cases, old age was sad, even pitiful. The elderly's only consolation was to have cultivated lifelong virtue: a life 'sober, moderate, simple, laborious'. Jaucourt imagined that this had always been the ideal. But the final attribute of *his* virtuous life – laborious (*laborieuse*) – would have shocked the elderly of earlier days. Carrying out one's duties in the Senate – as Cato had done, or dedicating herself to God and the poor as the pious Béatrice Gavandarie at Montpellier had pledged to do – had not been considered forms of labour but rather services carried out by people dedicated to a higher cause.

The logical terminus of Jaucourt's mechanistic thinking is exemplified by four paintings by David Allan (d. 1796) that trace the manufacture of lead bullion in *Lead Processing at Leadhills*.[15] Here the four ages of man are transformed into the four stages of industrial production. In the first of the series, the ore is pounded into powder; in the second, it is washed; in the third, it is smelted in the furnace; and in the last, it is moulded into ingots to be sold. The labourers are anonymous. The ore is the artist's focus as it 'matures', via labour, from raw to cooked.

Despite this artist's romanticization of lead manufacturing, the work was unhealthy and continuous. But it helped to fuel what Jan de Vries has dubbed the 'Industrious Revolution' – people working harder to afford new items on the market.[16] The fine faience made at Delft was glazed with lead produced by industrious workers at places such as Leadhills. It was then sold to Dutch consumers, who used it to hold their hot coffee or tea (relatively new and exotic imports). Around 1685–1700 they took to stirring in some sugar. Accompanied by wheat bread, the 'Continental breakfast' was born, while in England the afternoon tea took shape. To afford the pleasures of faience, glamorous hot drinks, sugar and soon many other fashionable things, householders devoted more hours to work. In short, a new work ethic was not simply *imposed* on labourers; it was the price they were willing to pay for fashion, comfort and elegance. De Vries dates the start of this revolution to the beginning of the seventeenth century, but subsequent researchers give a later date, and others, noting that inventories of household goods increased in the late sixteenth century rather than later, suggest that the industrious revolution began then.[17]

John Locke, the same man who proposed that children be schooled to labour, provided a theoretical justification for all this industriousness. He argued that labour was the foundation of private property, and he judged private property to be the 'chief end of civil society' (2.85, 323). While 'the earth and all inferior creatures be common to all men', he wrote, 'yet every man has a property in his own person... [Therefore] the labour of his body and the work of his hands, we may say, are properly his' (2.27, 287–8).[18] Once a man's labour is joined to something (gathering acorns in the woods, say, as long as the woods are not the property of someone else), that something (the acorns) becomes the private property of the man who has added his work (gathering) to them. Thus, he who cultivates wild or common land makes it his own private property – as long as he can enjoy its fruits and the byproducts of those fruits. If he raises more crops than he can use and brings the surplus to market, the money he makes there is also his to enjoy.

Private property benefits all, Locke said, for the improvement of land or raw materials such as lead ore is an advancement for everyone. The 'vacant places of America', therefore, are virtually crying out to be improved, not by gathering acorns but rather through the toil that will yield the best value (2.36, 295). Cultivation of grain is better than acorn-gathering, and milling the grain and transforming it into bread is best of all. If slaves are used to plant or reap the grain, the benefits are due their owner, for enslaved people, 'being captives taken in a just war', have given up their right to property, even in their person (2.85, 322).

By giving labour so important a role in generating value, Locke devalued all people unable to work. Those most certainly included the old. In the same memo in which he advocated the establishment of 'working schools' for poor children, he proposed that 'those who are not able to work at all . . . be lodged three or four or more in one room'. Why? To save money, because when they are herded together, 'one fire may serve [all] and one attendant may provide for many'. No wonder that not very long afterward Jonathan Swift (d. 1745) proposed, in a bitter caricature of such attitudes, that poor Irish families sell their babies to the rich. Those little ones, suitably fattened up, would make flavourful dishes and contribute to the betterment of the commonwealth to boot. As for 'that vast number of poor people who are aged, diseased, or maimed', Swift had the briskly satirical answer to pay them no mind, for 'they are every day dying and rotting by cold and famine, and filth and vermin, as fast as can be reasonably expected.'[19]

The 'vacant places of America'

Locke knew that the Americas were not really 'vacant', but he also knew that the land was not parcelled out among owners. Since, in his view, private property was the foundation of civil society, the peoples who lived in the Americas must have been as 'corrupt in manners' and 'lax in discipline' as the idle and useless poor of England. But by saying that 'civil society' was based on 'private property, production, and acquisition', Locke knew very well that he was challenging older definitions that were not founded on marketplace economics.[20] Nor were his ideas accepted by all. Indeed, around the time in which he was writing, other thinkers were arguing that civil society was founded not on individual self-interest but on *communities* of men with similar goals or sentiments, rather like emotional communities. These could be associations such as those constituted by the nobles, clerics and bourgeoisie within the French monarchy, as Montesquieu (d. 1755) advocated. Or they could be formed from enlightened self-interest, such as communities of buyers and sellers or those of parishes and the poor, as David Hume (d. 1776) thought. Or (as neither Montesquieu or Hume dared to imagine) civil society could be founded on communities of Indigenous Americans organized by functions, roles and ages under the leadership of a chief.

Consider the tribes speaking Anishinaabemowin (Ojibwe dialects), one of the language groups termed Algonquian by the French. By the early 1600s they were settled in the upper Great Lakes region. (Today this describes the mid-western lands of southern Canada and the northern United States.) In these communities of the seventeenth and early eighteenth centuries, natives and Europeans lived together in what Richard White has called a 'middle ground' – a melded culture. Even as late as the mid-nineteenth century, as Michael Witgen has argued, the Indigenous Great Lakes cultures retained a distinctly Native New World unrecognized by those who lived within their own myth of 'European discovery, conquest, and national reinvention'.[21] Nor did that Native reality give way entirely to increased control by Britain, France and their successors, the United States and Canada. Mixed populations and traditions in the region persist to this day.

Nevertheless, it is hard to deny the transformative effect of state forces and market interests, which wrested forests, territories and fisheries from Indigenous peoples. By the 1870s, many Native communities had been relocated involuntarily onto reservations – lands that, for the most part, had already been impoverished of their natural resources. At that point, missionaries and bureaucrats tried to disrupt Indigenous family structures by taking children away from their parents and forcing them to attend schools that undermined Native religions, ceremonies and languages. In the twentieth century, the situation changed yet again, this time in nearly opposite ways: while many Indians voluntarily moved away from reservations to urban areas, many (sometimes the same ones) returned to their Native traditions, though not always on reservations.

Among the peoples of the Great Lakes were and are the Ojibweg (singular: Ojibwe), whose culture has been studied by a variety of scholars today, some of them Ojibweg themselves. Michael D. McNally's sympathetic account of the roles of Ojibweg elderly is meant to offer lessons for us today. The Ojibweg, he observes, consider old age to be the high point of a life well spent, the culmination of a long and arduous moral development. Only an old man or woman has the power and authority necessary to impart the traditions of the tribe. Only they have mastered the skills and possess the time to pass their expertise along to the younger generation. They know when to milk the sap of the trees, spear the fish, hunt the animals, tend the garden and harvest the wild rice. They have established 'right relations with all other persons – which in [their] taxonomy includes nonhuman persons of the natural world (animals, plants, geological and weather phenomena) and of the spiritual world (ancestors, spirits, myths)'.[22] The younger generations, McNally observes, value the knowledge and wisdom imparted by their elders. Similarly, Ojibwe author Anton Treuer speaks of the reverence due the elderly in his society. 'The word for an old woman, *mindimooye*, literally means "one who holds things together", [and] even the gender-neutral term for elder in Ojibweg, *gichiaya'aa*, literally means "great being".'[23]

Ojibweg culture used to be oral and remains so to some degree even now. We must therefore be cautious about assuming that it was the same centuries ago as it is today. Although oral traditions connect the present to the past, they do not do so straightforwardly, for they are subject to the embroideries of their narrators and the needs of their audiences. They change as the societies in which they are embedded change, for they teach the norms, emotions and rituals that help the next generations to make sense of their *present* lives.

The challenge, then, is to look backward yet keep modern observations in mind. In the 1600s, when Locke was writing, French fur traders and Jesuit missionaries had only recently reached the Great Lakes and met the Indigenes living there. The traders came for the beaver fur that the Native Americans could supply; the Jesuits arrived to save Indian souls. In turn, the Indians looked to the newcomers to help them in their wars. For a while, neither was strong enough to gain what they desired by force, so both had to tread cautiously. During this period European and Native cultures merged in what White calls 'a process of mutual and creative misunderstanding'. That was the 'middle ground', a hybrid culture that was not quite one or the other.[24] At the same time, they remained apart in many ways, creating two different New Worlds, one 'Native', the other 'Atlantic'. Both were keen on empire and trade, but they were based on entirely different assumptions about social and political organization. The Indigene imaginary recognized communities that might form and change shape as needed, while the Atlantic-European could think only in terms of hierarchy, class, individuality and private property.

For this transitional period, we know how the Native elderly *felt* and were felt *about* only from European observers. Some were in effect proto-ethnographers, keenly curious and anxious to understand what they saw. Even so, they were also ready to call the natives 'savages', 'wild men' and the like. Pierre-Esprit Radisson (d. *c.* 1710) was a French fur trader who ventured into Algonquin territory from a perch in New France (more or less Quebec province today). Bacqueville de La Potherie (d. 1736) was a historian and French civil servant. He spent the years 1698–1701 in New France gathering information from various eyewitnesses. One of those was Nicolas Perrot, a seventeenth-century fur trader who lived among (and had the confidence of) the Anishinaabe for much of his life. Both described the 'customs' of the Indigenes living in the Great Lakes region.

What they observed was not exactly the 'Native' culture there. In fact, the tribes they dealt with were refugees from their former bases along the northeast coast of North America. They had moved west to the Great Lakes region to escape attacks from the gun-toting Iroquois Confederacy, which had recently learned about and obtained firearms from the French. As the refugees settled in, they coalesced into groups ranging from fairly large chiefdoms to small hunting bands. Their loyalties and identities were not tribal now (if they had ever been). Rather their allegiances were more local, centring on their villages in which a mix of tribes might live. A process of ethnogenesis, in which new groups formed and older ones disintegrated (or became absorbed into others), characterized this period in flux.

The chroniclers of these Upper Great Lakes cultures had little to say about elderly Anishinaabe *women*. That may have been because of their European understanding, which always privileged the male perspective. But Radisson, who ventured into Mohawk (Iroquois) territory at the age of twelve or a bit later, had the vantage point of a child and noticed the women there.

Indeed, he was protected from certain death by an 'old woman', who soon adopted him. She even came to his aid again after he attempted to escape and was recaptured: 'With all the authority of a Mohawk matron, [she] sang, danced, and distributed strings of wampum' in order to reconcile him once again with the tribe.[25] Even older Mohawk women had important roles:

> when the corn is green [the Mohawk] gather so much as need requires ... A dozen more-or-less old women meet together alike, of whom the greatest part want teeth and see not a jot, and their cheeks hang down like an old hunting dog, their eyes full of water and bloodshot. Each takes an ear of corn and puts it in their mouths, which is properly as milk [when chewed by them] (157).

The Mohawk were a matrilineal society, and Radisson's description of his 'mother' and of old Mohawk women at work suggests that physical debility did not prevent them from having a clear social and economic role.

But when he visited the Anishinaabe, Radisson had nothing to say about old women and rather little about the elderly in general. Other observers were less reticent, at least about the men. They noted that elderly male Ojibwe acted in numerous capacities and associated with various village groups for particular purposes. At times they were classed with the women and children. At others, they took a leading role in important male tribal rituals. The key village groupings were threefold: women and children; young men of warrior-hunter status; and chiefs. Somewhere in the interstices of these three were the old men, liminal creatures who 'floated' from one group to another.

When the elderly died, their souls often struggle (said the Ojibwe) to overcome the many obstacles on the path that all souls have to follow to get to the 'land of the dead'. The final hurdle is a passage blocked by 'two pestles of prodigious size, which in turn rise and fall without ceasing' (1.90–91).[26] If they are quick enough to get through without being crushed, they reach the promised land. If they fail (as happened to many little children), they die. Bacqueville de La Potherie remarked that it was absurd to speak of death in connection with the immortal soul, but he nonetheless reported what he heard.

Although the story of the pestles shows that the Algonquin were aware that old people were slow and weak, everything else points to the vibrant parts that they played within their society. Radisson reports that the corpse of the dead (now considered simply the container of the soul) was brought to the funeral by the old men. Then

> the elders who have brought her [the soul] there cover her with a very large white skin and color her legs with vermilion ... Then one of the elders makes a long speech to encourage the young people to go a-hunting to kill some meat to make a feast for [the] entertainment of the soul of their countrymen.[27]

Above all, the elders were involved in peacemaking. When one man killed another outside of his village, noted La Potherie, the old men of the offending village 'come together, make up among themselves a considerable present, and send it by deputies' to the injured tribe, which is without doubt keen on vengeance. In addition to giving gifts, the deputies remind the offended villagers of the long-standing alliance and peace between their peoples. If the relatives of the murdered man are still not mollified, it is the turn of the old men of *their own* village to 'intervene with presents, in order to become mediators'. They argue that vengeance will lead to war, 'with most grievous consequences' for all.[28] The aged heroes of the Homeric

26 Louis Nicolas (?), *Captain of the Nation*, c. 1700, pen and ink drawing of the moment recorded in Fr. Jacques Marquette's account of his meeting the chief of the Peouarea (Peoria), a branch of the Illinois tribe, in 1673: 'When we reached the village of the great captain, we saw him at the entrance of his cabin between two old men, all three erect and naked, and holding their calumet turned toward the sun.' The artist here decorously clothed the chief and (evidence of his European prejudices?) left out the two old men.

Greeks, such as Priam and Nestor, mediated individually, but the elders of the Great Lakes generally mediated within and as the voice of a collectivity.

Thus, when Perrot came to visit the Potawatomy, 'the old men solemnly smoked a calumet and came into his presence, offering it to [Perrot] as homage that they rendered to him' (illus. 26). In this instance, the elders helped seal an alliance with the French. At another time, the Potawatomi were worried about the fate of some of their people who had gone to Montreal with their chief to trade: 'they feared that the French might treat them badly or that they would be defeated by the Iroquois'. Then the old men begged Perrot to 'relieve them from their anxiety', channelling the fears of the entire community. Perrot made an educated guess about when the traders would return. When they indeed arrived as predicted, it was again the *old* men who greeted them, telling them that Perrot had been their protector. Carrying Perrot on their shoulders, the tribesmen 'arrived at the cabin of the chief... where all the old men were assembled, and a great feast of sturgeon was served' (1.314–16).

The elderly also mediated between the male villagers and the gods. La Potherie reported that when a divinity appeared to a tribesman in a dream, it did so as a fearful animal. To calm his alarm, the dreamer would hold a feast and invite the old men to hear his vision. 'Then one of the old men makes a speech and, naming the creature to whom the feast is dedicated, addresses to it the following words: 'Have pity', he says, 'on him who offers to you (and here he names each article of food); have pity on his family, and grant him what he needs' (1.49–50).

As today so too in the past, the elderly were bearers of tribal traditions. When the French could not understand why the Indians made a terrible clamour with gunshots in response to an eclipse of the moon, the natives explained, 'our old men have taught us that when the moon is sick it is necessary to assist her by discharging arrows and making a great deal of noise in order to cause terror in the spirits who are trying to cause her death. Then she regains her strength... If men did not aid her, she would die' (2.134).

No wonder Europeans and Indigenous peoples did not understand each other. Imagine Lear transported to a Great Lakes village with no kingdom to divide and no way to 'shake all cares and business', since Algonquin elderly had nothing to divide and no way to 'retire'. Or picture Locke conveyed to the American wilderness, where labour could not create private property because everyone in the village hunted together on the same lands and fished together on the same rivers. Living on the Great Lakes in the seventeenth century was hardly peaceful or ideal. On the other hand, the elderly men there were not beset by the heartbreak of the exploited Daniel Defoe nor by the misery of the impoverished Edward Messenger. French essayist Michel de Montaigne (d. 1592) reported that some natives of Brazil brought to France were 'amazed' that one half of the people were fat and sated, while the other half 'were beggars at their doors, emaciated with hunger'.[29]

No elderly Indians directly told the Europeans who met them how being old felt to them. But insofar as the feelings of others affect our feelings about ourselves, the old among the Algonquin must have felt honoured, essential and perhaps even beloved. At the same time, the story about their journey to the land of the dead suggests that they also felt enfeebled.

The Elderly Sentimentalized

Did the honour in which the Anishinaabe held their elders affect European attitudes? French philosophe Jean-Jacques Rousseau (d. 1778) took at least one short lesson from them to heart. In his *Social Contract*, he argued that 'the first societies' (he had in mind the Greeks and Romans) were governed by men of long experience: 'hence come the words priest, elders, senate, gerontes. The savages of North America are still governed in this way today, and are governed very well.' But, he continued, government by old men is 'only suited to simple societies'.[30]

Nevertheless, Rousseau was solicitous of the feelings of those advanced in age. When Jean Le Rond d'Alembert proposed establishing a public theatre in Geneva, Rousseau objected at length. Dramas, he said, threatened the well-being and self-respect of the elderly: 'Who can doubt that the habit of always seeing old persons in the theater as odious characters helps them to be rejected in society, and that, in accustoming us to confound those who are seen in society with the babblers and dotards of comedy, they all end up being equally despised?'[31] He was thinking of comedies by writers such as Molière (d. 1673), which featured miserly old fathers barring the paths to happiness of youthful lovers. Those plays were patterned on the Italian *commedia dell'arte* of Moliere's day, and (in turn) that *commedia* itself borrowed much from the tropes and jokes of Plautus and other early Roman playwrights.

Yet by Rousseau's day, that fashion had begun to dissipate – and he helped to undermine it along with many memoirists, dramatists and artists who depicted old people in newly sympathetic and sentimental fashion. Their creations reflected the increasing importance of the French middle class and its high opinion of lifelong marriages and filial piety. Some painters even did away with wrinkles and sagging flesh to show the serenity and grace of the elderly (illus. 22). The old woman in Voltaire's *Candide* was in fact not just a good laundress but also a healer, faithful companion and wise adviser.

This sympathetic treatment did not mean that the Enlightenment denied the deleterious symptoms of old age. Rather, it considered compassion for the elderly as morally advanced, the product of education, whether through life experiences, as in Candide, or via parental and political schooling, or by studying examples of good morality, as in Jean-Baptiste Greuze's sentimental depictions of Filial Piety (illus. 23). Just as the French chroniclers told vivid narratives about old Indians, so Greuze's paintings illustrated intergenerational familial harmony.

In the theatre, too, French playwrights of the later eighteenth century started to give the elderly benevolent roles. Consider the comedy *The Old Boy* (*Le vieux Garçon*) by Paul Ulric Dubuisson (d. 1794). Here Gercour (whose name means 'old heart') is a 'sad old boy' at the age of sixty (1,1).[32] At the start of the play he is the archetype of all the clichés about elderly curmudgeons. He dislikes his friends, is loathsome to his servants, disparages marriages, and scorns all women as 'wearying, impetuous, capricious, haughty, and disgusting' (1,2). He's the old codger straight out of all the ageist comedies lamented by Rousseau: utterly clueless, at the mercy of his servants and wrongly mistrustful of the people who care about him. When he meets the lovers Sophie and Sainfar, he is once again clueless, mistaking Sainfar's hesitation to wed (out of secret, honourable motives) for the scruples of a confirmed bachelor like himself. But when Gercour overhears Sophie's father try to convince the young man of the joys of married life, the old misogynist begins to waver: 'This scene struck at my heart,/ I see it, I feel it: I am unhappy!' (3,6). Gercour contemplates taking the place of Sainfar in Sophie's affections, saying that he now realizes that the liberty of the single man is useless in old age. Moreover, he hates to be alone. Why couldn't he, Sophie and her father all live together as a happy threesome?

Sophie quickly disabuses him of the thought. Married couples must grow old together. Gercour sees the wisdom of her words, 'At her age, an old man is not what she needs' (4,2). He hurries to find Sainfar to share that new insight. Together they discover that Sainfar is not only a bastard (the real motive for his not wishing to marry Sophie), but (happily!) the offspring of Gercour's one true, long-lost love. Gercour now has the very solace that marriage gives the old: a son to love him. In the end, the 'heart's nobility' conquers social prejudice against 'natural' (bastard) children. Gercour makes Sophie his heir, and the happy young couple gladly agree to the now tender-hearted old man's request: 'permit me to live out the rest of my life near you' (4,5).

Gercour's transformation from spiteful old man to tender father foreshadowed the desire of French revolutionaries to honour the elderly and even make them part of their new calendar. As Gilbert Romme wrote in his Report to the National Convention (established by the revolutionaries in 1792), at the end of each year six special holidays were to be celebrated. One was for old age. It could be a grand affair: for example, at one taking place in Paris in 1797 the presiding official declared that 'honouring old age, bringing to it the tribute of veneration and respect that are due to it, is a sweet duty to fulfil, for it is commanded by nature and chosen by reason'. No citizen, he maintained, is 'unaffected by a profound sentiment of respect and veneration' when seeing an old person, none who does not find in him or her 'the wise counsel of experience'.[33] He urged all young people hearing him to think of Rome – *Republican* Rome, which was ruled by the elders in the Senate. In those days, he said, the old were honoured almost as if they were gods. And all should ponder the example of Sparta, where the young sprang to their feet in order to let the old take their seats. Addressing two old men at the ceremony, he praised the honesty, fidelity and virtue of one; the artistic contributions of the other. Two old women were then singled out: 'you were faithful spouses, tender mothers.' Their lives, too, had been a long train of virtues. And finally: 'Receive, venerable citizens, the crowns offered by your magistrates.'

Thus, the drumbeat of toiling old age faded out (though never quite ceased) at the end of the eighteenth century. In England, some even voiced the opinion that old age should claim 'ease and repose'.[34] Put aside a tidy nest egg, young people were advised, and live on it when you retire. In effect Matthew 6:34 was turned on its head, as the young were admonished to 'take *every* thought for the morrow.' Private insurance companies sprang up to guarantee middle-class investors a comfortable old age, while landed elites were assured of the same from the income generated by their estates. 'Friendly societies' all across

England helped men and women save for retirement by charging dues that were disbursed according to need, and by 1803 the kingdom's Civil Service was providing pensions to its officers once they reached age sixty. In France, too, old soldiers began to receive pensions in the eighteenth century, and philosophes wrote that the elderly should sit back and enjoy the affection of friends and family.

Yet such solicitous views of the elderly had limited impact. For example, when the French revolutionary government set up outdoor workshops for indigent men and indoor proto-factories for poor women, it did not hesitate to employ old people. Given that most of the female workers at one cotton-spinning workshop 'were sixty to seventy years old or older', it is clear why such ateliers produced very little.[35] But perhaps the *image* of industriousness was the main point.

The so-called *Mémoires* of the actor P. L. Dubus-Préville (d. 1799) portrayed him as a smashing success, drawing smiles from 'the most serious' and tears from 'the most insensitive' members of his audience. But Dubus-Préville didn't know 'the value of money' and never saved a penny. When the Revolution came (reducing pensions, telling the elderly to keep working for the glory of the state and advising young people to save for retirement) Préville was caught short. Having left the stage, he tried to make a comeback, but, suffering from the 'many inconveniences of his age', he even mistook painted scenery for a real forest. At that point neither hard work or a retirement fund saved him. Rather, the ideal of the sentimental family came to his aid.

> A good husband, a good father, in the last years of his life Préville found tender care among his children . . . If heaven had not accorded to the best of fathers the best of children, perhaps this excellent man, to whom a most laborious life ought to have promised an old age

free of all disquiet, would have experienced the habitual privations that make for true neediness.[36]

In short, even after the Revolution, the family remained the chief support for the elderly in France.

Exploring the Self

Préville's *Mémoires* were not his personal records but rather another writer's biography of the actor based on some of Préville's notes. But at the same time, private explorations of the self and of feelings were becoming increasingly popular. To be sure, autobiographical accounts were not invented in the early modern period. Fronto's deeply felt letter to Emperor Marcus Aurelius was written in the second century; Petrarch's *Letters of Old Age* was penned in the fourteenth.

Nevertheless, it remains true that there was an explosion of self-reflection in the seventeenth and eighteenth centuries, and women were as involved in it as the men. Two detonators set off the boom. The late medieval and Protestant passion for spiritual self-examination gave the new fashion its form; the religious wars of the period induced people to withdraw – into themselves and other protected spaces.

Autobiography eventually took on a life of its own. Just as European identity was increasingly tied to exploration and exploitation of every landscape, so self-identity now depended on looking at another unknown country – the heart. The 'interior of the mind' gained exceptional importance as the locus of insight into the 'true person'. In the eighteenth century, the discipline of psychology began to break from theology to make feelings and emotions subjects of scientific investigation.

That was already true for René Descartes (d. 1650), who looked within himself to come up with his revolutionary claim

'I am thinking, therefore I exist.'[37] He was probably in his twenties when he wrote that, and he did not return to the topic of the self until, around two years before his death, he started to think about sentiments. The resulting book, *The Passions of the Soul*, offered a new theory of the emotions, one still debated today.

It said nothing about feeling *old*, for Descartes wanted to present universal truths, not an exposition of his own sentimental journey. But his book did have something to do with his own experiences. Most striking was Descartes' theory of 'habituation', which made our life-experiences crucial to individualizing us from one another emotionally. For Descartes, habituation is the most important way in which the emotions given to us by nature are modified. It begins very simply via surprise. Descartes gives an example: 'when someone unexpectedly comes upon something very foul in food he is eating with relish, the surprise of this encounter can so change the disposition of the brain, that he will no longer be able to see any such food afterwards without abhorrence, whereas previously he used to eat it with pleasure' (50).[38] Habituation, then, adjusts feelings (such as abhorrence or pleasure) by associating good things with pleasure and bad with abhorrence. This procedure is so basic that even dogs can be trained using it. It is the way to educate children as well, habituating them to make the right associations. Then, as they grow older, they will learn to school themselves by using their reason and good judgment, so that they will feel the right feelings about the right things.

Having listed and explained the nature of the many passions instilled by nature, Descartes summed up his discussion: 'Now that we understand them all, we have much less reason to fear them than we had before. For we see that they are all in their nature good, and that we have nothing to avoid but misuses or excesses of them' (211). Any dangers may be overcome by proper habituation and also (here Descartes adheres closely to Stoic teachings) by thinking thoughts that resist bad passions. In the end, 'wisdom . . . teaches us to render ourselves such masters of [the passions] and to manage them with such ingenuity, that the evils they cause can be easily borne, and we even derive joy from them all.'

Although he did not say so, Descartes' theory opened up a new way to consider the ageing process. Briefly, it denied that getting old was (as most hitherto had imagined) simply an inevitable decline of our senses and cognitive abilities. Nor was it just the relentless physical change from hot to cold and from wet to dry, both of which tended to produce vindictive, miserly, foolish old people. Rather, *in spite* of the inevitable physical enfeeblement that becoming old entails, it might also mean more and better habituations.

Descartes' treatise on the passions told his contemporaries to manage and enjoy all their emotions. It represented another aspect of the will to control and dominate that operated at so many other levels in the Europe in his day. But did ageing people 'habituate' and learn to 'manage their passions'?

We may trace something close to such an emotional transformation in the diary of Lady Sarah Cowper (1644–1720).[39] She began to write it when she was 56, at a difficult time in her life. She had always felt totally alienated from her husband, and now one of their sons had just been brought to trial for murder. After he was acquitted, she nevertheless continued to write, and she persisted even after her husband died and she could no longer complain about him. She did not stop writing until two years before her death, and then only because her hand shook excessively. At first glance, perhaps, her diary seems to be a miscellany of complaints, critical judgments and pious resolutions. Yet as a whole it coheres.

Born into a family of merchants, Cowper entered the English gentry by marrying the heir to a baronetcy. Throughout her life she constantly indulged in – and fought mightily against – feeling more pious than nearly everyone else. She considered her husband inferior on that score, and she once likened living with him to being in Hell. Yet, directly after writing those damning words, she admonished herself, quoting the words of Ecclesiasticus 8:11: 'Rise not up in anger at the presence of an injurious person.'

That sequence described her middle-aged emotional life in general: first displeasure, anger and misery (generally caused by her husband or sons); then remorse followed by comfort and reassurance (ordinarily derived from Scripture or other religious work). The pattern – ire, remorse, comfort – was, on the surface, quite similar to those of her contemporary Puritans, though Cowper was staunchly Anglican.[40] But Puritans directed their fury toward themselves, whereas Cowper most often felt angry at and hurt by others. Her husband's 'tongue cuts like a sharp razor', and the 'particulars [of her sons'] unkind neglect may not be enumerated or rehearsed' (125).

Her ire and grief had much to do with both her class and gender. In her day, husbands such as Sir William Cowper made all the decisions, hired all the servants and held all the purse strings. When they died, their sons did much the same. Thus, as soon as she was widowed, at the age of 63, she 'thought to have ordered my way of living so as to attain more peace and quiet of mind than formerly I had known. But alas. By sad experience I find that things without us will not give it [peace], but that it springs from what's within us' (145). Her oldest son doled out her stipend stingily (she thought) and her children continued to neglect her. To cheer herself up, she thought about Heaven and reminded herself to be more virtuous.

By that time, Cowper considered herself old, and virtuously so. She often thought about death and declared, in words echoing Saint Augustine, that she longed for that 'quiet harbour, an end of our journey that brings us from exile to our native home' (140). She congratulated herself for acting her age, not like 'Madam Hall, [who is] as old as I at least, yet so bedecked with gems all over, displaying her crop and bubbys [throat and breasts] that it would make one puke to see them' (137). Yet she observed that, however outworn old women's bodies might look, 'their mind continues the same. They still have the same passions and desires of pleasure' (142). How unlike the declarations of the old men of the classical world, who claimed to be beyond the impulses of their younger years and were glad of it! Cowper faced a different set of feelings even though she knew 'the importunity of years, the unwelcomeness of wrinkles, and such like mind-troubling accidents' (145). All that was vanity, of course, as she reminded herself.

Cowper's *Diary* allows us to glimpse how her feelings changed over time. After making a trip to visit her son, she was surprised by how fatigued she was. At the same time, she felt (to her surprise) warmly welcomed by her son and daughter-in-law, 'which comforts me much'. The old sequence that started with anger was dissipating. In Descartes' terms, she was getting 'habituated'. By now her son William was a great success, having been recently made the first (ever) Lord High Chancellor of Great Britain. At that point, Cowper professed to be 'weary' of the obligations of her role as mother of the High Chancellor – not because she belittled such duties as vanities (which she would have done at a younger age) but because she was too tired to enjoy them.

She became more self-aware. She had once thought that, as a widow, she might like to live with other bereaved women. Now she realizes that she likes to live alone. She used to blame her husband and sons for not caring for her company, but now she discovers that she is not a social creature. She notices that she fears death and does her best 'to inform myself of the words and manners of dying persons' (156). She wasn't afraid of Hell, she thought, but rather of the pain of dying. She calmed herself by reading a Protestant divine who maintained that death was painless.

Her fury, so predominant previously, relaxed. While she still got angry at her servants, she also took considerable interest in their lives. She laughed at herself a bit; old people would be odious to themselves if they did not become senile and thus forget from one minute to the next what they had just said. That half-serious, half-humorous rumination about old age was characteristic of her later entries. When her son came to her home to dine with her, she mused that 'there is not a greater pleasure to old age than seeing that we are not quite laid aside in the world' (185). Eventually she agreed to live near 'my dear son and lady'. By then her strength was fast fading, and she was grateful for the kindness of her son and his wife. But note: he too had changed. Earlier he had been an ambitious man on the rise with no time for his difficult mother. Now he could be caring. Or perhaps he could be less cold because she herself was less annoying.

Cowper's son did not keep a diary, but some young people did write down their feelings about their elders. Consider the *Conversations* between the aspiring German poet Johann Peter Eckermann (d. 1854) and the aged poet, writer and polymath Johann Wolfgang von Goethe (d. 1832).[41] Their relationship began when Eckermann was 31 and Goethe 74.

The younger man was poor and largely self-taught, since he could not afford to go to a university. But he was in thrall to literature, a budding poet himself and a keen admirer of Goethe. Resolved to make himself known to the great man, he began by wooing him with short poems – sent through intermediaries – and eventually followed up with a longer manuscript. Then he visited Goethe at his home in Weimar.

It was as if Goethe had been waiting for him! When the two met (in 1823), the 'august personage' virtually refused to let the young man go (434). He took Eckermann under his wing (their relationship continued for nine years, until Goethe's death), turning him into his (unpaid) editor, secretary and confidant. In turn, Eckermann had the great joy and privilege of being the worthy 'habitation for Goethean thoughts and sentiments' (434). He recorded their conversations by date, revised them for publication and brought them to the attention of the European literati in 1836, with a final section published in 1848.

Eckermann presented Goethe as a man of boundless energy, wise advice and brilliant observations. Their time together was rarely troubled by emotional turbulence or the ills of Goethe's age. The old man was always involved, passionate and enthusiastic. Their discussions were wide-ranging: from comments on Byron (whom Goethe greatly admired) to the faults of literary critics, to the domain of the 'daemonic' (the instincts and unconscious) in poetry. Goethe presented himself as the authority on everything and as surprised by nothing. For him, ageing involved no new 'habituations'.

Indeed, Goethe's persona was ever youthful. In his seventies he fell in love with a young woman and proposed to her. She turned him down, but that did not stop his flow of feeling, which he transformed into a poem composed in one day: 'And while a person is muted in his sorrow/ A god gave me the gift to speak what I was suffering'.[42]

To my mind, their *Conversations* show Goethe to have been controlling, full of himself and insensitive to the material and sentimental needs of the younger man. But Eckermann himself thought differently. He wanted and needed the elder's tutelage and sage advice. He drank in Goethe's astute analyses of poetry, art and nature, the fruit of the older man's lifelong and intense study. Through Goethe, Eckermann got to know all the best people, refined his aesthetic tastes and had the priceless pleasure of enjoying long dinners and equally lengthy discussions with the great poet. He was happy to rework, reorganize and critique many of Goethe's writings productively, and the poet appreciated all that.

They were, in effect, acting out the ideal of Cicero's elderly Cato and his young admirers, albeit transposed from a Roman Senatorial context to the German Enlightenment literary scene. Like Cato, Goethe continued to be active in his field. He read, wrote and critiqued others until the day he died. Like Cato, he made clear that his youth had prepared him for his mature pursuits, and, although he at times regretted not dedicating himself exclusively to poetry, he was pleased that he had studied painting and scientific topics, had been the director of a theatre company and had taken on various official duties at the ducal court. As a result, he could discourse on nearly every topic. Again, like Cato, he had *auctoritas*; his friendship was sought by artists, musicians, princes, poets – even Napoleon! About being old, he said little. He observed that 'every time of life has its own advantages and disadvantages . . . Now, in my eightieth year, I possess advantages that I would not willingly trade for those [in my forties]' (304). Yes, he had some sorrows – above all, he hated losing old and dear friends. But after he finished his masterwork, *Faust*, he remarked that 'any time remaining to me I can now regard as a bonus, and what I do now, if I do anything, is really of no consequence' (424). Like so many of the elderly people of the past, he looked back on his life and pronounced it good.

Those Less Lucky

What a pleasure it must have been to be an old and honoured poet in Germany! But what about less exalted people there? Did they, too, bask in honour or accomplishments as they grew old? The question is badly posed: in Goethe's time, there was no 'Germany'. Rather, German-speaking lands were organized as a conglomeration of loosely federated states and seriously divided by religion. The tiny duchy of Saxe-Weimar, where Goethe lived, was one of the most enlightened, for the duke there 'was like a renaissance princeling', who brought to his court and capital city the current German literati.[43] These well-educated men (all were men) admired Shakespeare for his expression of emotions, and they freed themselves from what they considered the excesses of both the religious piety and the classical restraint of their era. They included Goethe, of course; Christoph Wieland (d. 1833), who translated Shakespeare, tutored the duke-to-be Karl August, and wrote poetry, satire and romances; and Friedrich Schiller (d. 1805), a forwardlooking playwright who worked with Goethe at the Weimar theatre.

They were also social critics and took to heart the welfare of the 'people'. Goethe himself observed the plight of the poor when he served in the duke's government. But he also was forced to recognize that there was no fundamental way to help them: his hands were tied given the tyranny of custom and the fragmented jurisdictions in Saxe-Weimar alone. In the town of Ruhla, for example, once a prosperous place, the inhabitants now eked out a bare living through farming and pipe production. The duke's tax collector was met by stiff resistance from Ruhla's householders, who refused to pay the chicken, poppy seeds and land tax that they owed. With a stroke of his pen (for Goethe was a favourite of the duke and could do such things), he tried to mitigate the burden: 'Where are the arrangements for giving them hopes and prospects? If these cannot be provided, at least leave them unmolested with what they have.'[44] Yet taxes had to be paid or the whole duchy would go under. Goethe compromised, lifting the tax on the chickens and poppy seeds. But he had to retain the land tax.

The population of Germany was increasing (as it was everywhere in Europe), growing about 50 per cent between 1750 and 1800, but the German economy could not absorb more people. The rural sector, where about 90 per cent of the population lived, had always suffered from food shortages; now there were still more mouths to feed. The unemployed clamoured for work but few jobs were available. Wages fell and frequent famines hit hard. Shortly after Napoleon was defeated and a new political order was established (Germany was still divided, but now dominated by Prussia), it was clear to anyone who thought about it that the German poor needed relief more than ever.

No German reformer thought of separating impoverished elderly into their own category. If capable of working, even the old were expected to do so. If they could not, then they were helped (as in England) by their parishes, which organized funds for the poor, gave out loans, improved local poorhouses and hospitals, and organized new charitable foundations. Protestant states added to this a focus on education, for (in their view) helping the poor should go hand in hand with teaching them what they owed to God. Every state had its own demands. In Hesse, for example, hospitals were established to care for men and women age sixty and above. But to be accepted, applicants had to submit a petition that showed that they were pious, incurably ill, impoverished and without other means to support themselves. Consider the petition of Jacob Schöneweiss to enter one of its hospitals.[45] He described himself as 'poor, old, and now almost blind'. He had been a cowherd, but could no longer continue working. His wife, too, was 'old and advanced years [and] without accommodation, shelter, or food'. Previously he had been able to beg, but he could no longer do even that.

From testimony such as this, it appears that hospitals (at least in Hesse) were the elderly's last resort. In the countryside (as statistical studies derived from tax lists suggest), prior to around 1850 most old men and women lived with their families. In the cities they tended to live by themselves. And then, to be sure, there were old people like Goethe, very well-to-do, who continued to reside in their own homes. Goethe lived on the first floor; his son and his son's family lived on the floor above. Goethe did not depend on the younger generation. Indeed, in his home, his son was the needy one, both mentally and physically, and died in 1830, two years before his father.

The situation of the elderly in Italy may be usefully compared with Germany because it, too, was politically fragmented prior to unification in 1861, and, as in Germany, its various regions varied in their care for elderly. Unlike Germany, however, it was not divided by religious confessions since almost everyone adhered to Catholicism. The post-Tridentine papacy, rulers of Rome and of a belt of states across Italy's centre, took a keen interest in the welfare of the aged. A good example is the Apostolic Hospice of the Poor Invalids at Rome, established in 1692. Initially, it opened its doors to indigent old people once they reached the age of seventy; a bit later that was changed to age sixty, perhaps due to demand. But, of course, not *all* elderly men and women were welcome there. As in Hesse, they had to demonstrate that they were pious and deserving, that they could not support themselves by their own labour (even by begging), and that they had no family members to help them.

Work until you drop: that was the ideal. When one hospice at Rome decided to admit an 85-year-old man, it was not because of his age per se but due to his weaknesses and infirmities, 'on account of which he can no longer acquire the necessities of life by working' (14).[46] Once admitted, he was expected (like other residents at the hospice) to contribute to it by carrying out tasks suited to his abilities. Roman hospices ran on the labour of a whole raft of former tailors, shoemakers, cooks, barbers, weavers and carpenters. Some of these old people were enlisted to help those even less able-bodied. The elevation of work to iconic status was as evident in papal Rome as it was in Lear's England, Voltaire's France and Goethe's Germany.

Lack of family support was another prerequisite for admission to the hospices of Rome. During the seventeenth century, and even more so in the eighteenth, the papacy *required* relatives to care for their incapacitated elderly members. 'His Holiness does not intend for [the Apostolic Hospice] to relieve children of their burden of maintaining their parents which falls on them, regardless of the poverty of the children.' And the weight fell not just on the children but on spouses and siblings as well. The papacy established a tribunal to swiftly penalize recalcitrant family members, of which, apparently, there were quite a few. An old person had to prove beyond doubt that there was no one he or she could turn to. Thus, Margarita Narcisi, who never married, supported herself until she could no longer do so. Initially, she said, she relied on her widowed sister and nieces for support, but when they themselves did not have enough to live on, she requested admission to a hospice.[47] Before that could happen, her claims were no doubt checked by papal 'visitors' dispatched to her neighbourhood to question her parish priest and the neighbours. Were Narcisi's sister and nieces truly indigent? Let us hope so for her sake.

More flexible than papal Rome was Turin, in Piedmont, northern Italy. Under secular jurisdiction (Turin was the capital of the House of Savoy, the eventual kings of a united Italy), its Hospice of Charity worked in tandem with relatives. Sometimes, like the Apostolic Hospice, it took over when families could no longer manage; but often it was willing to supplement what the family could do. Every six months it updated its list of those requesting relief, dropping some names, adding new ones and reinstating others as needed. Although its statute of 1700 included a provision to house the elderly who 'are not able to gain their livelihood and do not have funds, income and other goods . . . or a family member . . . in condition to offer them relief', unlike the papacy, it did not *require* families to help out.[48] Moreover, people might cycle in and out of the hospice, depending on their needs.

Perhaps Turin's more elastic solutions for the poor and the elderly influenced the policies of Camillo Benso, count of Cavour (d. 1861), the first prime minister of a united Italy. Long before that post was even dreamt of, Cavour took a stand against the elitist sympathies of his family. Among his many concerns was the welfare of the poor and elderly, including his paternal grandmother.

The youngest son of noble parents, Cavour spent his very early childhood in the family palace at Turin along with all his relatives, including his grandmother – who was also his godmother and thus doubly important in his life. He began writing letters to her from the military academy to which he was sent at the age of five for schooling, and their correspondence continued for thirty-four years, until her death at age 87. 'We haven't seen each other for a month', he lamented in one letter written to her when he was thirteen (and she 61). He continued, 'that's a long time, and I hope on Sunday to compensate myself for the unhappiness I have felt' (74).[49] Even after finishing school, he continued to write to her – sometimes to voice his liberal political ideas (which she shared), at other times to speak of more frivolous matters, such as his delight at seeing the pretty girls of Ventimiglia (where his father had sent him to oversee some roadworks). When his mother died much later, Cavour wrote to a cousin about his still-living grandmother: 'In spite of her age', he maintained, 'she retains all the ardent feelings of a young girl, and in spite of that she still has the strength to console us [his family] and help us in our sorrow' (78).

Is it possible that Cavour's childhood concern for his elderly relative paved the way for the reforms that he later undertook? We hardly need early childhood experts to tell us that it may be so. Cavour became aware of the many serious social problems of his day while he was in his twenties. During a short sojourn in Genoa (which belonged to the Savoyard kingdom, as did Ventimiglia), he became interested in the way in which its hospices and prisons treated the poor. Once back in Piedmont, on his family's estates near Turin, he turned to the issue of poverty more generally. He was acquainted with the English Poor Laws, and right after they were updated in 1834, he prepared a report comparing them to the situation of the impoverished living in Piedmont, also part of the Savoyard kingdom. While there was a general movement at the time to legislate on behalf of the poor and infirm, Cavour singled out the *elderly* from the impoverished and sick in general. His question-and-answer format made their misery palpable. His concern about the aged was prescient, but, as illustration 13 suggests, it was a preoccupation of many social observers by the end of the nineteenth century.

> 1. Are there any hospices that take in those whom age has rendered unable to earn their living by working? – No establishment exists for this purpose. Still, as there are many hospices for those incurably ill, a few will sometimes receive poor people whose only 'illness' is the weakness of their advanced age.
> 2. Are they given help at home in the form of food and the like, or money? – The government and municipal authorities never give them any of these.
> 3. Are they given a pension? – Never from public institutions and very rarely from charity.
> 4. What help are their relatives required to give them? – Their children are supposed to provide for their parents'

subsistence. This holy obligation is only too often fulfilled imperfectly.[50]

In 1851, Cavour became minister of finance for the Savoyard king Victor Emmanuel ii, who, with the help of Garibaldi, was soon to become the king of a united Italy. Determined to ameliorate the plight of the old, he looked into pension schemes in other European countries, and his 'Retirement Fund for the Elderly' was adopted by the state legislature in 1859. Citizens were to contribute to the fund, which was guaranteed by the state. The 'holy obligation' that Cavour had earlier assigned to the family was now assumed by the government. While Cavour's plan was not implemented, it was a template for later legislation.

KING LEAR WANTED to retire not only with his status and dignity intact but in a bubble of unqualified love. Neither was to be. The love he got was imperfect; his status and dignity were contingent on his office. Homeless, rejected – and suddenly confronted with others equally miserable and disillusioned – he bewailed the human condition. Had he read the English Poor Laws promulgated while Shakespeare was writing his play, he would have had yet more to lament. Those laws would have put him to work.

'Work hard when you're young, and you can relax when you're old,' my grandmother told me. She clearly did not live in early modern Europe, when constant work was a moral, religious, even patriotic imperative. The body was a 'machine', and the more efficient and productive, the better. When it applied its labour – to land, to manufacturing, to changing ore into ingots, to making money – it was doing what Adam and Eve were meant to do when they were driven out of the Garden of Eden. The superior labour, tools and machines of Europe justified conquest and colonization elsewhere.

Adam and Eve's progeny had to contemplate why they had been expelled from the Garden. They looked within, excavated their inner selves and recorded their progress to salvation. Those practices dovetailed with the scientific desire to map the mind, as we saw with Descartes. They also answered the need of those who were alienated by interminable religious and civil wars and wanted to look within rather than at the devastation around them. The result was a new literature of self-exploration. None of these diaries, confessions and probes dwelt on old age per se, but inadvertently some of them revealed how it felt. As Sarah Cowper aged and became more dependent, she softened, appreciating the help of those around her. At the same time, her family cared more to be with her. As Goethe aged, he was happy to have finished the crowning work of his life (*Faust*), after which anything more, he thought, was gravy. Both accepted being old.

But Samuel Johnson (d. 1784) did not. When he was an old man of 69, he thought (like Cato) that 'it is a man's own fault, it is from want of use, if his mind grows torpid in old age' (661).[51] After a splendid dinner, he and his biographer (James Boswell [d. 1795]) argued about whether to admire the youthfulness of their host, age 65:

> JOHNSON: 'Why, yes, Sir, it is to be admired. I value myself upon this, that there is nothing of the old man in my conversation. I am now sixty-eight [in fact 69], and I have no more of it than at twenty-eight.'
>
> BOSWELL: 'But Sir would you not wish to know old age? He who is never an old man, does not know the whole of human life'. . .

JOHNSON: 'What, Sir, would you know what it is to feel the evils of old age? Would you have the gout? Would you have decrepitude?' – Seeing him heated, I would not argue any farther. (705)

Boswell, Johnson's younger biographer, hoped to be a Nestor one day. Johnson did not. As we shall see in the next chapter, Johnson was more modern in disparaging old age than was his disciple.

Five

Dignity

One of the achievements of the New Deal's Writers' Project of the 1930s was to collect more than 2,000 interviews with elderly formerly enslaved men and women. The purpose of these records was to provide information about plantation life before slavery was abolished in 1865. But they inadvertently shed light on the feelings of a whole group of very old people who shared an agonized past. Altogether they constitute what might be called an emotional community of pain – a youthful community that had for the most part dispersed and moved on by the time of the interviews.

The feelings of these elderly people cannot, of course, be separated from their recollections of life on the plantation, the focus of the interviews. But we need not do so. As we have seen over and over in this book, old people often think about their past, whether to reminisce or to commend or blame their life course. Indeed, the emotions that arise from looking back are among our most significant winter dreams. They may be unreliable about the facts of the past, but they are nevertheless precious for the historian of feelings.

As oral histories, however, the New Deal project had many faults. Consider some of the ways in which the materials were gathered in Georgia.[1] The interviewers came armed with a set of questions to which they wanted answers. Walking up to the door of their informant's home unannounced, they relied on 'southern hospitality' to let them in. Many interviewers were white, all were literate, and – given that they themselves were Georgians – they had preconceived notions of plantation life there. When Nancy Boudry, who thought she must be one hundred years old, talked about the cruelty of her enslaver, her interviewers, Maude Barragan and Leila Harris, interrupted: 'Nancy, wasn't your mistress kind to you?' Boudry was not intimidated. 'I ain't going to tell no story. I had a heap to undergo with' (114). Because the interviewers played an important role in shaping the responses, I look (above all) at the moments when the informants departed from the expected script – when they evinced unelicited feelings of enthusiasm or outrage and when they expressed by word or deed a sense of dignity or the opposite.

Why did now free people open their doors? Some enjoyed company and were glad to talk. 'I is powerful glad somebody is willing to stop long enough to pay some heed whilst I talks about something,' remarked Jasper Battle to the white lady who came by to interview him (62). Others were less welcoming. Alec Bostwick said bluntly that he regretted talking with his interviewer once he realized that she was not 'one of those pension ladies what come for to fetch me some money. I sure wish they would come' (112).

Basic necessities were often on their minds. Some ate while they were being interviewed. Many recalled with relish the foods of their childhood: 'Us sure ate good those days. Now us just eats whatsoever us can get' (41). Sadie Hornsby remembered the horror of her childhood bedding:

> [They] didn't have no slats or metal springs neither. They used stout cord for springs. The cloth that they made the ticks of them old hay mattresses and pillows out of was so coarse that it scratched us little children almost to death . . . I can still feel them old hay mattresses under

me now. Every time I moved at night, it sounded like the wind blowing through them peach trees and bamboos around the front of the house where I lives now.

The physical pain of the past still scratched at her mentally in her seventies.

So did other memories. Nancy Boudry had been a field slave and recollected only 'overwork, childbearing, poor food and long working hours' (113). At 86, John Cole (the man in illus. 27) was melancholy about Black life in general. 'Better for any nigger, anywhere, to bow low down to death' (230). Julia Brown (a.k.a. Aunt Sally) could still feel the pains of enslavement (142–53). 'I had such a hard time,' she said. She pitied the babies and mothers she saw torn from each other, and she felt for the husbands and wives who had to live on separate plantations. She was sensitive to the ways in which the values of the enslavers might become part of the mental equipment of the enslaved, in an early version of Stockholm syndrome. She saw it in herself: as she recounted, she had stolen a waffle from the stack that she was supposed to take up to the house of the 'white folks'. 'I just couldn't keep from taking one, and it was the hardest waffle for me to eat before I got to the big house I ever saw. I just couldn't get rid of that waffle because my conscience whipped me so.' Many decried their cruel overseers – white men who were hired by plantation owners to discipline the enslaved. Indeed, the interviewees often went off-script to express their resentment. Alec Bostwick, 76 years old, said of one overseer, 'All he done was sit around all day with a gun and make the niggers works. But I is going [to] tell you the truth: he sure was poor white trash with a house full of snotty-nose children . . . I mean this: if them days comes back, I hope the good Lord takes me first' (109). Rachel Adams sighed about her grandmother, who lived to age 115. She 'had done wore herself

27 John Cole, 86, former slave interviewed c. 1936. Looking back on his life, Cole judged that his 'freedom' had been a sham. Without support he had no way to start a new life, and he had to continue to work for his former master.

out in slavery time. Grandpa, he was sold off somewhere. Both of them was field hands.'

But some interviewees had happier thoughts as well. Rachel Adams was proud of her six children, nine grandchildren and nineteen great-grandchildren. She still cared for a grandson, who 'is done been blind since he was three weeks old. I sent him off to the blind school and now he can get around almost as good as I can. He has made his home with me ever since his Mammy died.' She was still responsible for him and excused herself at the end of her interview in order to give him 'something to eat' (1–8). Like Adams, Arrie Binns (about 86 years old) looked back on his life with pride. 'I'm so glad I always worked hard and been honest – it sure paid me time and time again' (79). Marshal Butler was glad of his strong muscles, his hard work and (if sheepishly) his school-educated grandson, who taught him to see slavery as a form of feudalism (162).

They recalled the old people of their childhoods with some ambivalence. Celestia Avery proudly retold her grandmother's stories. Georgia Baker, age 87, remembered 'grandpa Stafford well enough. I can see him now. He was an old man what slept on a trundle bed in the kitchen, and all he done was to sit by the fire all day with a switch in his hand and tend the children while their mammies was at work.' She concluded, 'Children minded better them days than they does now. Grandpa Stafford never had to holler at them but one time. They knowed they would get the switch next if they didn't behave' (40).

These people not only continued to feel the deprivations of their past – their harsh treatment by masters and overseers, their beds of straw, their families torn apart – but of their present lives. Most of them were barely getting by (hence the disappointment of one that an interviewer was not a 'pension lady'). On the other hand, many felt a dignity – derived from hard work, honesty, pride in their ancestors and their children. They contradicted the persistent assumption (we saw it already in Socrates) that wealth alone gives old people a sense of self-worth.

Snatched from Their Roots

The authority held by 'grandpa' Stafford, however vividly it was recalled, was but a shadow of the significant power of elderly men in African societies. The U.S. Congress prohibited the importation of slaves into the United States in 1808, but the practice died out only very slowly thereafter. It is therefore entirely possible that in the 1930s some free men and women could recall grandparents who had been wrested from Africa as youths.

Elderly people had played key roles in precolonial West and West Central African societies, whence many enslaved people came. As a result of living long and cannily cultivating advantageous kinship ties, some became rich. These prestigious old men formed councils of elders, taking care of practical and material matters such as infrastructures and markets. Or they acted as teachers of morality, instructing the young in good conduct and revered traditions. An old man was thought to be close to the spiritually empowered ancestor; he had the right to advise his community's kings and queens. Old women in African societies had prestige from other sources. They might be senior wives, beloved mothers or fearful witches with magical knowledge. European observers reported that old people in Africa basked in honour and authority while they lived and were celebrated in special rituals when they died. From their high perches on the social ladder, elders heaped much-resented insults on the young.

To get beyond the reports of outsiders, we may turn, if only briefly, to the African epic *Sunjata*. This work of oral literature, which dates back to the thirteenth century, may well not be historically accurate, but the *emotions* in its stories continue to resonate in the present and in that sense are true. Even today, *Sunjata* is repeated privately, in public performances and on radio broadcasts in Ghana and Mali.

The characters that populate this epic are exemplary models and heroes, larger than life and possessors of magical powers. They are understood to be the ancestors of the Manding peoples from time immemorial to today. Standing for the community's strength and pride, they also prove their underlying kinship. From *Sunjata*, Manding children learn that fathers want offspring, and they hear about the evil effects of jealousy among brothers, sisters and co-wives.

The first part of *Sunjata* is centred on the apparition of an old woman who terrorizes the countryside of her brother's kingdom in the form of a buffalo because he refuses to share his realm with her. The old woman is eventually won over by two pious

Muslim hunter-traders who show her kindness and hope to win her to gentler ways. She eventually not only regrets her many crimes but reveals to them that Sogolon, her little sister and the ugliest of all women, should be overpowered, wed and impregnated. She will be the mother of the hero Sunjata, a mother so beloved that, in one version of the story, the eponymous hero, faced with the choice of becoming king of his people or remaining with his ill mother, chooses to stay, telling her,

> Before dawn breaks
> Tomorrow, if you die,
> I am to be king of Manding.
> As long as you remain ill,
> I am not to be king of Manding,
> Because I will not leave you here in illness.[2]

A good son thus will renounce the throne to care for his sick mother. (However, she does die, and he becomes king.)

Enslavers did their best to sever captured Africans from such traditions. They were looking for workers, not fathers of kings or women with otherworldly powers, and they certainly fought against those who resisted. They turned the vaunted powers of Sogolon and her husband into the myth of 'strong' Black men and women who could be worked to death. They recast enslaved men as 'studs' rather than fathers. John Cole, (illus. 27), had vivid memories of this:

> If a hand were noted for raising up strong black bucks ... he would be sent out as a species of circuit-rider to the other plantations – to plantations where there was overplus of 'worthless young nigger gals'. There he would be 'married off' again – time and again. This was thrifty and saved any actual purchase of new stock (228).

Welfare

Cole was embittered. He knew what it meant to be exploited both during and after slavery. Once 1865 arrived, he got only broken pledges. 'Freedom' for him meant 'he had no way to go anywhere. He was rooted in the soil and would stay fast rooted. He worked on with his master for twenty years, without pay' (229). If the promises of the federal government had been kept, he would have had land of his own: soon after emancipation was proclaimed, the leader of the victorious Union army, General Sherman, issued an order in January 1865 (Special Field Order No. 15) to redistribute the land of former enslavers. About 400,000 acres was confiscated in order to be divided into 40-acre parcels to support newly free families. Sherman had consulted with Black leaders; he knew what was needed. But the reallocation was soon revoked.

Nor was any other support system established for the well-being of formerly enslaved people. Although various pension systems for them were proposed, none was passed by Congress. Around 1900, Blacks took the situation into their own hands, forming groups such as the National Ex-Slave Mutual Relief, Bounty and Pension Association to advocate for benefits. They called for a sliding scale of pensions that would be most generous to formerly enslaved people more than seventy years old and progressively diminish in size for younger men and women. This programme was similar to one long in place for Civil War veterans. But Congress did not pass the bill, and several federal agencies, including the Post Office, launched ugly campaigns to undermine the reputations of the movement's leaders.

That dolorous history is why many of the formerly enslaved people interviewed made clear the precarity of their situation. For support, they relied mainly on family members and handouts. For example, Alice Battle and her husband, who were 'too old and feeble to work', lived with one of their sons and 'were objects of charity' (59). George Brooks, well over one hundred, was supported by other Black people, who intended 'to look after the old man until he passes on' (131). Julia Brown got some food and cash from the state, but the amounts (she noted) were steadily decreasing, and the person who was supposed to help her get a pension never followed through. Lizzie Colquitt 'put in for one of them old age pensions, but they ain't give me nothing yet, so I just work when I can and hope that it won't be long before I has plenty again' (124). Susan Castle, more fortunate than most, got a pension: 'I is too old to work now and I is thankful for the old age pension. If it weren't for that, since this misery took up with me [perhaps arthritis], I would be done burned up, I sure would' (183). Della Briscoe, who believed she was more than ninety years old and had 'been unable to work for twenty-eight years' lived with her granddaughter, who paid the rent. She received some financial help from the Macon Department of Public Welfare (132).

With the possible exception of the Macon welfare department, Georgia, the state in which these men and women lived, offered negligible assistance to the elderly. It is true that the national Social Security Act, passed as part of Roosevelt's New Deal in 1935, was intended to offer a pension to all aged citizens. But the Act excluded farm and domestic workers, an omission demanded by southern congressmen. Even after the first Social Security cheque was issued, five years after passage of the Act, southern states delayed implementing it. The primary reason for this delay was racism – the reluctance to 'give' money to Blacks – even if most of them were farmers (who would not benefit) and even though many non-Black people would benefit. In fact, many poor white homesteaders were bankrupted after the Civil War. Some of them were relegated to 'poor farms'

– rural workhouses for children, jobless adults and the elderly. Others who were luckier found shelter with able and willing family members (illus. 24).

But perhaps the most important factor delaying the Act's implementation was the long-standing idea that poverty was the result of moral failure as well as the newer notion (we saw its birth in Chapter Four) that anyone who didn't work was lazy. This was a period in which 'grandfather' was supposed to operate like the wind-up clock in a popular song: it continued to tick faithfully for ninety years, until it 'stopp'd short – never to go again – When the old man died'.[3]

In other states, the provisions of the 1935 Act were implemented quickly. It provided supplements for state welfare programmes and (more significantly) it imposed a tax on both workers and employers to fund an 'Old-Age Reserve Account', which would provide all qualified people with a monthly sum when they turned 65 that would continue until their death. Benefits were largely limited to factory and salaried workers, and almost all of those were men. Four years later the spouses and dependent children of retired workers were added. In that way, an employee-based system became a family benefits programme. In 1965 health coverage for most Americans over age 65 began when a Medicare programme was passed by Congress.

European welfare programmes, responding to organized pressure groups, began about thirty years before they were implemented in the United States. The programmes in Europe were designed to meet the demands of industrialists, who were eager to promote a free labour market; of agrarian parties, which were keen to preserve rural interests; of workers' unions, which were bent on collective action; and of socialist organizations, which hoped to foment radical reform or even revolution. Germany, unified under Otto von Bismarck (d. 1898), was the first nation to institute a series of social insurance programmes

– sick leave, accident insurance and (via its pension law of 1889) small sums for workers once they turned seventy. These initiatives were funded through taxes on both employers and labourers.

By 1900 or so, most West European states were echoing the German welfare model, although almost invariably with modifications. Austria instituted only sickness insurance, while England and Denmark embraced old-age pensions that were financed by *general* taxes and dispersed to all indigent men over the age of sixty (in the case of Denmark) or seventy (in England). Older forms of relief from families and charities (both private and religious) continued, generally working hand in hand with municipal and state administrations. This was particularly the case in France, where the ageing population exploded earlier than elsewhere due to a low birth rate. The proportion of the French population sixty years old or more grew from 10.8 per cent in 1861 to 18.9 per cent in 1989.[4]

While in other countries men were the main recipients of aid to the elderly, in France both sexes were recognized by 1915. In the small town of Combourg in northwestern France (population 5,075), for example, 1.3 per cent of the population (20 men and 47 women age seventy or older) received small monthly allowances and, when needed, hospital care. Most of this money came from the local administrative district (*département*).[5]

No one country may be described as typical, but Italy offers a useful model, since it combined both the northern (wealthier) and southern (more impoverished) European experience. Recall that Cavour had noted the plight of the elderly poor in the north. His plan was meant to cover the entire Savoyard kingdom. That programme was never enacted, but regional societies of mutual aid (*società di mutuo soccorso*) in the north, mainly unaffiliated with church or state, did start to offer welfare to needy elders. Active in the major towns and villages, most of these so-called 'friendly societies' included members from different sectors of the labour force, including workers on farms and in the fledgling factories of the day. They were funded by membership dues and wealthy 'honorary members'. A bit like guilds (see Chapter Three), their purpose was to protect sick, indigent and elderly members from economic and physical ruin. Many offered a small lump-sum pension to retirees (at age 65) and subsidies for funeral expenses.

Italy's Mezzogiorno was far less developed and in the early years of the 1900s, in the wake of crop failures, unemployment and poverty were rife. Although there were a few self-help institutions there, one important solution to economic woe was immigration. From Italy's south came most of the four million Italians who arrived in the United States between the years 1880 and 1920. They had been sharecroppers or day labourers in Italy, supplementing their meagre farm earnings with part-time work in construction, mining and fishing. In the U.S. they sought jobs that did not disturb their customary work rhythm, even if farming was no longer available to them. They found employment as unskilled labourers in small shops, and they augmented their income with jobs in construction and coal mining.

Few *old* people immigrated, but in due course those who arrived inevitably aged. In 1905, for example, a bit less than 3 per cent of Italian-born males working in Buffalo (New York) were over the age of sixty. Some of them had prospered over time: 18 per cent of the older population could boast ownership of small retail shops. On the other hand, about 63 per cent of the rest were labourers.[6] Although in Buffalo, as in Italy and indeed in all of Western Europe, two-generation families were increasingly the norm, even so young and old in Buffalo did not lose touch. The daily *Buffalo Express* observed grandmothers in Buffalo's 'Little Italy' neighbourhood: 'Here you may see a grandmother, with a shawl over her head and a little two-year-old boy sprawled out asleep in her lap, knitting while she exchanges the latest gossip with her next-door neighbor.'[7] But autobiographies born of the immigrant experience suggest that a painful abyss would quickly form between *nonne* and their grandchildren once they went to school and learned English. As for the old men, having spent their lives working non-stop, they could feel defeated by old age's idleness more than anything else. In the words of Pio Federico, a 75-year-old Italian who had come from Abruzzo (east of Rome) to New York in 1909 and lived his final years in Los Angeles, 'When you are not in condition to create a family, a new factory, to speculate in the buying and selling ... to enjoy the pleasures of life, how can you say you are alive? What is worth living long if this is all in the past?'[8]

Back in Italy, with the end of the First World War (1914–18), disability and old-age pensions (at age 65 for those who had worked a minimum of twelve years) became mandatory for all private employees (public ones already had or would soon receive similar benefits). Some of those benefits went to women, many of whom had started to work in factories while men fought in the war. The Fascist regime (1922–43), which aimed to control all aspects of Italian life, attempted to turn back the clock by stressing women's maternal roles. Nevertheless, it founded the main Italian assistance institution that persists to this day, the National Institute of Social Welfare. The amount of aid has expanded steadily as Italy's economy has grown. In 1950, for example, only 39 per cent of elderly Italians received benefits, but by 1970 that percentage had swelled to 99.

In Germany, by contrast, the Nazis offered little financial aid to the elderly; its robust welfare system began only after the war. Instead, the Nazis nurtured the fantasy of the three-generation family even though in Germany, as elsewhere, two-generation families with grandparents living separately from their children, were already the norm. With 'blood and soil' as their nationalistic slogan, the Nazis adhered to a myth of 'pure-blood' ancestry rooted in the very soil of their forebears. As painted by Nazi artist Adolf Wissel the older generation – here the grandmother – linked the untainted past of Germany's farming families to the nation's glorious future, symbolized by the serious little boy in the middle of the picture.[9]

Happy Old Age?

Welfare for the elderly wrought a revolution. Hitherto, most old people were poor. Today, most elderly people (in developed countries) have some form of social security and are not in dire poverty. In 2024, as I write, perhaps 10.2 per cent of the U.S. population aged 65 and older lives below the poverty line. That means that they cannot afford basic essentials such as food, housing and clothing.[10] Are the remaining 90 or so per cent now happy to be old? *World Happiness Reports*, which began publication in 2012, ranks nations from most to least happy. Studded with images of smiling or laughing people of every age, it bases its ratings largely on states' GDP per capita, the social services they offer, the life expectancy of their population and similar metrics. It appears to ratify the assumption that happiness comes from being well off and well cared for.

Similarly, according to historian Élise Feller, the feelings of and about the elderly in France changed for the better after the Second World War as their pensions grew. At the start of the twentieth century, she points out,

> those designated as 'renters/retired', were grouped with 'those living exclusively from their savings and those without remunerated profession' along with 'nomads, prisoners, the hospitalized and the insane', as much as

if to say that they belonged among the marginalized and unclassifiable.[11]

But by the 1940s, a majority of the French population over the age of 65 was receiving a pension, and 'retired' became a high-status category. Everyone aspired to it. For example, in the city of Colmar, 'most of the people questioned [in 1946] appeared to see retirement as a "sacrosanct institution" that one gained by working during one's active life. It was an absolute right acquired by every old worker.' This attitude continued. When French presidents Nicolas Sarkozy and Emmanuel Macron (2007–12 and 2017–27 respectively) proposed raising the retirement age in France, long and bitter (though ultimately unsuccessful) popular protests broke out in numerous cities. According to Feller, the elderly in France gained a new status over time: from shameful 'old person' to proud 'retiree'.

Even so, in 1970, when the French pension system was in full bloom, feminist writer and activist philosopher Simone de Beauvoir maintained that old people in France and everywhere else were treated as 'criminals' and 'outcasts' (1–7).[12] Old age was a 'shameful secret', a condition that people kept under wraps in order to maintain their dignity. She described old people as 'condemned to poverty, decrepitude, wretchedness and despair', blaming happiness as among 'the myths and the clichés of bourgeois culture'. We ought at least to feel compassion for the aged, since they are ugly and weak, she argued; but capitalism, founded on profit, values only the 'working stock'. For Beauvoir, the elderly formed an unrecognized 'caste' oblivious of its own condition. She called for a revolution to liberate them, as Gandhi had freed the untouchables in India and the Communists had emancipated women in China.

To me, Beauvoir seems to be talking about the situation of her parents rather than of her own time. But many of my female friends have told me that the book was eye-opening for them. They were reading it at the beginning of the women's liberation movement in the United States, and they found Beauvoir's description of the position of old people uncomfortably close to the status of women. Like old people on pensions, many young women stopped working when they married, and then (quoting Beauvoir on retirees), 'the fact is that biologically, economically and socially their status has declined. All the tests to which they are submitted show a self-disgust' (462).

Beauvoir did not say which tests she was thinking of, but certainly today many gerontologists do administer tests to the elderly to discover how they feel. However, they discover not self-disgust but the very opposite! Already in the 1960s, some gerontologists discovered that old people claimed that they were happy. The word 'gerontology' (derived from the Greek *geron*) was coined around 1900, but it was only in the 1950s that the term took off, with a long trail of scientific publications on the topic since then. 'The science of gerontology has the practical purpose of... helping people to enjoy life, and to get satisfaction from life', wrote Robert Havighurst, an early researcher in the field. A 'successful' old age was seen as one of joy and satisfaction *appropriate to advanced age*. Why did Havighurst choose the criterion of 'success'? It may well be that he was following Erik Erikson, who argued (see my Introduction) that each 'age of man' has its own particular task. That of the elderly is to accept their lives as inevitable and right.

Like Erikson, Havighurst argued that successful old people do not allow themselves to despair. To measure their psychological well-being on a large scale, he created a questionnaire that allowed for one of two choices for each item. The answers could be tabulated and made to yield statistically valid results. Here is an example of one item on his major survey form (Life Satisfaction Index-A [LSI-A], which is still in use):

I am just as happy as I was when I was younger.
Response options: 0 Disagree, 1 Agree.[13]

After many rounds of interviews, almost all of the elderly subjects who remained with the study and filled out this self-reporting instrument agreed.

More recent studies have added sophistication to this method. Laura L. Carstensen and colleagues, for example, sampled adults over a ten-year period. Their participants represented a variety of ages, ethnicities and genders. Further, the researchers added questions about a range of emotions. Seeing nuance in the emotional lives of the elderly, they suggested that 'as the end of life slowly but steadily nears, emotional experience grows more complex and overall more positive'.[14] In another study they asked about new experiences. Were old people less open (as the researchers at first assumed) to novelty than younger adults? To their surprise, they found the opposite to be true. Both young and old might find novelty stressful, but the old tended to be less anxious and more resilient. This finding, as the researchers summed it up, 'highlight age-related benefits in emotional well-being ... and further implies that older adults may not be novelty averse'.[15]

Such sunny conclusions may need to be tempered by the fact that the researchers included only participants who declared themselves 'in good or better [health] than most people their age'. Ill health is not, however, 'abnormal' in the case of the old.[16] A study of the elderly in Sweden that *included* people in bad health found that life satisfaction as measured by LSI-A *decreased* with age.[17]

Rather than ask, 'How does it feel to get old in such-and-such a political, social, cultural, religious context?', or at least 'What does it feel like to get old?', most researchers today sacrifice specifics for statistics. But there are exceptions. Seeking 'subjective dimensions, which touch on the core of a person's sense of meaning and self-definition', L. Eugene Thomas and Kim O. Chambers conducted a cross-cultural study of two groups of elderly men, one in Delhi, India, the other in London, England.[18] Using LSI-A among other 'standard measures', they also conducted 'in-depth open-ended interviews'. The usual statistical methods yielded few dissimilarities between groups, both of which were 'happy'. But the interviews revealed gaping differences. The Londoners dreaded becoming incapacitated, useless and dependent on others and were happy that they were none of those things. The Indian men, by contrast, were pleased that they had raised successful children, that their children respected them and that they had carried out their religious duties well. Old people *want* to feel good about themselves and to present a positive picture to others within the context of their own cultures, but their cultures shape what they feel good about. Beauvoir wasn't exactly wrong about the miseries of the elderly, but she didn't consider that people's sense of self depends on more than 'objective' circumstances.

A study of the elderly in residential care highlighted the tactical efforts that both staff and patients made to preserve their dignity and good spirits. When potentially embarrassing situations came up (for example, helping an old person go to the toilet), it was often handled through jokes. As for happiness per se, Ed, a resident, had a revelatory conversation with his caregiver Keira:

ED: I'm not doing too well [laughs]
... Getting breathless more often and oh what else there's everything else. [laughs]
KEIRA: oh Ed
ED: well dear Keira I have to note that I'm, I'm eighty seven that's not (easy?)

KEIRA: it's a good age, it's not (bad?)
ED: It's a good age yes
KEIRA: and you're happy with the life you've led so (far?)
ED: (untranscribable) oh oh I've had a good, pretty good time . . .[19]

At the start of this conversation, Ed wasn't doing too well. But as he joked with his sympathetic caretaker, Keira, he became more cheerful. By the end he was reassuring her – and perhaps himself – that he was pretty happy, all in all. Happiness and sadness are embedded in human relations. Before Keira arrived, Ed was sad. Maybe interviews and questionnaires, too, are experienced as interventions by caring people. Happiness is today's key word. But as even these few examples demonstrate, happiness means many different things.

Let us listen to 89-year-old José Mujica, a former president of Uruguay, who was interviewed just as I was finishing this book.[20] Old people want to be happy, he maintains, but they need to find happiness in the right things. The wrong things are those to which our capitalist culture lures us. We don't need lots of shoes, cars or refrigerators. Rather, we need to discover and cultivate our life's purpose. Mujica's own purpose was political struggle. Even though it meant that he would spend many years in jail, he went right back to political organizing as soon as he was free:

> Man . . . has the ability to find a purpose. Or not. If you don't find it, the market will have you paying bills the rest of your life. If you find it, you will have something to live for. Those who investigate, those who play music, those who love sports, anything. Something that fills your life.

Recently diagnosed with oesophageal cancer and weakened by radiation therapy, he knows the pains of growing old and what it means to face death. 'I love life,' he says, but he knows his time is running out. For those who seek serenity, he has lots of advice: stop working so hard and, instead, enjoy nature, read books and converse with others. He echoes Cephalus on the pleasures of conversation, Petrarch on the joy of reading and Cato on the wonders of nature. He loves his chrysanthemums, his dogs, and above all his wife, his companion of nearly forty years. He is fascinated by human complexity – by our emotions, which (he maintains) are more important than our reason; and by our interconnectedness not only with one another but even with the lowly bacteria that help us digest the food in our guts. Of his dear wife, just ten years younger than he, he says, 'Love has ages. When you're young, it's a bonfire. When you are an old man, it's a sweet habit. I'm alive because of her.' It's a lovely winter dream.

Visions of the Elderly Woman

Mujica's paean to his wife is unusual. Usually old women, following tradition, are presented as hags. Here is William Faulkner (d. 1962) writing as if he were a young man observing old Rosa Coldfield as he and she sit in her airless 'office' in spite of the stifling heat outside. Dry as the dust motes that float in the room, she smells 'of old flesh long embattled in virginity'. She keeps the young man captive (but not captivated) for a long time in order to hear the history of the family they both share. He stares at her legs, which hang from her chair like sticks, and at her wan and haggard face.[21] We have already seen her: in the poetry of the ancient Roman writer Horace, telling us of an old, nameless, 'half-rotten' crone; and in the satire by the thirteenth-century poet Rustico Filippi, laughing at a 'stinky old woman'. But should we expect it in the work of an author writing in Mississippi in the 1930s, at about the same time as formerly enslaved men and women were asserting the dignity of their lives in nearby Georgia? Traditional tropes, like prejudices, die hard.

It should not be surprising, then, that old women continue to be seen as witches. Writing around the same time as Faulkner, but some 4,000 miles away in England, novelist Elizabeth Bowen (d. 1973) writes of an old lady who looks perfectly normal but manipulates everyone else in strange and sinister ways.[22] Behind *The House in Paris*'s subtle psychology and evocative imagery is the wicked cackle of Horace's Canidia and numerous other 'witches' throughout history working their magic on innocent youths.

Although superficially a tragic love story, with Karen and Max its young protagonists, Bowen's novel is more surely a study of the cruel and conniving Madame Fisher. An enterprising woman in hard times, she runs a sort of boarding house in Paris, limited at any one time to only two paying guests, invariably young English women. Too young to wed but old enough to try their wings away from their mothers, they are sent to live under the watchful eye of Madame Fisher – or, rather, as girls soon learn, they are to live under the hypnotic presence of the old woman. She refuses to act as their mother-substitute, escort, friend or disciplinarian. Rather, she plays the role of guilty conscience, a constant force, a nameless and ceaseless power. They dare not get out of line – or, if they do, Madame Fisher quietly sends them home.

Karen was once one of those girls, studying art in Paris. There she first encountered Max, a young man of about twenty at the time, who regularly visited Madame Fisher in the evenings. He was striking, brilliant, Jewish, exotic. Those days, whenever Karen met him on the stairs or in the hall, she trembled, was confused, felt upset. She thought she hated him. He, for his part, noticed her but said little, for he was very careful around all the young ladies. After all, he was there in order to have long conversations with Madame Fisher. Why did he bother with the old lady every evening? Clearly, it was her sorcery. As he recognized even at the time, yet could not quite put into words, she was fashioning him into a man – *her* man. She was in love with him; she 'seduced' him to depend on her and to know himself through her.

Madame Fisher's daughter, Naomi, was around Karen's age. The two young ladies became close friends, never quite losing contact. Mousy and thin, Naomi was (like Max) in thrall to her mother. She never separated from Madame Fisher, never became her own person. Years later (the novel moves across about two decades) she inherits a fortune from her aunt. Max, badly in debt, asks her to marry him, the fulfilment of *her* long-held, silent dream. Madame Fisher makes clear that she disapproves and undermines the engagement by telling Max that *Karen* loves him. She is all too correct, but she refuses to accept that coupling as well. Confronting Max, the old lady takes control of his feelings. Tormented, he slits his wrists in front of her and bleeds to death. The evil witch has had her way. But at a cost. Thereafter, she becomes a sick old woman. 'Waxy skin strained over her temples, jaws and cheek-bones; grey hair fell in wisps round an unwomanly forehead . . . her mouth was graven round with ironic lines. [She was like] someone cast, still alive, as an effigy for their own tomb' (40). This is how we meet her; this is how she remains for ten years. Her curse has recoiled upon herself.

More recently, visions of old women have lightened up. If they look like witches, it is because they *want* to look that way. They wear purple dresses together with red hats just for fun, as 'Warning' (1961), a poem by Jenny Joseph (d. 2018), happily proclaims.[23] Her jolly old-lady persona kicks off the traces: she'll 'learn to spit' and get fat if she wants. She is the modern female version of Procleon, except that she has no political concerns and no one to try to keep her in line. Joseph herself was 29 years old when she wrote 'Warning', as readers might guess from the fact that the poem is written in the future tense: 'I shall'. The here-and-now of the poet is prosaic: sober, serious, decorous. She is simply making plans, though (she hints) perhaps she should give eccentricity a try even now.

'Warning' was twice 'voted Britain's favourite modern poem' in BBC polls, and decades after its publication it inspired the formation of the Red Hat Society (1998).[24] 'Little did I know', wrote one member on that society's website, that old age 'was the time to "kick up my heels, travel, make new friends across the globe and have a ball!" Thanks, RHS for my second childhood!!!!'[25] Nor is the idea only for poems or websites. I met an older woman at my doctor's office who had gorgeous rose tattoos up and down her arms. After I exclaimed in surprise and admiration, she was happy to explain: 'When I turned 65, I decided to do what I had always wanted to do.'

Thus, it is true, as the Netflix series *Grace and Frankie* (2015–21) demonstrates, that for some people old age is the time to write a 'new chapter' of life. But as it unfolds, the moral of that television sitcom is less that we start anew in old age than that we return to our early twenties, with all the zany and heartbreaking things we did then, but this time with osteoporosis and lapses of memory. So Grace (played by Jane Fonda) falls down and breaks her hip, but in no time at all, it seems, she is back on her feet and ready for more adventures.

The Elderly Man Envisaged

The novel *Père Goriot* by Honoré de Balzac (d. 1850) tells us that old men think that they are happy, but they are fooling themselves.[26] To those around him old Goriot seems the saddest man alive. But he thinks that he is the happiest, for he has two wonderful daughters, and nothing else matters. When we first meet him, he is living in a shabby room in a run-down boarding house in a Paris slum. To save money he has cut back on his meals. His clothes are in rags. Balzac wrote the novel in the years 1834–5, precisely when Cavour compiled his report on the elderly indigent of Piedmont. Like Cavour, he meant to evoke pity. Unlike Cavour, he also wanted to induce fear: Goriot's fate could be our own.

In his younger days, Goriot was a pasta importer who made a fortune from the famine precipitated by the French Revolution by selling flour 'at ten times what it cost him' (69). In cahoots with the Committee of Public Safety, famous for its unrestrained use of the guillotine, he was exactly the sort of nouveau riche that Balzac, a convinced royalist, detested. Fittingly, then, Goriot's ambition was also his undoing. He lived for the success of his two daughters, and his love for them was so absolute that it doomed him. Giving each of them huge dowries so they might marry well, he kept only a small annuity of around 10,000 francs per year for himself. Like King Lear, he imagined that after his daughters were settled, he would have 'two places where he would be able to live, two houses where he would be adored and spoilt' (69).

That winter dream is not to be. His sons-in-law and even his daughters (as it turns out) are ashamed of this 'vermicelli-merchant' of a father and banish him from their homes. In 1820 or so, when the novel takes place, an annuity of 10,000 francs was 'equivalent to the annual income of a low-paid manual worker'.[27] That sum could possibly have supported Goriot during his remaining years. A man of sixty at the time could expect to live another thirteen years, and Goriot was already in his mid- to late sixties when the novel's events take place. But he is not allowed to live out his life on this pittance because at least one of his daughters is always cadging more money from him. This, however, does not discourage him. Rather, as he turns his beloved silver-gilt breakfast set into ingots to pawn on her behalf, he weeps for the 'poor child', not for himself. He is only occasionally aware of his desperate and compromised situation.

Another character in the same book, the rich high-society matron Madame de Beauséant, knows that Goriot had toppled from riches to rags. But as a member of the beau monde, she has the sort of compassion for the old man akin to what one feels about a natural disaster: it is 'dreadful, and yet we see it every day'. Meanwhile Goriot's fellow boarders are either immobilized, like 'oysters on a rock', or they flee the decrepit place as soon as they can for the 'the special allurements of Parisian life'. After they depart, they forget 'all about the poor old man they mocked' (26).

Two students are the exception to the general corruption, the most important of them being the law student Eugène de Rastignac. Young, poor, naïve and virtuous, he cares about Goriot. Yet he, too, is drawn to the shining path of deceit, as Balzac makes clear in subsequent books.

Goriot had preyed on the weak and poor when he was young; now his daughters prey on him. Yet, as he himself confesses, he *courted* their ill treatment. He is 'happy' just to glimpse them in their fancy carriages as they drive by. On his deathbed, utterly penniless, ignored by his daughters, he rants and raves, riding an emotional roller coaster from fury to love: 'I want my daughters! I made them! They are mine! . . . I shall be dead, dead in a fit of rage, rage rage . . . I curse them . . . I adore them!' (248–9). He dies thinking that the two young students who lift him up – so that his bedsheet can be changed – are his daughters. From beginning to end, the happiness of his old age is founded on delusion.

Even if Goriot had lived in a welfare state, his sorrows would not have been salved. His problem was not penury per se but rather the indifference of others. If Cicero offered the model of an honoured and respected old age, then Balzac presented its antithesis: an old age accorded so little dignity that it did not even rate the clean sheet due the dying. For, as it happens, even that final bedsheet was dirty. The moral: it is self-deception to be contented with our past; we are lucky if we die without recognizing the truth. Meanwhile, the indifferent world will continue, with all its own illusions intact.

Italo Svevo's loosely connected stories about ageing, unfinished in 1928 when he was killed in a traffic accident at the age of 67, were both bleaker and funnier. He was writing in tumultuous times. Living in Trieste, which had been part of the Habsburg (Austrian) Empire but transferred to Italy after the First World War (1914–18), Svevo witnessed the impact of fascism on this hitherto prosperous, polyglot and multi-ethnic city.

Zeno Cosini, the protagonist of Svevo's *A Very Old Man* also lives in Trieste. He finds his true self only in what he writes, not in 'horrid real life'.[28] In his notebooks he can be honest about himself (no one will ever see them, so why not?), whereas in life he wears a mask. Yet, from the evidence of those very stories, no one around him is ever fooled. Above all, he gets angry – even furious – at others, while he is 'full of sympathy' for himself (8). He objects to his son, Alfio, a self-taught artist, and he thinks (probably rightly) that Alfio 'doesn't hold me in great esteem' (32). He tries to pretend to love his son, but his words come out as rebukes. He is humiliated by his younger employee, Olivi, who runs Cosini's business better than he does. He disdains his son-in-law, Valentino, whom he finds boring, physically disgusting and bothersome. Although he probably means well, Valentino seems to be taking over Cosini's life. The old man simply can't stand these young men telling him what to do.

Dignity

Nor can he understand why his beautiful, virtuous daughter, Antonia, married Valentino, on whom she clearly dotes. When Valentino dies of a rare case of premature old age, Antonia wails and mourns endlessly, wearing her widow's weeds like trophies. Soon Cosini won't like her either.

There are three people who charm him out of his general pique: his wife, Augusta, who is dumpy and doesn't understand him at all but is unfailingly supportive; his little grandson, Umbertino, whose childish antics give him great pleasure; and his nephew, Carlo, who knows how to humour him, and who is an excellent doctor as well. Indeed, Carlo's prescribed diet for Cosini has worked so well that he's never felt better in his life. Or so he says, as he counts up his ailments and potential ailments: his liver might fail him, his kidneys too.

When he learns that Mother Nature loves not abstinence but rather the sex drive, Cosini decides to 'trick Mother Nature' and take a mistress. She costs a hefty penny, but he tries to think of it as filling a prescription for better health. Even so, when he realizes that his mistress is entertaining another old man as well, he leaves her. Only as the affair recedes in time does he accept that, as an old man, 'I am not worth more than what I pay' (114). Without his mistress, he must now find pretty girls to leer at. It's not that he is lecherous, he reassures himself; it's just his way to outwit death. He can pretend that the youthful sap is still running in his veins.

All in all, he's unlucky. When he was young, old men were respected and the young kept silent in their presence. Now he is old, but 'only the young are respected' (61). In effect, Svevo is enacting, on the intimate level of Cosini's conflicts with Olivi and Alfio, the generational clash that was already developing in pre-fascist Italy leading up to the war. In his novel, Svevo has Cosini bet on Austria, where he hoped to be a war profiteer. But there, too, he has no luck. Although he is not impoverished by Austria's defeat, Cosini has to suffer the revolution of the youths, whose blood has been stirred by the likes of Benito Mussolini (d. 1945), the eventual ruler of fascist Italy. 'It's to you, young Italians,' Mussolini wrote at the start of the First World War, before Italy had given up its neutrality, 'you youths of the factories and universities, you youths in age and spirit, you who are destined to "make" history: it's to you that I launch my cry . . . War!'[29]

But while the ravages of war in early twentieth-century Europe made an old man superfluous, the cholera of the same era in South America at last fulfilled the lifelong dream of Florentino Ariza, the flawed but admirable hero of a novel by Gabriel García Márquez.[30] As a young man in love with Fermina Daza, he is separated from her after her father opposes their marriage and she marries someone else. Ariza never gives up. Yes, he has lovers aplenty. But he remains passionately in love with Daza and, as it were, transforms and grooms himself to be hers one day. At an age that most people consider too old to love, the two fall into a blissful, old-person's love, both giving off 'the sour smell of old age' and not caring at all (335). On a cruise ship unexpectedly stranded on a river in Colombia, 'they spent unimaginable hours holding hands in the armchairs by the railing, they exchanged unhurried kisses, they enjoyed the rapture of caresses without the pitfalls of impatience' (338). And in the 'magic' of Márquez's 'realism', their ship will 'keep going, going, going'.

Taken together, the winter dreams of the recent era seem to have evolved in the direction of happiness. And why not? Cushioned by their pensions and savings, old people today would seem to have it all. Enough to live on. Leisure time to travel. Friends and family to visit. An article in *Forbes* cannot resist a joke as it chronicles the growing rates of sexually transmitted diseases among the elderly: 'It would seem retirement homes might not be such dull places after all.'[31] Yet when I raised the issue among my friends in their sixties and seventies, asking them if old people didn't have many compensations for their pains, they laughed bitterly. By objective standards they should be enjoying their lives – they go to plays and concerts, entertain friends, volunteer for worthy causes, read books and continue to work if they want to. From the outside, their lives seem to be privileged, and they know it. So why do they not echo Mujica's contentedness? Well, a few do concede that they are lucky. But others point out that they spend much of their time going to doctors' appointments, undergoing surgeries, hobbling around on weak knees, and watching (with painful frequency) dear friends and spouses die. Perhaps my informal survey needs to be repeated when these friends are in their eighties and nineties to get more tranquil answers.

What Happens to People?

Shakespeare claimed that the old were 'sans everything' – less than a shadow, 'mere oblivion'. 'Would that it were so,' said the daughters of Goriot, considering their now penniless father nothing more than burden. 'Would that it were so,' say modern state-pension systems, panicked by the disparity between the birth rate and the increasing longevity and number of old citizens. For it is clear that old people are *not nothing*. They are, at the very least, living organisms: they need food and shelter and, because they are still people (even if many can no longer speak, walk or remember), they have feelings.

What happens to people both physically and mentally has long been known. Sappho sang about her white hair and weak knees. Solon knew that the elderly needed care and assigned the job to sons while warning against intergenerational resentments. The actor playing Pheres (the old father in Euripides' *Alcestis*, who refuses to die in place of his son) had to convey both dotage *and* a zest for life. The one performing Trojan Queen Hecuba as a prisoner of war had to take 'halting footsteps' even as she carried out her revenge. Aristotle was aware of the failing eyesight and hearing of the old, along with their tendencies to be miserly, fearful and suspicious of others. In the third or second century BCE, with the decline of classical norms, artists played up wrinkles, whether to evoke disgust, ridicule or admiration (see illus. 9).

The ancient physician Galen's explanation for these characteristics was the natural process of heat and moisture loss – the body simply dried up and cooled off until eventually it plummeted like a dry leaf in winter. His prescription for postponing that fate included eating the right foods, exercising, sleeping well and taking care to get massages and purgatories.

Much of that sort of advice persists today, whether in advice columns, books or websites. But *explanations* for the symptoms of the elderly entirely reject Galen's scheme. Today, scientists studying ageing can peer into the body by using a variety of scanning and measuring devices. They now know many more 'symptoms' of ageing beyond white hair and wrinkles and many more reasons for the ageing process. Consider the brain, where some of the most exciting work of this sort is being done. For example, we know that the size of our brains tends to diminish as we get older. Nevertheless (at least as *some* scientists see the matter), two regions of the brain, the amygdala and the ventromedial prefrontal cortex, seem to keep their volume as people age. These are the regions that many scientists believe are associated with affect.

The real-life consequences of these findings are unclear. It is by no means certain what shrunken brains imply about human emotions, and the same is true of proportionally larger regions of the brain. Moreover, the brain is not the only part of the body that generates feelings. Think of the heart and the gut.[32] Galenic medicine had a faulty theory, many fewer tools and far less funding than its modern counterpart. But it was not so full of uncertainties.

Microbiology offers one of the most promising areas of research into the ageing process because it has discovered a correlation between the life of the cell (and thus of life in general) and the shortening of telomeres in the process of cell division. To explain, I must digress a bit.

The DNA molecule, which contains the genetic code and famously looks like a double helix, is very long.[33] To fit into the tight space of a cell nucleus, DNA is wound around protein spools called histones. In cells these structures (DNA and histones) condense into chromosomes when the cell is ready to divide. Chromosomes look something like an X, each end of which is capped by a telomere made up of more DNA, but structured as loops that hide their own ends. Telomeres act like the aglets at the ends of shoelaces, keeping the chromosomes stable and ready for cell division. But telomeres shorten with each cell division. Eventually (after fifty divisions or so) they lose their special abilities to hold the cell together and enable it to divide. The cell becomes 'senescent' – a word not by hazard related to *senex*. One sort of cell, however, does not have this problem: germline cells, the cells that form eggs and sperm. That is because they alone contain telomerase, which solves the problem of telomere shortening. As the embryo grows, the telomerase is suppressed.

Our own senescence is built into this scheme. Cell division stops when the telomeres get too short. It's good that this happens. When it doesn't, then cancerous, 'immortal' tumours may result. So, while some geneticists argue that telomeres 'cause ageing', they do not suggest keeping the telomeres long, for that would ignite the very conditions that favour the development of tumours.

There are, however, other ways to keep us quasi-immortal. Some animals, for example, are more or less immortalized through cloning. Furthermore, it is now known that any differentiated cell (for example a human skin cell) may be turned into a pluripotent stem cell (the sort found in very early embryos) to form *any* kind of cell in the body.

The main goal of genetic science is to cure diseases, keep people well and prolong lives. Some scientists consider old age a sort of disease and seek to medicate it. Others think they have found the diet that will keep people youthful. Consider one advocated by Valter Longo. He claims to 'exploit our body's innate ability to regenerate itself', blaming 'the constant consumption of the modern life-style' for turning off these innate mechanisms (xii).[34] He advocates following a 'daily nutritional regimen' punctuated by four- to five-day periods of semi-fasting during the year. He speaks of 'semi-fasting' because if you eat Longo's special plant- and nut-based food during it, you will not feel hungry (xiv). He wants people to start his 'fasting mimicking diet' young and continue it for life (xviii). Like Galen's regimen, Longo's solution to ageing demands constant vigilance, self-control and quite a bit of money. And, of course, people die for all sorts of reasons other than getting old. It is not for nothing that parents warn their children to 'look both ways' when crossing the street, whether or not they are following a life-prolonging diet.

A modern riff on the ancient Greek myth of Tithonus is Oscar Wilde's tormented *The Picture of Dorian Gray*. Here the young hero's portrait is painted as he was: 'the most marvelous youth'.[35] A friend laments that poor Dorian can only go downhill from there. One day he will be 'old and wrinkled and ugly'. He will have to bow to the inevitable: 'what the gods give they quickly take away' (32–3). Terrified of this fate, Dorian gives in to impulse and utters 'a mad wish that he himself might remain young, and the portrait grow old' (102). But he forgets to ask that his moral innocence continue. In the course of his life he deceives, tortures and murders. But he leaves no evidence of his misdeeds except in the picture, which turns bloody and loathsome. Horrified by this image, Dorian picks up a knife, stabs the picture and dies as he does so.

Dorian's wish is echoed by many today. While Valter Longo doesn't claim that followers of his diet will *look* young, he implies that it's possible, since they will 'maintain [their] vigor and functionality' (22). Many people today want still more: they want to look and be young forever. Once upon a time, Cato declared himself delighted that he was no longer bothered by sensual desires. But today, many old people enjoy sex. One couple profiled by journalist Maggie Jones, David and Anna, both in their eighties, found new (for them) techniques to get ready for intercourse: he uses Viagra and she a vibrator. 'Thank you, God, for one more time', they say afterward.[36] Cato's social strata distrusted eros; modern Western society can't get enough of it.

The American Society of Plastic Surgeons reported in 2022 that 'cosmetic surgery procedures have grown by 19 per cent since 2019' (3).[37] Even more striking is the fact that youthful looks are so desirable that even very young people are turning to medical treatments to stave off ever looking old. In 2019, *The Guardian* reported that 'girls of 13 are lining up for Botox'.[38] Thereafter, between 2019 and 2022, the number of neuromodulator injections (among them the botulinum toxin) rose by 75 per cent in the United States among people nineteen years old and younger. Why is this happening? Fingers point to the rise of celebrity culture, deep-rooted notions of beauty and the financial benefits sought by plastic surgeons and cosmetics companies, which blitz the media with their airbrushed images. Let me add that remaining young-looking is a way to deny (out of sight, out of mind) the gradual but inevitable deterioration of a beautiful body into a corpse. Every reminder of decay is avoided today; even Halloween costumes of skeletons seem to be losing their appeal.[39]

Crises

The dignity of the elderly was honoured by Solon, demanded by Roman patriarchs and recognized by medieval charity. But it was largely left behind by the early modern work ethic, and it has been recovered today only half-heartedly. Hard-won social security is meagre compensation when society tells old people that they look disgusting, that there are too many of them and – most recently – that their longevity is causing a crisis for everyone else.

It is indeed true that more of the world's population is old than ever before, and if the trend continues, people sixty years and above will comprise nearly 30 per cent of the people on earth in 2100. By that same year, the birth rate and percentage of young people is projected to decline by over 8 per cent.[40] Industrialized nations have some form of social security, but in many instances, it is inadequate to keep elderly bodies and souls together without other sources of support. We should also keep in mind that 'the overwhelming majority of the world's population is still without some form of income security in old age or disability'.[41]

There seem to be two obvious ways to reorder matters in industrialized countries. Either change the grounds of support systems such as social security, which now depend on the work of younger generations, or find ways to increase the work force. But the will to change is limited, and if resources are reallocated, someone or some interest will suffer.

In the United States, the social security tax on income is capped. For example, in 2024, salaries beyond $168,600 were exempt. Why not set the cap higher or eliminate it altogether?[42] Because, counters the right-leaning Republican Study Committee, American workers are already overburdened by taxes. Instead, this group advocates gradually diminishing the stipend paid out to retirees and letting workers bow out of Social Security taxes entirely, using the money 'to invest in private retirement options.'[43] In effect, this would gut the entire system within a few years and old Americans would be left to fend for themselves as they were before the New Deal.

Alternatively, the workforce that pays into social security might be expanded by, for example, considering immigrants as a source of labour rather than as 'mooching layabouts and rapists'.[44] Already in 2005, 'the seven million or so illegal immigrant workers [in the United States provided the Social Security] system with a subsidy of as much as $7 billion a year', although they had no hope of receiving benefits when they retired.[45] In the state of Maine, with a large and growing population of elderly people and a billion-dollar industry in catching and processing lobsters, 'companies are turning to foreign-born workers to bridge the divide'.[46]

Increasing the birth rate would also expand the workforce over the long term. But that would require both state support and a culture attentive not only to the care of children but to the right of both parents to work. In Bolzano, Italy, where these conditions are in place, the birth rate is steadily high, and mothers and fathers benefit from flexible work schedules.[47] Alternatively, pensions could come out of general federal taxes, bypassing the need for young workers to pay into the system.

In short, solutions to the growing population of elderly exist, but they require an unwonted toleration of new taxes or newly positive feelings toward people who do not work, or do not speak the prevailing language, or do not have the means to advocate for themselves.

The senile, the terminally disabled: their numbers, too, are growing as the population ages. They too are part of the 'crisis'. It is one thing to deal with elderly people who, like Zeno Cosini, can still gad about; or who, like Cato, can continue to go to the Senate; or, who, like Ojibwa elders, retain control over important domains of knowledge. It is quite another to come to terms with elderly people who are like Gilbert of Sens – the man who, before his miraculous cure, could not feed himself. Many older people cannot walk or bathe or go to the toilet by themselves; they cannot talk or, if they can, repeat themselves endlessly. They are weak and often angry and unpleasant. They are burdens on everyone – their children, their healthier spouses, their caregivers, their societies. They are the 'old old'. And they don't want to hear those words applied to them by anyone. The very designation is degrading. Think of how Lear's daughters Goneril and Regan wielded the term 'infirm' to debase him. When I was finishing this chapter, Joe Biden, at age 81, withdrew from running for a second term as President of the United States because everyone who mattered said that he was 'too old' to serve. Is 81 'too' old? All of us can think of people in their eighties who continue to be active, creative, energetic, involved and smart. For that matter, there are centenarians like that as well. But there are also fifty-year-olds who can no longer walk.

The real issue is not chronological age but something else, the deterioration of mind and body that leaves a person unable to care for herself. This is senility, and it is nothing new. Cato talked about it and blamed it on people who had been wayward and undisciplined in their youth. Seneca was less judgmental, and he was ready to abandon ship if he became infirm. But would he have had the presence of mind or strength to do so when the time came? World statistics show that people aged seventy or more have the highest suicide rate of any age group. Yet the numbers for that category have declined more than 30 per cent in the last three decades even though the population of elderly (65 and over) has increased by more than 60 per cent in the last forty years.[48] These statistics, for all their incomparability, suggest a decrease in the suicide rate of elderly people. Seneca's 'solution' is certainly not popular.

Painful Transitions

In northern Ghana, old women (and sometimes old men) are routinely accused of witchcraft and driven out of their villages. They find shelter nearby, in so-called 'witches' camps'. In 2021, over 85 per cent of them were sixty or more years old, and 21 per cent were eighty and older. When researchers administered a battery of questionnaires to 277 people in the camps to assess their mental and physical well-being, they found that most were in ill health and lacked both energy and hope.

To be sure, those researchers were looking for symptoms of depression, just as Havighurst (the researcher who created the Life Satisfaction Index) and subsequent gerontologists were looking for happiness. But if, as those who studied the 'witches' wrote, 'depression is the commonest mental health condition in the general population worldwide', then, to distinguish the sad feelings of the 'witches' from the prevailing global malaise, we need to find out *why* they were sad and what sorts of sorrows they felt.[49] Were they depressed by camp conditions? By the rejection of family and neighbours in their native villages? By the fact of being old?

It seems that rejection hurt the most. They arrived at the camps as 'morally compromised strangers' and had to go through humiliating cleansing rituals to wash away their shame.[50] It is true that when they were in dire need in the camps, their families might send a child or maid to help them. Even so, as one accused woman said of her children, they 'have abandoned the very person who brought them to this world. They want me to die' (263). When the witches are sick and failing, their kinsmen often delay coming to see them. After they die, 'they [are] not memorialized... and [can] never be listed as "ancestors" worthy of veneration' (293). The Ghanian health service has also effectively abandoned them, even though by law it is obliged to offer free medical services to impoverished old people.

In highly industrialized nations, elderly people are not left to die in witches' camps. But when they become utterly dependent on the help of others, when they are (or are seen to be) on the edge of death, then ambivalent feelings are stirred up that sometimes lead to the equivalent of such camps. During the COVID-19 pandemic, the elderly in hospitals and old-age homes were the most vulnerable and the least attended-to of any group. Caregiving, whether by families or strangers, is a largely thankless and poorly rewarded task. It is not by chance that accused Gambian witches are often those who served as caregivers themselves and then were blamed for the ills of those in their charge.

The pandemic was abnormal in leaving vulnerable people institutionalized and without recourse to other help. Normally, even today, families rather than institutions are the caregivers: spouses for each other, sons and daughters for parents. Women provide much of this care, but, in the United States, at least, 'men make up nearly 40 per cent of unpaid family care'.[51] Family caregivers are often themselves in anguish. They want to help, have to make difficult choices, and need to save themselves from despair by 'toughening up'. They are overwhelmed even as they are glad to be of service. And the feeble for whom they care feel both intensely grateful and acutely frustrated. Experiencing the deterioration of oneself or another leaves both sides feeling isolated and impotent.

AND YET CARE for the elderly is worth the effort. Mortality and vulnerability are built into our genomes and lurk in the world we live in. They greet us from the moment we are born. What we need to ensure is not that we will never get old and die but that we will retain our dignity throughout – in our own eyes if we are alert enough to know what is happening to us, and certainly in the eyes of others.

This is not easy. An incontinent old lady and an incontinent infant do not and cannot feel the same way about themselves, nor do they provoke the same feelings in others. The baby will be toilet trained. The old lady who wears diapers is unlikely to regain her control. Nor are the elderly the same as disabled people, for they frequently deny their limits and refuse help.

Old age is unlike any other stage of life, and yet it is (barring mortal illnesses and accidents) inevitable. And the percentage of the elderly within the world population is increasing. But this is not a crisis until we choose to make it so. The real crisis is our newly urgent need to know how to feel about it, how to cope with it. Once we know how to face it, the practical, ethical and personal solutions will follow.

More caregivers will be needed, and they will need help dealing with many old people who are extremely ill; who have lost the ability to feed themselves or control their bodily functions; who are furious with themselves and others, or so sweet that you want to cry; who communicate only through roars or (seeming) nonsense.

It seems heartless to question why societies should spend their precious resources on such people. Yet we had better confront this question, because it is being posed all around us in disguise. We remain hostages of the worldview of John Locke, convinced that productivity and work are the measure of man. (A woman has a more complicated role in that schema, but by the time she becomes old old, she, like her male counterpart, is no longer 'useful' in the normal sense.) Old people in general are a burden. Why, then 'give' them social security?

We should by now have an answer that supplements the ethical one (we ought to do so) and the affective one (we love them so we care). Old people offer us something that is unique and socially precious, if only we knew how to receive, appreciate and enjoy it. Their winter dreams introduce us to what Dasha Kiper has called 'unimaginable lands'.[52] Through those dreams we see and understand the measured feelings expressed by formerly enslaved people in Georgia; the irascibility of Svevo's unsuccessful war profiteer; the love of Márquez's elderly couple floating eternally down a river; and the fury of the sick and sepulchral Madame Fisher at the end of her life. Only the elderly have winter dreams. Frightening, erratic, stubborn, odd and unrealistic as some of them may seem, nevertheless, taken together, they offer a rich array of the feelings that can help us face and exit this otherwise unforgiving world with dignity.

Conclusion

Toward the end, my mother said things that I took to be nonsense. My friend at the retirement home – the one living there happily while I was writing Chapter Two – could only scream in wordless frustration during her last days, as sadly arrived while I was writing the last chapter. Another dear friend's elderly wife cannot talk, spends most of her time sleeping and rarely seems to know who he is.

Yet those seemingly unresponsive people were not and are not 'sans everything'. What I have learned from writing this historical guide is that beneath what may seem as unyielding as frozen earth and wintry cold are emotional depths. They are not gone, even if they can hardly be observed or expressed. Think of them like the roots of dormant plants, still active and growing, sending out feelers, responding to unseen stimuli.

To be sure, such feelings need not be underground, inarticulate or irrational. They may simply be the emotions of people in the final season of their lives. They are sometimes Janus-faced, such as the hope of the *Odyssey*'s 'noble swineherd' who looked forward to having land of his own and an enviable wife even as he thought back to his life of hard labour. Or they may be forward-looking, as was the fantasy of my mother as she imagined marrying her make-believe lover. Or as was Procleon's promise to live together with his sweet 'little honey-pot' when his son died. Or as were the feelings of joy expressed by Robert

Browning (d. 1889) in a poem that assumed the persona of Andalusian poet Abraham ibn Ezra (d. 1164/7): 'Grow old along with me!/ The best is yet to be,/ The last of life, for which the first was made'.[1] As Eliphaz told Job in the Bible, only when you are old can you see God's plan. When you are young, you 'seek and find and feast'. That's normal and fine. But when you are old you see the wisdom of God, and you praise the maker of both your body and soul.

Browning's Ben Ezra assesses his past and accepts it, even though he recognizes some of his errors: his rage on one occasion was only *mostly* right; his compliance on another was useless. That kind of critical self-assessment may recall the Roman Stoic Seneca or the diarist Sarah Cowper. They cherished an ideal self and were not sure that they measured up. But unlike the others, ben Ezra was not worried, for in the light of God's plan, all – even his foibles – made sense.

Such feelings sound simple and easy to characterize. But as soon as we put them into their cultural contexts, the categories fall apart and the feelings become highly particular. Browning's nineteenth-century version of ben Ezra praised old age for the wisdom it granted, a wisdom that depended on trust in God. But Cicero's first-century BCE ideal of Cato made his wisdom derive from trust in himself.

Or consider the notion of happiness in old age. In the exceptionally competitive society of Homer's warriors, its bliss, its winter dreams included being envied by others for one's bride and land and having the moral authority to soothe the wrath of warriors. But in the cocoon of romantic expectations (at its height in movies of the 1940s), my mother's future fulfilment involved only loving and being loved. For Procleon, protected by Solon's laws, the winter dream was cohabitation with a flute girl. Similarly, in the context of the wealthy and striving members of the Athenian elite, Cephalus' contentedness came from having paid his debts. Cato's at Rome derived from sober living and *auctoritas*. The self-doubt of Seneca was based on a set of philosophical principles that demanded calm in the face of fearful events such as death. The happiness of the monk Egbert came from having sufficiently mortified himself all through his life to expect bliss in heaven; and those who associated with him by giving him gifts also shared in some of his joy. Richard Whittington's bequest did that too, if more formally. By founding a charity, he alleviated his worries about the afterlife. But Petrarch found happiness in the companionship afforded him by the works of the ancients.

The emotions and experiences of the aged are variously countered or reinforced by everyone around them. Prejudices about impotent old men were bolstered by Ariosto's limp old hermit and Gower's confrontation with Venus. On the other hand, these biases were challenged by Boccaccio's defence of old Master Alberto and the Viagra-aided David of today. Svevo's hero incorporated both of these feelings about old men: Cosini hired a prostitute to keep him 'healthy' but was embarrassed by his wrinkles. Hostility toward witchy old women was both amplified and undermined by Ovid's Dipsas, who was ugly yet as crafty as the poet himself. But such animosity was utterly defeated by the enduring love of Florentino Ariza for Fermina Daza, her age be damned.

The chapter titles in this book represent the major experiences of the elderly that pull together many of the threads of a particular period of time. Some less-featured winter dreams died out or, to the contrary, continued long into the future. A *constant* theme, for example, is how horrible and ugly and miserable it is to be old. It was already articulated in ancient Greece, as when Homer's Laertes needed the help of Athena to be vigorous, and Sappho complained of her creaking knees. It was thereafter savagely depicted by Roman poets such as

Juvenal, repeated by medieval poets such as Gower, and revived with zest by authors of the French Enlightenment such as Louis de Jaucourt, who prefaced his *Encyclopédie* article on the physiology of old age with a poem written by Voltaire. But, while Voltaire wrote about being ill, Jaucourt turned his very words into a lament about being old: 'It's the age when human beings are dead to pleasures ... All that remains to us in this state is a useless blend of confused feelings/ An unhappy present, a gloomy future'.[2] Today the fear of physical deterioration leads even teenage girls to start Botox treatments right away.

Although there are points of comparison and continuity, the feelings of old age are not the same today as they were in the past. To the contrary. I see two major caesuras in Western history. With Christianity and Islam, the elderly poor were incorporated into a circle of charity that benefited the giver as well as the recipient, softening feelings toward them. Then, with the Industrious and Industrial Revolutions, old people lost traction within a society bent on work. It is possible that the advent of social security and retirement may prove to be another turning point. However, it may also be that valuing the elderly is a blip in an otherwise steady deterioration in their status in the West, with the exception of certain sub-communities such as among Native and Black Americans.

Across these inflection points are two nearly universal issues. The most obvious is the love and the resentment children feel about their parents, and the love and often outsize expectations of reciprocity that their parents harbour in turn. Parents think they have given all to their children – as Pheres thought he had done for Admetus – but everyone else thought that that old man should have been happy to sacrifice his own life to save his son from death.

Some children think they owe everything to their parents – like Aeneas, who carried his elderly father on his back out of a city in flames. Or the ancient Chinese as they tried to balance duty to parents with their obligations to the emperor. Other children resist filial responsibility, like old Goriot's daughters, who disdained their pasta-peddler of a father. Svevo's discontented and withdrawn Cosini wanted his son, his employee and his daughter to respect and love him. They didn't, or not sufficiently, and he concluded that he had been born in the wrong era. It would have been different before the war. But (truth to tell) even before the war, few, apart from Goethe, commanded the absolute respect of the young – and let us remember that Eckermann was not the poet's son. Grandparents, however, sometimes escape the generational tension, as Cavour's ardent letters to his grandmother made clear.

When, in a novel by Ivan Turgenev (d. 1883), young Bazarov visits his elderly parents after a three-year absence, his mother covers him with kisses and tears while his father tries unsuccessfully to hide his own sobs. Their emotional community is embarrassed by outbursts, and so even their coachman looks away. Bazarov, who loves them both, can hardly bear their stifling eagerness. He yawns, he shrugs, nothing of their lives interests him, and after a couple of days he takes off. Profoundly hurt, his parents wave goodbye. "'Left us, he's left us', [his father] sobbed, "he's left us, he was bored here. And now I'm all alone, as lonely as this finger.'" But Bazarov's mother now shows her mettle: 'What can we do, Vasya? A son is a piece of you that's cut free. Like a falcon – he wanted to come, so he flew here to us, and he wanted to go, so he flew away; and you and I are like mushrooms on a tree stump, we sit here side by side and don't go anywhere.' At least they had each other, unlike Papiria Tertia (see illus. 7), who lost both her husband and her son.

The other nearly universal feeling that crosses the historical divides is the desire to live as long as possible and as healthily as possible. Those hopes were encouraged by physicians at least since the time of Galen. And although medical knowledge has gained enormous sophistication since his day, helping to keep many people healthy into advanced old age, nevertheless the advice of doctors has remained remarkably constant: ageing well depends on proper exercise, rest, intake (of food and prescribed medications) and the like *throughout one's life*. Galen called this therapy hygiene; gerontologists today speak of lifestyle. Such advice is most easily adopted by elites with the leisure, wealth and non-toxic environments in which to follow it.

At the moment, the prospects for fulfilling that universal desire do not seem entirely rosy. The age of antibiotics appears to be coming to an end without obvious substitutes on the way as yet; nine-tenths of the world's population lives with unacceptably high levels of air pollution; over a quarter of that population drinks unsafe water; and disease forecasters predict a 27.5 per cent chance of 'a pandemic as deadly as Covid-19 in the next decade', unless a vaccine is developed for the new pathogen within one hundred days. Those forecasters do not take the anti-vax movement into account.[3] Should we really worry about the elderly population overwhelming the globe? The crisis is rather one of population balance. But old, rich nations seem more determined than ever to keep young, poor non-nationals from entering them.

The old will remain, one way or another, and not even another pandemic will cancel out their winter dreams, though the content of those dreams will always change. In the age of 'industriousness', they had to do with contributing to the community through some form of work, like the old woman in *Candide*; while in the sentimental age of Rousseau, characters such as Gercour wanted to be loved as part of a warm family circle. Today, they ride on the hopes of science.

But I need to stop listing a few examples as if they might possibly represent the entire panoply of elderly feelings. All, in their full complexity, demand our attention, understanding and deference, whether they be felt silently or loudly cry to be heard. As we pore over the variety that constitutes their history, we may try some of these feelings on for size, or let them reassure us that we are not alone in *our* winter dreams. We may also learn not to be embarrassed and flummoxed by those expressed by our dear ones, as I once was by my mother. For the epigraph to this book, I chose a sentence from Italo Svevo: it's hard to notice old age because it's so calm. I hope that I have shown that *within* that 'calm' are feelings – from enjoyment to acceptance, from reciprocity to work and dignity – that belong to all of us.

REFERENCES

Introduction

1 Fabian Guénolé et al., 'Le rêve au cours du vieillissement normal et pathologique', *Annales de Gérontologie*, VIII/2 (2010), pp. 87–96.
2 See the chart under 'Variation over time' at 'Life Expectancy', https://en.wikipedia.org, accessed 25 October 2024.
3 Jo Appleby, 'Ageing and the Body in Archaeology', *Cambridge Archaeological Journal*, XXVIII/1 (2017), pp. 145–63.
4 Michael Gurven and Hillard Kaplan, 'Longevity among Hunter-Gatherers: A Cross-Cultural Examination', *Population and Development Review*, XXXIII/2 (2007), pp. 321–65 at 323 and 334.
5 Ovid, *Metamorphoses*, trans. Z. Philip Ambrose (Newburyport, MA, 2004), cited by book and line numbers.
6 Erik H. Erikson, *Childhood and Society* (New York, 1950), p. 232.
7 See Jan Plamper, *The History of Emotions: An Introduction* (Oxford, 2012).

One Enjoyment

1 Homer, *The Odyssey*, trans. Emily Wilson (New York, 2018), cited as *Od.* followed by book and line numbers. For 'old age', Eumaeus used the Greek word *geras* (whence our terms such as geriatric).
2 Homer, *The Iliad*, trans. Peter Green (Oakland, CA, 2015), cited as *Il.* followed by book and line numbers.
3 Trans. Ellen Greene in 'Sappho 58: Philosophical Reflections on Death and Aging', in *The New Sappho on Old Age: Textual and Philosophical Issues*, ed. Ellen Greene and Marilyn Skinner (Washington, DC, 2009), ch. 11, at https://chs.harvard.edu (used by permission of the translator).
4 Delfim F. Leão and P. J. Rhodes, *The Laws of Solon: A New Edition with Introduction and Commentary* (London, 2015), pp. 93–4.
5 Eva Cantarella, 'Greek Law and the Family', in *A Companion to Families in the Greek and Roman Worlds*, ed. Beryl Rawson (Malden, MA, and Oxford, 2011), pp. 333–45, esp. 336–7.

6 Hesiod, *Works and Days*, ll. 185–8, in Hesiod, *Theogony and Works and Days*, trans. Catherine Schlegel and Henry Weinfield (Ann Arbor, MI, 2006), p. 63.
7 Xenophon, *Memorabilia* 3.5, §15, trans. E. C. Marchant, at www.perseus.tufts.edu.
8 Plutarch, *Lycurgus* 26.3, in *Plutarch's Lives*, trans. Bernadotte Perrin, at www.perseus.tufts.edu, cited by chapter and section.
9 Tyrtaeus, *Fragment 12*, in *Greek Elegiac Poetry: From the Seventh to the Fifth Centuries BC*, ed. and trans. Douglas E. Gerber, Loeb Classical Library 258 (Cambridge, 1999), p. 61.
10 Tyrtaeus, *Fragment 10*, in *Greek Elegiac Poetry*, p. 53.
11 Henry Rosemont Jr and Roger T. Ames, *The Chinese Classic of Family Reverence: A Philosophical Translation of the Xiaojing* (Honolulu, HI, 2009), p. 111.
12 Confucius, *Analects* 1.2, in *Analects: With Selections from Traditional Commentaries*, trans. Edward Slingerland (Indianapolis, IN, 2003), cited by book and paragraph number.
13 Cong Ellen Zhang, *Performing Filial Piety in Northern Song China: Family, State, and Native Place* (Honolulu, HI, 2020), pp. 1–4, 52–82.
14 Thucydides, *The Peloponnesian War* 2.50.
15 Peter J. Rhodes, *The Athenian Constitution Written in the School of Aristotle* (Liverpool, 2017), p. 145 (§55.3).
16 Euripides, *Alcestis*, in *Alcestis, Medea, Hippolytus*, trans. Diane Arnson Svarlien and Robin Mitchell-Boyask (Indianapolis, IN, 2007), cited by line number.
17 Euripides, *Hecuba*, trans. William Arrowsmith in *Euripides II: Andromache, Hecuba, The Suppliant Woman*, ed. David Grene, Richmond Lattimore, Mark Griffith and Glenn W. Most, 3rd edn (Chicago, IL, 2012), cited by line number.
18 *Heracles*, trans. William Arrowsmith in *Euripides III: Heracles, The Trojan Women, Iphigenia among the Taurians, Ion*, ed. David Grene, Richmond Lattimore, Mark Griffith and Glenn W. Most, 3rd edn (Chicago, IL, 2013), cited by line number.
19 Aristophanes, *Acharnians*, in *Against Demagogues: What Aristophanes Can Teach Us about the Perils of Populism and the Fate of Democracy*, trans. Robert C. Bartlett (Oakland, CA, 2020), cited by line number.
20 Aristophanes, *Wasps*, in *Aristophanes I: Clouds, Wasps, Birds*, trans. Peter Meineck (Indianapolis, IN, 1998), cited by line number.
21 Aristophanes, *Women of the Assembly*, 1001–11, in Aristophanes, *Four Plays: Clouds, Birds, Lysistrata, Women of the Assembly*, trans. Aaron Poochigian (New York, 2021), cited by line number.
22 Aristophanes, *Clouds*, trans. Peter Meineck in *Aristophanes I: Clouds, Wasps, Birds*, cited by line number. Chaerephon was a close associate of the philosopher Socrates.
23 Plato, *Republic*, trans. G.M.A. Grube, revd C.D.C. Reeve in *Plato: Complete Works*, ed. John M. Cooper (Indianapolis, IN, 1997).

The whole of the Cephalus episode is comprised in lines 328b–331d. All citations by Stephanus number.
24 Plato, *Apology*, trans. G.M.A. Grube in *Plato: Complete Works*.
25 Plato, *Crito*, trans. G.M.A. Grube in *Plato: Complete Works*.
26 Plato, *Phaedo*, trans. G.M.A. Grube in *Plato: Complete Works*.
27 Xenophon, *Apology of Socrates* 6–8, at www.perseus.tufts.edu.
28 Aristotle, *Nicomachean Ethics*, trans. Robert C. Bartlett and Susan D. Collins (Chicago, IL, 2011), cited by Bekker and line number.
29 Aristotle, *Rhetoric*, trans. Robert C. Bartlett, in *Aristotle's 'Art of Rhetoric'* (Chicago, IL, 2019), cited by Bekker number.
30 *Isocrates II*, in *The Oratory of Classical Greece*, vol. VII, trans. Terry L. Papillon (Austin, TX, 2004).
31 Sophocles, *Oedipus at Colonus*, in Sophocles, *The Theban Plays*, trans. Ruth Fainlight and Robert J. Littman (Baltimore, MD, 2009), cited by line number.

Two Acceptance

1 Virgil, *Aeneid*, trans. Stanley Lombardo (Indianapolis, IN, 2005), cited by book and line number.
2 Cicero, *On His House*, 109, quoted in Robert Turcan, *The Gods of Ancient Rome: Religion in Everyday Life from Archaic to Imperial Times* (Edinburgh, 2022), p. 14.
3 In the twelfth century, it was the least-often copied of the three major Ciceronian works; see Birger Munk Olsen, *I classici nel canone scolastico altomedievale* (Spoleto, 1991), p. 117.
4 Cicero, *On Old Age*, in Cicero, *Selected Works*, trans. Michael Grant (London, 1971), cited by page number.
5 Lucretius, *On the Nature of Things*, trans. Martin Ferguson Smith, revd edn (Indianapolis, IN, 2001), cited by page number.
6 Cicero, *Letter to Atticus* 14.21.3, 11 May 44, at www.perseus.tufts.edu.
7 Cicero, *Cato Maior de senectute*, ed. J.G.F. Powell (Cambridge, 1988), p. 3.
8 *Ad senatus consultum Macedonianum*, at www.uwyo.edu.
9 Cicero, *Pro Roscio Amerino* 38, in D. H. Berry, trans., *Cicero, Defence Speeches* (Oxford, 2000), p. 20.
10 Mike Brogden, *Geronticide: Killing the Elderly* (London, 2001).
11 Richard P. Saller, *Patriarchy, Property and Death in the Roman Family* (Cambridge, 1994).
12 Eva Cantarella, 'La famiglia romana tra demografia sociale, antropologia e diritto', in *Ubi tu Gaius. Modelli familiari, pratiche sociali e diritti delle persone nell'età del principato*, ed. Francesco Milazzo (Milan, 2014), pp. 3–21.
13 P. Ovidus Naso, *Amores* in *Ovid Amores: Text, Prolegomena and Commentary in Four Volumes. Text and Prolegomena* 1, ed. J. C. McKeown (Prenton, Merseyside, 1987) cited by book, poem number and line number.

14 Ovid, *Amores* in *Love Poems, Letters and Remedies of Ovid*, trans. David R. Slavitt (Cambridge, 2011).
15 Cicero, *De oratore* 3.217, in Cicero, *On the Ideal Orator: Book 3*, ed. James M. May and Jakob Wisse (Oxford, 2016), p. 28.
16 *Corpus Inscriptionum Latinarum* (henceforth CIL, cited by volume followed by inscription number) 6.28774. Most are at CIL Open Access, https://arachne.dainst.org.
17 Tacitus, *The Annals* 16.4.3, trans. A. J. Woodman (Indianapolis, IN, 2004), p. 336.
18 Seneca, *Consolation to Marcia* 21.4, trans. Harry M. Hine in *Seneca: Hardship and Happiness*, ed. and trans. Elaine Fantham, Harry M. Hine, James Ker and Gareth D. Williams (Chicago, IL, 2014), p. 29.
19 Seneca, *Letters on Ethics: To Lucilius*, trans. and ed. Margaret Graver and A. A. Long (Chicago, IL, 2025), cited as *Sen. Let.* followed by letter number and paragraph number.
20 Seneca, *Oedipus*, ed. and trans. A. J. Boyle (Oxford, 2011), cited as *Oed.* and line number.
21 All quotations from Fronto to Marcus, letter 53 in Fronto, *Selected Letters*, trans. Caillan Davenport and Jennifer Manley (London, 2014), pp. 200–203.
22 Juvenal, *The Satires*, trans. Niall Rudd, ed. William Barr (Oxford, 1991), cited by satire and line number.
23 Tim G. Parkin, *Demography and Roman Society* (Baltimore, MD, 1992), p. 92.
24 CIL 6.26901.
25 CIL 6.18086.
26 CIL 5.2435.
27 Galen, *Hygiene Books 5–6*, ed. and trans. Ian Johnston (Cambridge, 2018), cited by paragraph number.
28 Galen, *De Temperamentis* 581K–582K, in *Galen: Works on Human Nature*, vol. 1: *Mixtures (De Temperamentis)*, trans. P. N. Singer and Philip J. van der Eijk with Piero Tassinari (Cambridge, 2018), pp. 160–61.
29 Seneca, *De clementia* 2.6.3, trans. and ed. Susanna Braund, at www.oxfordscholarlyeditions.com.
30 CIL 8.7156, trans. into French and commented upon by Michel Griffe, Jean-Marie Lassère and Jean Soubiran, at www.persee.fr.

Three Reciprocity

1 Augustine, *The City of God*, 1.8, trans. Henry Bettenson (Harmondsworth, 1972), p. 13.
2 Baudri, archbishop of Dol, in *The Two Lives of Robert of Arbrissel, Founder of Fontevraud: Legends, Writings, and Testimonies*, ed. Geneviève Giordanengo et al. (Turnhout, 2006), p. 177.
3 *Regula Benedicti*, prol., at www.thelatinlibrary.com.

4. Wolfram von Eschenbach, *Willehalm*, trans. Marion E. Gibbs and Sidney M. Johnson (New York, 1984), cited by book and page number.
5. Thijs Porck, *Old Age in Early Medieval England: A Cultural History* (Woodbridge, 2019), esp. ch. 6.
6. *Beowulf*, ed. and trans. R. D. Fulk in *The Beowulf Manuscript* (Cambridge, 2010), cited by page number.
7. Usama ibn Munqidh, *The Book of Contemplation: Islam and the Crusades*, trans. Paul M. Cobb (London, 2008).
8. John Gower, *Confessio Amantis*, vol. I, ed. Russell A Peck, 2nd edn (Kalamazoo, MI, 2006), cited by line number.
9. Ludovico Ariosto, *Orlando Furioso* canto 8,49, trans. David R. Slavitt (Cambridge, 2009), pp. 139–40.
10. Rustico Filippi, *Dovunque vai, con teco porti il cesso*, trans. Riccardo Cristiani, at www.pubblicascuola.it.
11. Geoffrey Chaucer, *The Wife of Bath's Tale* (c. 1405–10), at https://chaucer.fas.harvard.edu, cited by line number.
12. Bertran de Born, *Belh m'es quan vey camjar lo senhoratge*, in *The Poems of the Troubadour Bertran de Born*, ed. William D. Paden Jr, Tilde Sankovitch and Patricia H. Stäblein (Berkeley, CA, 1986), pp. 296–8.
13. Giovanni Boccaccio, *Decameron*, ed. Vittorio Branca (Milan, 1992), pp. 304–6, at www.brown.edu.
14. Guido Guinizelli, *Al cor gentil rempaira sempre amore*, at https://online.scuola.zanichelli.it.
15. Abu Tammam quoted in Hasan Shuraydi, *The Raven and the Falcon: Youth versus Old Age in Medieval Arabic Literature* (Leiden, 2014), pp. 158–9.
16. Bartholomeus, *Glose super Isagogen Iohannitii*, ed. Faith Wallis (Florence, 2022), §15, p. 297.
17. Lothario dei Segni (Pope Innocent III), *On the Misery of the Human Condition* 1.10, ed. Donald R. Howard, trans. Margaret Mary Dietz (New York, 1969), p. 13.
18. Bede, *The Ecclesiastical History of the English People* 5.22; 3.27, ed. Judith McClure and Roger Collins (Oxford, 1994), pp. 286, 162–3.
19. Bertran, *Gerr'e trebailh vei et afan*, in *The Poems of the Troubadour Bertran de Born*, p. 460.
20. See Guillaume de Saint-Pathus, *Les miracles de saint Louis* (Paris, 1931), pp. 31–2. See also the discussion in Sharon Farmer, *Surviving Poverty in Medieval Paris: Gender, Ideology, and the Daily Lives of the Poor* (Ithaca, NY, 2002), pp. 102–3.
21. Lucie Laumonier, *Solitudes et Solidarités en ville: Montpellier mi XIIIe–fin XVe siècles* (Turnhout, 2015), cited by page number.
22. Discussed in Lucie Laumonier, 'Manières de parenté. Les formes de l'adoption dans la région de Monpellier au XVe siècle', *Annales du midi*, CXXVII/289 (2015), pp. 7–24.
23. Leon Battista Alberti, *Della famiglia*, bk 3, trans. Renée Neu Watkins (Long Grove, SC, 1969), pp. 54–5.

24 Reproduced on the web at bit.ly/3NkhKOb.
25 Arie van Steensel, 'Varieties of Guild Welfare: Florence, Ghent and London, c. 1300–1550', paper delivered at Warwick for the Economic History Society Annual Conference, 28–30 March 2014. Consulted by kind permission of the author.
26 Jean Imray, *The Charity of Richard Whittington: A History of the Trust Administered by the Mercers' Company, 1424–1966* (London, 1968), p. 109.
27 Quoted and discussed in Syrinx von Hees, 'Mamluk Soldiers in Their Old Age: The Case of the *Tarhan* Status', in *La guerre dans le Proche-Orient médiéval (xe–xve s.) État de la question, lieux communs, nouvelles approches*, ed. M. Eychenne and A. Zouache (Cairo, 2015), pp. 111–41.
28 Usama, *Book of Contemplation*, pp. 174–5.
29 Usama ibn Munqidh, *Dwelling and Abodes* 3–4, trans. in Paul M. Cobb, *Usama ibn Munqidh: Warrior Poet of the Age of Crusades* (Oxford, 2005), p. 54.
30 Usama, *Book of Contemplation*, p. 179.
31 Boncompagno da Signa, *De male senectutis et senii. Un manuale duecentesco sulla vecchiaia*, ed. and trans. (into Italian) Paolo Garbini (Florence, 2004).
32 Robert M. Durling, ed. and trans., *Petrarch's Lyric Poems: The 'Rime Sparse' and Other Lyrics* (Cambridge, MA, 1976), 46–7, poem 12.
33 Francesco Petrarch, *Letters of Old Age, Books I–IX, X–XVIII*, trans. Aldo S. Bernardo, Saul Levin and Reta A. Bernard (New York, 2005), cited by book and letter numbers.
34 Peter Brown, *Through the Eye of a Needle: Wealth, the Fall of Rome, and the Making of Christianity in the West, 350–550 AD* (Princeton, NJ, 2012), pp. 78–9.

Four Work

1 William Shakespeare, *King Lear*, ed. R. A. Foakes (London, 1997), cited by act, scene, line number.
2 Daniel Defoe, *The Letters of Daniel Defoe*, ed. George Harris Healey (Oxford, 1955, published online 2017), letter 251. To Henry Baker, 12 August 1730.
3 Pat Thane, *Old Age in English History: Past Experiences, Present Issues* (Oxford, 2000), p. 120.
4 Henry Cuffe, *The Differences of the Ages of Man's Life* (London, 1640), pp. 192–3.
5 *The 1601 Poor Relief Act*, ch. 2, at www.workhouses.org.uk.
6 Susannah R. Ottaway, *The Decline of Life: Old Age in Eighteenth-Century England* (Cambridge, 2004), p. 178.
7 Tim Wales, 'Poverty, Poor Relief and the Life-Cycle: Some Evidence from Seventeenth-Century Norfolk', in *Land, Kinship and Life-Cycle*, ed. Richard M. Smith (Cambridge, 1984), p. 360.

8 *Norwich Census of the Poor, 1570*, ed. John F. Pound (Norwich, 1970), p. 29.
9 Quoted in Wales, 'Poverty, Poor Relief and the Life-Cycle', p. 388.
10 Lorenzo Coccoli, 'Labour as a Form of Charity and Almsgiving in Early Modern Poor Relief', in *Rethinking the Work Ethic in Premodern Europe*, ed. Gábor Almási and Giorgio Lizzul (Cham, 2023), pp. 255–99.
11 John Locke, *An Essay on the Poor Law* (1697), at https://pols2900.wordpress.com. The proposal was not adopted.
12 Voltaire, *Candide* in *Candide and Other Stories*, trans. Roger Pearson (Oxford, 2006), p. 87.
13 Jaucourt, 'Vieillesse', Édition Numérique Collaborative et Critique de l'*Encyclopédie* (1765), at http://enccre.academie-sciences.fr, accessed 25 October 2024.
14 Amie Bolissian, 'Masculine Old Women or Feminine Old Men? Rethinking Gender and the Ageing Body in Early Modern English Medicine', *Gender and History*, XXXV/2 (2023), pp. 408–28.
15 National Galleries of Scotland, Edinburgh, at www.nationalgalleries.org, accessed 25 October 2024. Following this are nos 15, 16 and 17.
16 Jan de Vries, *The Industrious Revolution: Consumer Behavior and Household Economy, 1650 to the Present* (Cambridge, 2008).
17 Gerrit Verhoeven, 'Fashionably Late? Time, Work and the Industrious Revolution in Early Modern Antwerp', *Continuity and Change*, XXXV (2020), pp. 255–79 at 262.
18 John Locke, *Two Treatises on Government*, ed. Peter Laslett (Cambridge, 1988). Cited by treatise number, paragraph number and page numbers.
19 Jonathan Swift, *A Modest Proposal and Other Short Pieces Including A Tale of a Tub*, ed. Jim Manis (Hazleton, PA, 2008), p. 9, at https://aulico.wordpress.com.
20 John Ehrenberg, *Civil Society: The Critical History of an Idea*, 2nd edn (New York, 2017), p. 6.
21 Michael John Witgen, *An Infinity of Nations: How the Native New World Shaped Early North America* (Philadelphia, PA, 2012), p. 7.
22 Michael D. McNally, *Honoring Elders: Aging, Authority, and Ojibwe Religion* (New York, 2009).
23 Anton Treuer, *Everything You Wanted to Know about Indians but Were Afraid to Ask* (St Paul, MN, 2012), p. 85.
24 Richard White, *The Middle Ground: Indians, Empires, and Republics in the Great Lakes Region, 1650–1815* (Cambridge, 2011), p. xii.
25 Pierre-Esprit Radisson, *The Collected Writings*, vol. I: *Voyages*, ed. Germaine Warkentin (Montreal, QC, 2012), p. 31.
26 Claude Charles le Roy, sieur de Bacqueville de La Potherie, *History of the Savage Peoples Who Are Allies of New France*, in *The Indian Tribes of the Upper Mississippi Valley and Region of the Great Lakes*, ed. Emma Helen Blair, 2 vols (Cleveland, OH, 1911). Cited henceforth as Blair followed by vol. and page number.

27 Radisson, *The Collected Writings*, p. 299.
28 Blair, 1.139–40.
29 Michel de Montaigne, 'Of Cannibals', in *The Complete Works*, trans. Donald M. Frame (New York, 2003), p. 193.
30 Jean-Jacques Rousseau, *Discourse on Political Economy* and *The Social Contract* 3.5, trans. Christopher Betts (Oxford, 1994), pp. 102–3.
31 Jean-Jacques Rousseau, *Letter to D'Alembert and Writings for the Theater*, trans. Allan Bloom, Charles Butterworth and Christopher Kelly (Hanover, NH, 2004), p. 287.
32 Paul Ulric Dubuisson, *Le vieux garçon* (Paris, 1783), cited by act, scene.
33 Speech of T.-F. Huguet, président, IVe Administration municipale du canton de Paris, *Fête de la Vieillesse* (1797).
34 Ottaway, *Decline*, p. 73.
35 Lisa DiCaprio, 'Women, Work, and Welfare in Old Regime and Revolutionary Paris', *Social Politics*, V (1998), pp. 97–124.
36 K.S.H. [Henri-Alexis Cahaisse], ed., *Mémoires de Préville* (Paris, 1812), pp. 13, 14, 34, 48–9.
37 René Descartes, *A Discourse on the Method . . .*, trans. Ian Maclean (Oxford, 2006), pp. 12, 27–8.
38 René Descartes, *The Passions of the Soul*, trans. Stephen H. Voss (Indianapolis, IN, 1989), cited by article number.
39 *The Diary of Sarah, Lady Cowper*, ed. Anne Kugler, in *The History of Old Age in England, 1600–1800*, vol. VII (London, 2009), cited by page number.
40 Alec Ryrie and Tom Schwanda, eds, *Puritanism and Emotion in the Early Modern World* (London, 2016).
41 Johann Peter Eckermann, *Conversations with Goethe in the Last Years of his Life*, trans. Allan Blunden (London, 2022), cited by page number.
42 Goethe, 'Elegie' (1823), at www.gedichte7.de.
43 Roderick Cavaliero, *Genius, Power and Magic: A Cultural History of Germany from Goethe to Wagner* (London, 2013), p. 67.
44 Quoted in Richard Friedenthal, *Goethe: His Life and Times* (London, 1963), p. 200.
45 Quoted and summarized in Louise Gray, 'The Experience of Old Age in the Narratives of the Rural Poor in Early Modern Germany', in *Power and Poverty: Old Age in the Pre-Industrial Past*, ed. Susannah R. Ottaway, L. A. Botelho and Katherine Kittredge (Westport, CT, 2002), pp. 107–23.
46 Angela Groppi, '"Le devoir de travailler jusqu'à la fin de ses jours": Le travail des personnes âgées dans la Rome pontificale (XVIIIe–XIXe siècles)', in *Mélanges de l'École française de Rome. Italie et Méditerranée*, CXXIII/1 (2011), pp. 25–32.
47 Angela Groppi, 'Old People and the Flow of Resources between Generations in Papal Rome, Sixteenth to Nineteenth Centuries', in *Power and Poverty: Old Age in the Pre-Industrial Past*, p. 95.

48 Beatrice Zucca Micheletto, 'Family Solidarity vs. Institutional Relief? Interaction and Complementarity between Different Survival Strategies in 18th-Century Turin', in *Social Assistance and Solidarity in Europe from the 13th to the 18th Centuries*, ed. Francesco Ammannati (Florence, 2013), p. 524.
49 Letters of Cavour as quoted in Elena De Marchi and Claudia Alemani, *Per una storia delle nonne e dei nonni. Dall'Ottocento ai nostri giorni* (Rome, 2015), cited by page.
50 [Camille Cavour], 'État de la mendicité et des pauvres dans les États Sardes', in *Report from His Majesty's Commissioners for Inquiring into the Administration and Practical Operation of the Poor Laws* (Appendix F) (1834), p. 654F.
51 James Boswell, *The Life of Samuel Johnson*, ed. David Womersley (London, 2008), cited by page.

Five Dignity

1 *Slave Narratives: A Folk History of Slavery in the United States from Interviews with Former Slaves: Georgia*, vol. VI, part 1 (Washington, DC, 1941), www.loc.gov, cited by MS page number. I regularize the spelling, though not the grammar, of all quoted dialect; the interviewers were not trained linguists, and, although many were sympathetic to their elderly informants, they did not control for their stereotypes about Black language.
2 Bamba Suso, trans. Gordon Innes in *Sunjata: Gambian Versions of the Mande Epic* (London, 1999), p. 15, ll. 394–8.
3 Henry Clay Work, 'Grandfather's Clock', recorded in 1905, available at www.youtube.com.
4 Élise Feller, *Histoire de la vieillesse en France, 1900–1960. Du vieillard au retraité* (Paris, 2005), table 1.1, p. 26.
5 Ibid., table 6.2, p. 186.
6 See Virginia Yans-McLaughlin, *Family and Community: Italian Immigrants in Buffalo, 1880–1930* (Ithaca, NY, 1977), table 1, p. 45.
7 'Buffalo's Little Italy', *The Illustrated Buffalo Express* (May 1902), p. 4.
8 Quoted in Ilaria Serra, *The Value of Worthless Lives: Writing Italian American Immigrant Autobiographies* (New York, 2007), p. 59.
9 Wissel's painting, *Kalenberger Bauernfamilie (Farm Family from Kalenberg)* is reproduced at www.dhm.de/lemo/bestand/objekt/kalenberger-bauernfamilie-1939.
10 Center on Budget and Policy Priorities, 2024 report at www.cbpp.org. For the situation in Italy, where 'Individuals 65 or older living in a household with a HH [head of household] 65 or older have a poverty rate of 9.7%', see Daniele Franco, Maria Rosaria Marino and Pietro Tommasino, *Pension Policy and Poverty in Italy: Recent Developments and New Priorities, Giornale degli Economisti*, GDE (*Giornale degli*

Economisti e Annali di Economia), Bocconi University, LXVII/2 (2008), pp. 119–60.
11 Feller, *Histoire de la vieillesse en France*, p. 298.
12 Simone de Beauvoir, *The Coming of Age*, trans. Patrick O'Brian (New York, 1972 [orig. publ. in French, 1970]).
13 See the Life Satisfaction Index A at https://eprovide.mapi-trust.org/instruments/life-satisfaction-index-a, accessed 31 October 2024. The LSI-A is the scale most often used by researchers. See Bernice L. Neugarten, Robert J. Havighurst and Sheldon S. Tobin, 'The Measurement of Life Satisfaction', *Journal of Gerontology*, XVI/2 (1961), pp. 134–43. LSI-B has six open-ended questions.
14 Laura L. Carstensen et al., 'Emotional Experience Improves with Age: Evidence Based on over 10 Years of Experience Sampling', *Psychology and Aging*, XXVI/1 (2011), pp. 21–33.
15 Li Chu, Yochai Z. Shavit, Nilam Ram and Laura L. Carstensen, 'Age-Related Emotional Advantages in Encountering Novel Situation in Daily Life', *Psychology and Aging*, XXXIX/2 (2024), pp. 113–25.
16 Jane L. Tavares et al., 'Chronic Inequities. Measuring Disease Cost Burden among Old Adults in the U.S.: A Health and Retirement Study Analysis', *National Council on Aging* (April 2022), table 2, p. 3, at www.ncoa.org, finds that two chronic diseases affect about two-thirds and two others affect one-third of a large number of sampled individuals sixty and older in the United States.
17 Sölve Elmståhl et al., 'The Life Satisfaction Index-A (LSI-A): Normative Data for a General Swedish Population Ages 60 to 93 Years', *Clinical Interventions in Aging*, XV (2020), pp. 2031–9.
18 L. Eugene Thomas and Kim O. Chambers, 'Phenomenology of Life Satisfaction among Elderly Men: Quantitative and Qualitative Views', *Psychology and Aging*, IV/3 (1989), pp. 284–9.
19 Sharon Marsden and Janet Holmes, 'Talking to the Elderly in New Zealand Residential Care Settings', *Journal of Pragmatics*, LXIV (2014), pp. 17–34.
20 Jack Nicas, 'How to Be Truly Free: Lessons from a Philosopher President', *New York Times*, 23 August 2024, at www.nytimes.com.
21 William Faulkner, *Absalom, Absalom! The Corrected Text* (New York, 1986), pp. 3–4.
22 Elizabeth Bowen, *The House in Paris* (London, 1935).
23 Jenny Joseph, *Warning: When I Am an Old Woman I Shall Wear Purple* (1961), at www.scottishpoetrylibrary.org.uk.
24 BBC obituary, 'Jenny Joseph, "I Shall Wear Purple" Poet Dies' (2018), at www.bbc.com. For the Red Hat Society, https://redhatsociety.com, accessed 31 July 2024.
25 Red Hat Society, https://redhatsociety.com.
26 Honoré de Balzac, *Père Goriot*, trans. A. J. Krailsheimer (Oxford, 1991).

27 Jérôme Bourdieu and Lionel Kesztenbaum, 'Surviving Old Age in an Aging World: Old People in France, 1820–1948', *Population*, LXII/2 (2007), pp. 183–211, at www.cairn-int.info.
28 Italo Svevo, *A Very Old Man*, trans. Frederika Randall (New York, 2022).
29 Benito Mussolini, 'Audacia', *Popolo d'Italia*, I/1 (1914), at www.raicultura.it.
30 Gabriel García Márquez, *Love in the Time of Cholera*, trans. Edith Grossman (New York, 1988).
31 Clary Estes, 'Historic High Rates of STI's among Older Americans', *Forbes*, 26 February 2020, at www.forbes.com.
32 For the two-way communication between the heart and the brain that are among the 'neurophysiological substrates for the emotional experiences and affective processes that are major components of social behavior', see Stephen W. Porges, 'The Polyvagal Perspective', *Biological Psychology*, LXXIV (2007), pp. 116–43, at 121.
33 I have profited greatly from – and here simplified radically – the information in Titia de Lange's presentation about telomeres, '1. Telomeres and Human Disease', www.youtube.com, 11 January 2017.
34 Valter Longo, *The Longevity Diet: Slow Aging, Fight Disease, Optimize Weight* (New York, 2018), p. xii.
35 Oscar Wilde, *The Picture of Dorian Gray* [1891] (New York, 1931).
36 Maggie Jones, 'The Joys (and Challenges) of Sex after 70', *New York Times*, 12 January 2022.
37 American Society of Plastic Surgeons, '2022 Procedural Statistics Release', at bit.ly/4cFkIxp, accessed 25 August 2024.
38 Yomi Adegoke, 'Girls of 13 Are Lining Up for Botox. Here's Why', *The Guardian*, 25 March 2019, at www.theguardian.com.
39 James Powel, 'Here Are the Most Popular Halloween Costumes of 2023, According to Google', *USA Today*, 16 October 2023, at https://eu.usatoday.com.
40 See Einar H. Dyvik, 'Projected Distribution of the World's Population from 2022 to 2100, by Age Group', *Statista*, 4 July 2024, at www.statista.com.
41 Colin Gillion, 'The Development and Reform of Social Security Pensions', 20 January 2005, at https://webapps.ilo.org.
42 Kathleen Romig, 'Increasing Payroll Taxes Would Strengthen Social Security', 27 September 2016, at www.cbpp.org.
43 RSC, 'Blueprint to Save America: Fiscal Year 2023 Budget', 9 June 2022, p. 82, at https://banks.house.gov.
44 John Washington, *The Case for Open Borders* (Chicago, IL, 2023), p. 5.
45 Eduardo Porter, 'Illegal Immigrants Are Bolstering Social Security with Billions', *New York Times*, 5 April 2005, at www.nytimes.com.
46 Jeanna Smialek, 'Immigrants in Maine Are Filling a Labor Gap. It May Be a Prelude for the U.S.', *New York Times*, 12 April 2024, at www.nytimes.com.

47 Jason Horowitz and Gaia Pianigiani, 'What Happened When This Italian Province Invested in Babies', *New York Times*, 1 April 2024, at www.nytimes.com.
48 For the decline in world suicide rates by age, see https://ourworldindata.org. For the global increase in the elderly population, see *World Population Prospects 2022: Summary of Results*, United Nations Department of Economic and Social Affairs, Population Division (2022) = UN DESA/POP/2022/TR/NO. 3, p. 7. This latter source involves those aged 65 and over during the course of four years.
49 Lamnatu Adam et al., 'Depression and Quality of Life of People Accused of Witchcraft and Living in Alleged Witches' Camps in Northern Ghana', *Health and Social Care in the Community*, https://doi.org/10.1155/2023/6830762 (2023), p. 1.
50 Baba Iddrisu Musah and Mutaru Saibu, 'Old Age: A Painful Transition in Ghana', *African Journal of Aging Studies*, 1 (2023), p. 263.
51 Helen K. Black, John T. Groce and Charles E. Harmon, *The Hidden among the Hidden: African-American Elder Male Caregivers* (Oxford, 2017), p. xvii.
52 Dasha Kiper, *Travelers to Unimaginable Lands: Stories of Dementia, the Caregiver, and the Human Brain* (New York, 2023).

Conclusion

1 Robert Browning, 'Rabbi ben Ezra', in *Complete Works of Robert Browning*, vol. VI (Waco, TX, 1996), pp. 226–34.
2 Jaucourt, 'Vieillesse', Édition Numérique Collaborative et Critique de l'*Encyclopédie* (1765), at http://enccre.academie-sciences.fr.
3 WHO report, '9 Out of 10 People Worldwide Breathe Polluted Air, But More Countries Are Taking Action', 2 May 2018, at www.who.int; Airfinity report, 'A Strong Pandemic Defence System Could Reduce the Chance of Another COVID-like Pandemic in the Next Ten Years from 27.5% to 8%', 12 April 2023, at www.airfinity.com.

FURTHER READING

Introduction

For schemes of the ages of man (and, in spite of the title, dealing with far more than those created in the Middle Ages), see Elizabeth Sears, *The Ages of Man: Medieval Interpretations of the Life Cycle* (Princeton, NJ, 1986). For discussions of the field of the history of emotions, see Jan Plamper, *The History of Emotions: An Introduction* (Oxford, 2012) and Barbara H. Rosenwein and Riccardo Cristiani, *What Is the History of Emotions?* (Cambridge, 2018).

One Enjoyment

In general, see Thomas M. Falkner, *The Poetics of Old Age in Greek Epic, Lyric, and Tragedy* (Norman, OK, 1995). For Homeric society see especially the chapter on that topic by Kurt Raaflaub in *A New Companion to Homer*, ed. Ian Morris and Barry Powell (Leiden, 2011), pp. 624–48. David Ephraim, *Old Age in Sparta* (Amsterdam, 1991) makes good use of anthropological studies to propose informed guesses about the experiences of the old in Sparta. Ancient Greece and ancient China are treated together, but not with regard to the feelings of the elderly, in *Ancient Greece and China Compared*, ed. G.E.R. Lloyd and Jingyi Jenny Zhao with Qiaosheng Dong (Cambridge, MA, 2018).

Two Acceptance

In general, see Phyllis Culham, 'Women in the Roman Republic', in *The Cambridge Companion to the Roman Republic*, ed. Harriet I. Flower, 2nd edn (Cambridge, 2014), pp. 127–48; Karen Cokayne, *Experiencing Old Age in Ancient Rome* (London, 2003); and David Konstan, *Roman Comedy* (Ithaca, NY, 1983). For the Greek experience of Rome's expansion, Angelos Chaniotis, *Age of Conquests: The Greek World from Alexander to Hadrian* (Cambridge, MA, 2018), chs 7–8. For changing images of the old, see Jane Fejfer, *Roman Portraits in Context* (New York, 2008).

Three Reciprocity

For the lively ongoing debate about Roman cultural hegemony over the various regions and peoples of its empire, see Janet Huskinson, ed., *Experiencing Rome: Culture, Identity and Power in the Roman Empire* (London, 2000). Shulamith Shahar, *Growing Old in the Middle Ages: 'Winter Clothes Us in Shadow and Pain'*, trans. Yael Lotan (London, 1997) offers a general survey of the medieval period. See also George Minois, *History of Old Age: From Antiquity to the Renaissance*, trans. Sarah Hanbury Tenison (Chicago, IL, 1989). For old women in the crusades, see Helen J. Nicholson, *Women and the Crusades* (Oxford, 2023).

Four Work

David G. Troyansky, *Old Age in the Old Regime: Image and Experience in Eighteenth-Century France* (Ithaca, NY, 1989) offers a sensitive portrait of changing views of the elderly in France during the Enlightenment. On the early modern vogue for diaries, memoirs and other 'egodocuments', see James R. Farr and Guido Ruggiero, eds, *Historicizing Life-Writing and Egodocuments in Early Modern Europe* (London, 2022). For female self-exploration in France, see Joan Hinde Stewart, *The Enlightenment of Age: Women, Letters and Growing Old in Eighteenth-Century France* (Oxford, 2010). Essential for old age in England are the primary sources in *The History of Old Age in England, 1600–1800*, ed. Lynn Botelho and Susannah R. Ottaway, 8 vols (London, 2008–9). On the elderly among the Indigenous peoples along the North American eastern seacoast, see Jason Eden and Naomi Eden, *Age Norms and Intercultural Interaction in Colonial North America* (Lanham, MD, 2017).

Five Dignity

John W. Blassingame, 'Using the Testimony of Ex-Slaves: Approaches and Problems', *Journal of Southern History*, XLI/4 (1975), pp. 473–92, offers a comprehensive evaluation of the Federal Writers' Project interviews as primary sources. On American Black old age before and after the Civil War, see Frederick Knight, *Black Elders: The Meaning of Age in American Slavery and Freedom* (Philadelphia, PA, 2024). On American poor farms, see Megan Birk, *The Fundamental Institution: Poverty, Social Welfare, and Agriculture in American Poor Farms* (Urbana, IL, 2022). An eclectic set of studies of ageing across the globe is Jay Sokolovsky, ed., *The Cultural Context of Aging: Worldwide Perspectives* (Westport, CT, 2009). On family care for the frail or disabled, see Jason Danely, *Fragile Resonance: Caring for Older Family Members in Japan and England* (Ithaca, NY, 2022). The feelings of aged Italian women today are explored via literature in Rita C. Cavigioli, *Women of a Certain Age: Contemporary Italian Fictions of Female Aging* (Madison, WI, 2005).

ACKNOWLEDGEMENTS

Gratitude is one emotion I find hard to express in words, and hardest of all to those to whom I owe the most. But I will try. For this book, Riccardo Cristiani researched diverse topics and read every chapter many times, offering trenchant comments. Grazie, caro Riccardo. The late and much-mourned David Konstan read drafts of my first two chapters, gave me greatly needed encouragement and saved me from many errors. Similarly, Douglas Cairnes offered numerous corrections and suggestions. I am greatly indebted to the erudition of those two classicists, as I am to historian Susannah Ottaway, who read a draft of my fourth chapter and alerted me to many unresolved issues there. Art historian and friend Larry Silver read all the chapters; he is my model general critic. I have relied as well on the expertise of an anonymous reader for Reaktion, Julia Bray, Ida Caiazza, Karen Cherewatuk, Jennifer Cole, Ian Cornelius, Christopher John Davis, Matthieu Dupas, Robin Fleming, Tikia Hamilton, Lynn Hunt, Peter Kruschwitz, Mary MacKay, Frances Paden, William Paden, Nefeli Papoutsakis, Michael Sherman, Kathryn Starkey, Lynn M. Thomas and Edward Wheatley. I am immensely grateful to the universities of Radboud, Stockholm and Uppsala as well as the Arab-German Young Academy (Berlin) for hosting me while I presented aspects of this work, and to the exceptional welcome I received while doing so from Anneleen Arnout, Floris Meens and their students at Nijmegen; Wojtek Jezierski at Stockholm; Yiva Söderfeldt at Uppsala; and Konstantin Klein and his colleagues at AGYA. I thank Pascal Porcheron for his constant encouragement, patience and exceptional editorial skills.

I could not have written this book without the constant support of my husband, Tom, always ready to read drafts, call my attention to relevant items in the news and cheer me on. Finally, I thank my 'Elegant Three' for showing me diverse paths to old age and its many winter dreams.

PHOTO ACKNOWLEDGEMENTS

The author and publishers wish to express their thanks to the sources listed below for illustrative material and/or permission to reproduce it. Some locations of artworks are also given below, in the interest of brevity:

Antikensammlung, Staatliche Museen zu Berlin/Ingrid Geske (CC BY-SA 4.0): 4; Bayerische Staatsbibliothek, Munich (Cgm 193/III, fol. 4v): 15; Bodleian Library, University of Oxford (MS Bodl. 902, fol. 8r): 17; British Library, London (Arundel MS 83, fol. 126v): 16; The British Museum, London, photo Jastrow/Wikimedia Commons (public domain): 9; Castello della Manta, photo Bridgman Images: 19; Center for Epigraphical and Palaeographical Studies, The Ohio State University, Columbus: 7; Gallerie dell'Accademia, Venice: 20; Library of Congress, Manuscript Division, Washington, DC: 24, 27; The Metropolitan Museum of Art, New York: 12, 25; Musée des Beaux-Arts, Marseille, photo Josse/Bridgeman Images: 22; Musée d'Orsay, Paris: 13; Museo Chiaramonti, Vatican City: 5 (photo Till Niermann/Wikimedia Commons, CC BY-SA 3.0), 6 (photo Fabrizio Garrisi/Wikimedia Commons, CC BY-SA 4.0); Museum Boijmans Van Beuningen, Rotterdam: 1; National Archaeological Museum, Athens: 2 (photo Zde/Wikimedia Commons, CC BY-SA 4.0), 10 (photo Scala, Florence), 11 (photo Enrico Della Pietra/AdobeStock); oksmit/AdobeStock: 14; Palazzo Ducale di Mantova, su concessione del Ministero dei Beni e delle Attività Culturali e del Turismo: 3; Rijksmuseum, Amsterdam: 18; The State Hermitage Museum, St Petersburg: 23; Stourhead, Wiltshire, photo © National Trust Images/Matthew Hollow: 21; Thomas Gilcrease Institute of American History and Art, Tulsa, OK: 26; Toledo Museum of Art, OH: 8.

INDEX

Illustration numbers are indicated by *italics*

Abelard, Peter 105
ageing
　bodily decline in 19, 36, 38–9,
　　82, 104, 110, 138, 142, 149,
　　191, 207, 225–6, 228, 230, 236
　public roles and 25, 77, 81
　theories of 10–11, 12, 50–2,
　　88–92, 160, 223–5, 242–3, *1*, *16*
ageism 8, 104–5, 107–8
Ages of Man and Woman 1
Alberti, Leon Battista 132, 135
Allan, David 160
Ariosto, Ludovico, *Orlando Furioso*
　106–7
Aristophanes, *Acharnians, Clouds,*
　Wasps, Women of the Assembly
　41–5, 66, 91
Aristotle 29, 50–52, 55, 66, 68, 89,
　90, 111, 141–2, 222
Athens 10, 24–6, 29, 32–5, 41–3,
　45–6, 48–9, 53–5, 57, 67, 91–2,
　151
Augustine 97–8, 147, 179
Augustus (Octavian) 56, 59, 62,
　64, 70–71, 77, 79

Bacon, Roger 111, 137
Balzac, Honoré de, *Père Goriot*
　215–18
Bartholomew 109–10
Beauvoir, Simone de 207–8, 210

Beowulf 100–101, 149
Bertran de Born 107, 112, 136
Biden, Joe 63, 228
Boccaccio, Giovanni, *Decameron*
　108–9, 139, 146–7, 235
Boncompagno da Signa, *On the*
　Evil of Old Age and Senility 137,
　139–43, 146, 147, 149
Boswell, James 191–2
Bowen, Elizabeth, *The House in*
　Paris 213–14
Brown, Peter 148
Browning, Robert 234–5

Carstensen, Laura L. 209
Cavour, Camillo Benso 188–90,
　203, 216, 237
Chambers, Kim O. 210
Chaucer, Geoffrey 107
China 29–32
Cicero, *Cato the Elder: On Old Age*
　53, 57–65, 70, 73–7, 81–2, 85,
　90–92, 132, 135, 140, 144–5,
　148, 183, 218, 234, *3*
Claudia Toreuma 64, 74, 78, 84,
　90, 92, 95
Cluny 110
Cole, John 195, *196*, 199–200
Confucius 29–31, 55
Cowper, Sarah 178–81, 191, 234
Cuffe, Henry 152

Dandolo, Erico 104
death
  by suicide 78, 83, 228–9
  funerary rites and mourning 22–4, 40–41, 74, 76, 86–8, 92–3, 145–6, 152, 168, 181–2, 208
  ideas about 49–50, 60–63, 78, 80–86, 144–6, 199
  tombs and inscriptions 38, 40, 54, 64, 74, 76–7, 84, 87–8, 92–3, 110, 129, 156, 214, 4, 6, 7
Defoe, Daniel 151, 152, 171
Descartes, René 176–8, 180, 191
Dubuisson, Paul Ulric 172–3
Dubus-Préville, P. L. 175–6
Duparc, Françoise, *The Old Woman* 22

Eckermann, Johann Peter 181–3, 237
Encyclopédie 159, 236, 23
Ennius 73
Epicurus 61
Erikson, Erik 12, 208
Euripides, *Alcestis, Hecuba, Heracles* 34–41, 45, 52, 70, 221

Faulkner, William 212–13
Feller, Élise 206–7
Filippi, Rustico 106, 109, 144, 212
Florence 131–2, 140
France 173–5, 207–8
Friedan, Betty 9
Fronto, Marcus Cornelius 83–6, 88, 92, 101, 176

Galen 88–91, 110, 137, 159–60, 222–3, 224, 237–8
Germany 184–6
gerontology 208
Giorgione, *The Old Woman* 20
Goethe, Johann Wolfgang von 181–4, 186, 187, 191, 237
Gonglin, Li, *The Classic of Filial Piety* 12

Gower, John 106, 107, 109, 122, 141, 236
Grace and Frankie (TV series) 215
Greuze, Jean-Baptiste 172, 23
Guinizelli, Guido 108, 143
Gurven, Michael 9

Harvey, William 159
Havighurst, Robert 208, 229
Heloise 105
Hesiod 26, 41
Homer, *Iliad, Odyssey* 17–24, 62
Horace, *Epodes* 64–6, 86, 212, 213
Hume, David 163

Isocrates 52, 55
Italy 130–31, 186–8, 204–6

Jaquerio, Giacomo, *Fountain of Life* 19
Jaucourt, Louis de 159–60
Johnson, Samuel 191–2
Jones, Maggie 225
Joseph, Jenny 214–15
Juvenal 85–6, 139, 236

Kaplan, Hillard 9

La Potherie, Bacqueville de 166, 168, 170
Laumonier, Lucie 129
Leonardo da Vinci, *Last Supper* 132
Locke, John 157, 161–3, 165, 170, 231
London 134
Longo, Valter 224–5

McNally, Michael D. 164
Marcus Aurelius 83, 88, 176
Márquez, Gabriel García 220, 232
Menander 67, 68
Messenger, Edward 155–6, 171
Molière 172
Montaigne, Michel de 171

Montesquieu, Charles-Louis de Secondat de 163
Montpellier 130–32, 153, 160, 245
Morbelli, Angelo, *Feast Day at the Trivulzio Hospice* 13
Murillo, Bartolomé Esteban, *An Old Woman Holding a Distaff and a Spindle* 21
Mussolini, Benito 220

Nicolas, Louis, *Captain of the Nation* 26
Norwich 154–5

old age
  and emotional communities 13, 71, 92, 163, 193, 237
  and emotions: ambivalent (hope, pensiveness) 60–63, 80–82, 84–6, 86, 92, 109, 129, 135, 150, 187–8, 195, 199, 201, 227, 233; contented (happiness, joy, pleasure, self-satisfaction) 8, 15–16, 23, 27–30, 42, 47–8, 50, 60, 67, 80, 91, 97, 101, 112, 117, 147, 159, 177–8, 180–83, 206–8, 211–12, 219–20, 229, 233–5; discontented (despair, grief, humiliation, loneliness, resentment, sadness, sorrow) 12, 15–16, 20–23, 34, 37, 39–40, 60, 62, 69, 84, 86, 88, 98–9, 109, 131, 139–41, 144–5, 149, 151, 158, 179–80, 182–3, 188, 195, 207–8, 211, 218, 222, 230, 236; fearful (fear, shame) 11–12, 16, 47, 49, 52, 107, 131, 135–6, 138, 141–2, 177, 216, 229, 236; hostile (anger, disgust, envy) 16, 36, 39, 54, 72, 86, 87, 98–9, 101, 106, 109, 139, 147, 150, 156, 173, 179–80, 208; loving (compassion, gratitude, love) 7–8, 16, 28, 36–9, 41, 58, 64, 66, 71–3, 95, 98–9, 101–2, 105–6, 108–9, 136, 138, 142–3, 173, 182, 190, 208, 211–14, 216–18, 220, 232, 235–7
  and formerly enslaved men and women 193–7, 200–202
  and gender: females 24–5, 64, 66, 72, 74, 91–2, 106–8, 213–15; gendered stereotypes 64–6, 72, 74, 106–8, 199, 213–15; male figures and patriarchs 25, 56–7, 67, 130–31, 132–3, 198; and sexuality 13, 66, 72, 107–8, 213
  and generational conflict 26–7, 30–33, 35–6, 54–5, 91–2, 139, 151–2, 220
  and welfare: familial support (filial piety, pietas, *xiao*) 25–6, 30–31, 35–6, 55, 58, 69, 71, 85, 91–3, 132, 151, 172, 186–7, 230–31, 12, 23; institutional support (hospices, hospitals, pensions, retirement) 130–31, 133–6, 154–5, 175–6, 186–8, 190–91, 201–4, 207–9, 229–31, 13; legislation 26, 130–31, 133–5, 187, 190–91, 201–3, 227–8; social networks and community 9, 92, 186, 229–31
  and wisdom 49–50, 60–61, 84–5, 96–7, 164–6, 168–70, 173–4, 232–4
  celebration of, Paris (1797) 174
  in cultures: African 197–200; Chinese 15, 29–32, 55; Greek (Athens, Hellenistic, Sparta) 10, 24–30, 34–49, 53–5, 57, 67, 76–7, 91–2, 151; Islamicate (Muslim) 16, 103–4, 109; medieval (Christian) 96–7, 99–100, 104–5, 129–31, 146–8, 157–8; Native American (Anishinaabe, Mohawk, Ojibwe) 15–16, 163–73; Roman 56–9, 67–71, 73, 75–8, 83–4, 86–9, 92–5, 130–32, 186–8

population statistics and 10, 206–7, 226–9
words for 12–13, 25, 27, 59, 110, 152, 208, 223, 228, 231
Ovid 10, 71–6, 86, 105, 145, 235

Papiria Tertia 88, 92, 237, 7
Parkin, Tim 86–7
patria potestas (paternal power) 58, 69, 93
Perrot, Nicolas 166, 169–70
Peter the Venerable 109–10
Petrarch, Francis 14–16, 137, 143–7, 149, 176, 212, 235
Pietersz, Aert, *Rich Children, Poor Parents* 122
Plato 46–50, 52, 55, 60, 148
Plautus, *Pot of Gold* 67–9, 172
Plutarch 27–8, 63

Radisson, Pierre-Esprit 166–8
Robert of Arbrissel 99
Rome 56–9, 67–71, 73, 75–8, 83–4, 86–9, 92–5, 130–32, 186–8
Rousseau, Jean-Jacques 171–2, 173, 238

Sadeler, Raphael I 158, 25
Saller, Richard 70
Sappho 23–4
Schiller, Friedrich 184
Shakespeare, William, *King Lear* 10–11, 150–56, 184, 190, 221
Socrates 9–10, 44, 45–50, 52, 55, 61, 81, 142, 145, 148, 159, 197
Solon 25–6, 28, 29, 32, 34, 36, 41, 43, 55, 221, 226, 234
Sophocles 53–4, 142

Sparta 10, 26–30, 32, 43, 57, 92, 174
Sunjata 198–9
Svevo, Italo, *A Very Old Man* 15–16, 218–20, 232, 235, 237, 239
Swift, Jonathan 162

Tacitus 78
Thane, Pat 152
Thomas, L. Eugene 210
Thucydides 42
Treuer, Anton 164–5
Turgenev, Ivan 237
Turin 187–9
Tyrtaeus 28

United States of America 163–4, 202–3, 207, 226–8
Usama ibn Munqidh 103, 136–9, 149

Virgil 56
Voltaire 159, 172, 187, 236
Vries, Jan de 160–61

Wheel of Fortune 110
Wheel of Life 110–11, 16
White, Richard 163, 165
Whittington, Richard 134–5, 235
Wieland, Christoph 184
Wilde, Oscar 224
Wissel, Adolf 206
witch camps 229–30
Witgen, Michael 163
Wolfram von Eschenbach, *Willehalm* 100, 101–2, 136, 149, 15

Xenophon 27, 29, 50